THE
WORLD WAR II
QUIZ BOOK

THE
WORLD WAR II
QUIZ BOOK

OVER **1,700**
QUESTIONS AND **ANSWERS**
TO TEST YOUR **KNOWLEDGE** OF
HISTORY'S MOST
COMPELLING CONFLICT

ROBERT DAVENPORT

TAYLOR TRADE PUBLISHING
Lanham • New York • Boulder • Toronto • Plymouth, UK

Published by Taylor Trade Publishing
An imprint of The Rowman & Littlefield Publishing Group, Inc.
4501 Forbes Boulevard, Suite 200, Lanham, Maryland 20706
www.rlpgtrade.com

Estover Road, Plymouth PL6 7PY, United Kingdom

Distributed by NATIONAL BOOK NETWORK

Library of Congress Cataloging-in-Publication Data

Davenport, Robert Ralsey, 1950–
  The World War II quiz book : over 1,700 questions and answers to test your knowledge of history's most compelling conflict / Robert Davenport.
     p. cm.
  ISBN 978-1-58979-394-1 (pbk. : alk. paper) — ISBN 978-1-58979-446-7 (electronic)
  1. World War, 1939–1945—Miscellanea. I. Title.
  D743.6.D38 2009
  940.53—dc22

                                    2009004297

CONTENTS

ACKNOWLEDGMENTS

A very big thanks to Jake Elwell, my agent, and to Peter Burford, my editor, without whom I would have never done this book.

I would also like to thank those veterans of World War II with whom I grew up, and who saw this war firsthand, including my grandfather, Lieutenant Colonel Harry Augustus Davenport Jr., U.S. Army (South Pacific); my father, Commander Harry A. Davenport III, U.S. Coast Guard; my uncle Colonel Richard Morton Cosel Sr., U.S. Air Force (North Africa and Europe); my namesake uncle, Robert Ralsey Davenport, U.S. Air Force (Greenland); my aunt Lucille Davenport Boos (British War Relief); my uncle Christian Boos (U.S. Army, France); and my aunt Georgine Davenport Cosel (Red Cross, North Africa, Italy). With the exception of my father, they are all gone now.

I would also like to acknowledge my mentor Larry Gelbart, who brought to life the Korean War through his television show M*A*S*H.

INTRODUCTION

As a baby boomer, I grew up in the shadow of World War II. Everyone that I knew had been in the war. For example, when we lived in Florida, our next door neighbor was missing a leg. When I asked my father about it, he said that Dave had been on the Bataan Death March, and then in the prison camp at Cabanatuan. Because the Japanese did not feed the prisoners very well, they would sneak out of the camp, look for food, and then sneak back into the camp. He was shot in the leg trying to get back into the camp.

My father wrote a short piece recently for his high school reunion at Great Neck High School in New York, and I thought that it would be most fitting to include it here, since it comes directly from the greatest generation, and shows directly what it was like to grow up during the war:

> My father and uncles were all World War I veterans serving at sea and in the front lines of France. They knew what was coming. In '41 my father went to Persia and what is now Iraq to help build a road to Russia which was fighting for its life. All during my freshman and sophomore years the war preparations were an everyday conversation at home. Even as a freshman

in high school I "knew" I was going to Annapolis or Navy flight school. Of course Pearl Harbor changed everything. The classes of '42, '43 and '44 [Great Neck High School] enlisted en masse. The Merchant Marine Academy came to Great Neck. Civil Defense and air raid precautions were an everyday occurrence. My sister Lucille worked for the British War Relief and I remember volunteering there many times during 1942–3. Her husband wound up in France. My family disappeared into the war effort with Bob serving in Greenland, my Dad in the South Pacific for three years and my other sister in North Africa and Italy. I wound up in ROTC and the U. S. Coast Guard Academy. I'm sure it was the same for many, many others.

World War II is probably the most horrific war that will ever occur on this planet. It certainly touched every single family. I hope what follows is an entertaining, and challenging, series of questions on this, our greatest war.

PRIVATE
FIRST CLASS

These are the easiest of the questions. You should be able to work your way through most of this section without any difficulty.

1. The Italian dictator during the war was:
   a. Mussolini
   b. Delmanio
   c. King Emmanuel
   d. Tortellini

2. What is important about December 7, 1941?
   a. Atomic bombing of Hiroshima
   b. Allied victory over the Nazis
   c. Japanese bombing of Pearl Harbor
   d. Allied invasion of Normandy

3. What happened on September 1, 1939?
   a. Battle of Britain commenced
   b. Japanese bombing of Pearl Harbor
   c. German invasion of Poland
   d. Allied invasion of Normandy

4. Which country defended Iwo Jima against the Allies?

   a. Russia
   b. Germany
   c. Japan
   d. Italy

5. Where in France did the Allies invade on D-day?

   a. Île-de-France
   b. Provence
   c. Pas de Calais
   d. Normandy

6. The name of the four-month battle between the Royal Air Force and the Luftwaffe to control the skies over England is:

   a. Battle of Falaise
   b. Battle of Britain
   c. Battle of the Atlantic
   d. Operation Sea Lion

7. The original code name for the Allied research program on the atomic bomb referred to the town in which it was first headquartered. What was the code name?

   a. Minneapolis Engineering District
   b. Madison Engineering District
   c. Miami Engineering District
   d. Manhattan Engineering District

8. What U.S. general was elected president of the United States?

   a. Eisenhower
   b. Montgomery
   c. Bradley
   d. Bush

9. What happened on June 6, 1944?

   a. Allied invasion of Normandy
   b. Italy joined the Axis powers
   c. France fell to the Nazis
   d. Japan surrendered

10. The aircraft that dropped the atomic bomb on Hiroshima was:
    a. Enola Gay
    b. Dixie
    c. Sweetheart
    d. Blue Gal

11. Who was the emperor of Japan during the war?
    a. Hirohito
    b. Centerkan
    c. Himushi
    d. Zumauw

12. What was the Allied code name for the D-day landings?
    a. Operation Landlord
    b. Operation Lowlands
    c. Operation Highlord
    d. Operation Overlord

13. What began in 1929 that was a major cause of the war?
    a. Civil rights movement
    b. Industrial Revolution
    c. Great Depression
    d. French Revolution

14. Who was the leader of the U.S.S.R. at the beginning of the war?
    a. Lenin
    b. Stalin
    c. Khrushchev
    d. Yeltsin

15. Which country was invaded by Germany on September 1, 1939?
    a. Norway
    b. Poland
    c. France
    d. Czechoslovakia

16. What were Fat Man and Little Boy?

  a. Battleships
  b. Submarines
  c. Bombers
  d. Atomic bombs

17. This battleship was sunk during the attack on Pearl Harbor and had more fatalities than any other ship:

  a. U.S.S. *Utah*
  b. U.S.S. *Arizona*
  c. U.S.S. *Oklahoma*
  d. U.S.S. *Maryland*

18. Because of the high number of casualties being taken by Allied bombers over Europe, it became impossible to complete a tour of duty in theater. Crews were "flying until they died." In the face of this grim statistic, the Army Air Force announced a policy that any crew which completed twenty-five missons could go home. What was the first B-17 bomber to complete its twenty-fifth mission and to qualify under this policy to go home?

  a. Big Beautiful Gal
  b. Memphis Belle
  c. Ready Betty
  d. San Antonio Rose

19. The Russian capture of this city ended the war in 1945:

  a. Frankfurt
  b. Berlin
  c. Stuttgart
  d. Vienna

20. What was the nickname of the U.S. 101st Airborne Division?

  a. Screaming Eagles
  b. Golden Talon
  c. Hawks
  d. Spearhead

21. Which laws were on the books in the United States long before the bombing of Pearl Harbor?

    a. Ban on male immigrant workers from Japan
    b. Ban on Japanese women entering the United States to marry
    c. Ban on land ownership by Japanese immigrants
    d. All of the above

22. Which treaty ended World War I and was a cause of German resentment, which led to World War II?

    a. Geneva Conference
    b. Treaty of Paris
    c. Treaty of Versailles
    d. Treaty of Ghent

23. Who was the commander of the Japanese Combined Fleet at the attack on Pearl Harbor?

    a. Admiral Yamamoto
    b. Admiral Tanaka
    c. Admiral Togo
    d. Admiral Kondo

24. What sister ship to the KMS *Bismarck* was sunk in the Tromsofjord in Norway by an air attack from the British Navy?

    a. *Hindenburg*
    b. *Baden*
    c. *Tirpitz*
    d. *Hamburg*

25. What was unusual about the British Mosquito?

    a. Made from plywood with a balsa wood core, because it was believed that metal would be in short supply during the war
    b. Built after the war
    c. Britain's first heavy bomber
    d. Only aircraft used in the Battle of Britain

26. What was the secret of the B-17's precision bombing?

   a. Photographic intelligence

   b. Multiple runs

   c. Norden bombsight

   d. Laser targeting

27. Which aircraft is also known as the B-17?

   a. Liberator

   b. Lightning

   c. Flying Fortress

   d. Thunderbolt

28. What was name of the B-29 bomber that dropped the atomic bomb on Nagasaki in August 1945?

   a. Bock's Car

   b. Memphis Belle

   c. Great Artiste

   d. Nostromo

29. The offensive in France was called *Blitzkrieg* by the Germans. What does it translate to in English?

   a. Lightning war

   b. Panzer assault

   c. Mechanized war

   d. Combined forces

30. So many soldiers were killed in the invasion of Okinawa that it convinced President Truman to take what action?

   a. Execute Emperor Hirohito

   b. Full-scale Marine landings in Japan

   c. Use the atomic bomb

   d. Massive bombing runs on Tokyo

31. Who was the Desert Fox?

   a. Albert Speer

   b. Erwin Rommel

   c. George Patton

   d. Omar Bradley

32. Germany had Hitler. Italy had Mussolini. Japan had:

   a. Emperor Maximilian
   b. Emperor Hirolito
   c. Emperor Hirohito
   d. Emperor Hironito

33. Where were the war trials of Nazis held after the war?

   a. Nuremberg
   b. London
   c. Paris
   d. Berlin

34. What was the German standard-issue sidearm?

   a. Colt M1191
   b. 44 Magnum
   c. M19 revolver
   d. P38 Walther

35. What was Japan's main defensive system on Iwo Jima?

   a. Bunkers on the beaches
   b. Underground cave system
   c. Air superiority
   d. Naval superiority

36. What was the name of the final invasion of continental Europe by the Allies?

   a. Battle of Falaise
   b. Invasion of Normandy
   c. Operation White Coast
   d. Dieppe Raid

37. Who was the German field marshal in charge of the Atlantic Wall?

   a. Leni Riefenstahl
   b. Heinrich Heine
   c. Erwin Rommel
   d. Ernst Roehm

38. What battle provided a rallying point for the British people at the beginning of the war?

   a. Battle of Norway

   b. Battle of France

   c. Battle of Britain

   d. Battle of Germany

39. What country was not invaded by the Nazis?

   a. Netherlands

   b. France

   c. Spain

   d. Denmark

40. What happened immediately after Germany invaded Poland?

   a. Germany declared war on Russia

   b. France and Britain declared war on Germany

   c. Russia declared war on Germany

   d. Germany declared war on France

41. Britain's largest battle cruiser, which was sunk by the German battleship *Bismarck* in the Denmark Strait on May 24, 1941, was:

   a. HMS *Hood*

   b. HMS *Ark Royal*

   c. HMS *King George IV*

   d. HMS *Repulse*

42. In April 1942, U.S. Army B-25 medium bombers launched from the carrier *Hornet*, which was commanded by Jimmy Doolittle, dropped bombs on:

   a. Japan

   b. Aleutian Islands

   c. Wake Island

   d. Philippines

43. What theoretical physicist with little practical engineering experience was chosen as overall scientific leader of the Manhattan Project?

   a. Harold Urey
   b. Ralph Serber
   c. Richard Feynman
   d. J. Robert Oppenheimer

44. The largest battle of the war, a five-month siege that became the turning point of the war in Europe, took place in:

   a. Moscow
   b. Leningrad
   c. Stalingrad
   d. Kharkov

45. What city acquired international status at the end of World War I and became the focus of the Polish Corridor?

   a. Moscow
   b. London
   c. Berlin
   d. Danzig

46. What all-star movie portrays the D-day invasion?

   a. *From Here to Eternity*
   b. *The Longest Day*
   c. *Blitzkrieg*
   d. *Patton*

47. Which country did not fall under the control of an Axis power?

   a. Norway
   b. Netherlands
   c. Denmark
   d. Ireland

48. What was General George S. Patton's nickname?

    a. Old Blood and Gore

    b. Old Blood and Guts

    c. Old Guts and Grime

    d. Old Blood and Thunder

49. The choice of how to treat Germany after the war caused serious tension between which Allies?

    a. United States and France

    b. United States and Britain

    c. United States and U.S.S.R.

    d. Britain and France

50. What member of the Nazi Party saved over a thousand Jews by giving them work in his factory?

    a. Oskar Schindler

    b. Rudolf Hess

    c. Irwin Rommel

    d. Hermann Goering

51. Why was the P-51 Mustang such a successful fighter?

    a. Armament

    b. External fuel tanks

    c. Maneuverability

    d. All of the above

52. What is the name of the volcano on Iwo Jima?

    a. Mount Japan

    b. Mount Surbaki

    c. Mount Iwo Jima

    d. Mount Suribachi

53. Who killed themselves on the island of Saipan to encourage their troops to fight to the death?

    a. Admiral Nagumo and General Saito

    b. Admiral Donnelson and Lieutenant Patterson

    c. Admiral Nimitz and General Patton

    d. Admiral McLaughlin and Major General Williams

54. What type of ship was the *Yorktown*?

    a. Frigate

    b. Battleship

    c. Aircraft carrier

    d. Destroyer

55. What was unusual about the F4U Corsair's wing structure? It had:

    a. Three wings

    b. Four wings

    c. Inverted gull wing

    d. Overhead wing

56. The Luftwaffe called the P-38 the *Gabelschwanzteufel*, which means:

    a. Whistle of death

    b. Destroyer

    c. Twin demon

    d. Fork-tailed devil

57. The Fifth Rangers, 101st Airborne, and the 82nd Airborne were shocked by the:

    a. Russians killing prisoners in the Baltic

    b. Treasures at Berchtesgaden

    c. Concentration camps

    d. Surrender of 150,000 German troops

58. What was the ancestry of the Sullivan brothers, the five U.S. Navy seamen who died on the same day when their ship was sunk? Their loss resulted in regulations prohibiting brothers from serving together in the same unit, so that mothers would be less likely to lose all of their sons in the war. Their situation was later the inspiration for the film *Saving Private Ryan*.

    a. Italian

    b. Scottish

    c. Irish

    d. Dutch

59. The overall commander of all Allied forces in Europe at the end of the war was:

   a. General Bradley
   b. General Eisenhower
   c. Winston Churchill
   d. Archibald Wavell

60. On what city was the second atomic bomb dropped?

   a. Osaka
   b. Hiroshima
   c. Nagasaki
   d. Tokyo

61. Which nation used the Tiger tank?

   a. Japan
   b. Germany
   c. Italy
   d. France

62. When the U.S. flag was planted on Iwo Jima, where was the photograph taken?

   a. Pork Chop Hill
   b. Mount Ishii
   c. Mount Moriuri
   d. Mount Suribachi

63. The Allies decoded the cipher used by the Germans, giving the Allies a significant advantage in the war. What was the code name for the Germans' ciphering machine?

   a. Dolphin
   b. Heimisch
   c. Shark
   d. Enigma

64. The nickname given to the carrier *Enterprise* was:

    a. Little E

    b. Big E

    c. Lady E

    d. Miss E

65. What was the name of the German pocket battleship that faced three adversaries in 1939?

    a. KMS *Admiral Scheer*

    b. KMS *Prinz Eugen*

    c. KMS *Tirpitz*

    d. KMS *Admiral Graf Spee*

66. The location for the signing of the Japanese surrender was:

    a. Subway in Osaka

    b. Parliament House, Tokyo

    c. Aboard the U.S.S. *Missouri*

    d. War Centre, London

67. Who fled the Philippines in 1942, but said, "I shall return"?

    a. General Dwight D. Eisenhower

    b. General Douglas MacArthur

    c. General Mark Clark

    d. General Omar Bradley

68. Following the British evacuation of their land forces at Dunkirk, Hitler planned to swiftly invade England. The German code name for this planned invasion of Britain was:

    a. Operation Sea Leopard

    b. Operation Seal

    c. Operation Sea Lion

    d. Operation Walrus

69. Who was the commander of the British Eighth Army in Africa and Europe?

   a. Archibald Wavell
   b. Louis Mountbatten
   c. Neville Chamberlain
   d. Bernard Montgomery

70. Germany honored the neutrality of which European country?

   a. Austria
   b. Romania
   c. Switzerland
   d. Yugoslavia

71. Which of these Allies did not receive a German sector to control in postwar Germany?

   a. Britain
   b. Russia
   c. United States
   d. Italy

72. The Japanese high command was determined to defeat the U.S. Marines on Guadalcanal. The nightly runs by destroyers and transports to land troops and supplies, led by Admiral Tanaka, were called:

   a. Tanaka's Express
   b. Tojo's Night Run
   c. Tokyo Express
   d. Night Run

73. The Marines in the Pacific received early warning of the approach of Japanese air strikes and seaborne reinforcements by a dedicated group of observers known as the:

   a. Special Forces
   b. Beachcombers
   c. Coast Watchers
   d. Observers

74. What made Iwo Jima a strategic target in the war against Japan?

    a. Center of the munitions industry
    b. Submarine base
    c. Fighter base
    d. Major source of crude oil

75. On June 11, 1940, the day after Italy declared war on France and Britain, which nations declared war on Italy?

    a. United States, Spain, and Netherlands
    b. Australia, New Zealand, and South Africa
    c. Sweden, Finland, and Denmark
    d. India, Pakistan, and Iran

76. The HMS *Ark Royal* launched its torpedo aircraft against the *Bismarck*. They did not sink it, but they damaged what important part of the ship?

    a. Rudder
    b. Gunnery radar
    c. Propellers
    d. Fuel oil compartments

77. This Royal Sovereign–class battleship was hit by three torpedoes in Scapa Flow on October 14, 1939:

    a. HMS *Royal Oak*
    b. HMS *Vanguard*
    c. HMS *Black Swan*
    d. HMS *Royal Standard*

78. During actual bombing runs during the war, which crew member was in control of the aircraft?

    a. Copilot
    b. Bombardier
    c. Navigator
    d. Radio operator

79. The B-29 included many improvements over the B-17 bomber, including a pressurized cabin, a central fire-control system, and remote-controlled machine-gun turrets. What is the nickname for the B-29?

   a. Mitchell
   b. Flying Fortress
   c. Superfortress
   d. Liberator

80. George Patton's pistol handles were made of:

   a. Pearl
   b. Mahogany
   c. Ivory
   d. Cedar

81. The air battle between Germany and England was called:

   a. Battle for the English Channel
   b. Battle of Gibraltar
   c. Battle of Dover
   d. Battle of Britain

82. Which leader was nicknamed Uncle Joe?

   a. Joseph Stalin
   b. Franklin Delano Roosevelt
   c. Winston Churchill
   d. Adolph Hitler

83. In which branch of service did the Sullivan brothers serve?

   a. Marines
   b. Air Force
   c. Navy
   d. Army

84. Shortly after his eighteenth birthday, Audie Murphy, who was ultimately to become the most highly decorated member of the U.S. armed forces during World War II, joined the:

   a. U.S. Marine Corps
   b. U.S. Coast Guard
   c. U.S. Navy
   d. U.S. Army

85. What day was D-day?
    a. December 6, 1944
    b. June 7, 1944
    c. December 7, 1944
    d. June 6, 1944

86. The head of the SS was:
    a. Erwin Rommel
    b. Adolf Hitler
    c. Heinrich Himmler
    d. Ernst Roehm

87. On August 6, 1945, the first atomic bomb was dropped on what Japanese city?
    a. Tokyo
    b. Nagasaki
    c. Hiroshima
    d. Sakhalin

88. Even though he was a general in the German air force, as a field marshal he was the commander of all ground forces in Italy. He is quoted as saying, "Results will demonstrate an officer's fitness to be a field marshal, and no one will then ask about his origins, whether he came from the army or the air force. But one piece of advice I will give to all air field marshals: do not become a one-sided technician, but learn to think and lead in terms of all three services." Who was he?
    a. Ernst Udet
    b. Albrecht Kesselring
    c. Hugo Sperrle
    d. Erhard Milch

89. What organization was founded by Woodrow Wilson, although the United States never joined?
    a. United Nations
    b. League of Nations
    c. Geneva Convention
    d. World Trade Organization

90. On August 7, 1942, the First Marine division, led by General Vandergrift, landed on Guadalcanal, captured the airfield, and named it:

    a. Cactus
    b. Morrison
    c. Henderson
    d. Jefferson

91. When was the atomic bomb dropped on Nagasaki?

    a. August 9
    b. November 25
    c. August 6
    d. September 9

92. On January 17, 1941, infantry of the Australian Nineteenth Brigade, the Seventh Armored Support Group, and the Eleventh Hussars reached a strategic port 800 miles from Tripoli and threw a cordon around this city in what was to become a famous siege:

    a. El-Sheriffe
    b. Mogadishu
    c. Tobruk
    d. Cairo

93. The sinking of the U.S.S. *Indianapolis* was the worst single loss of life in the history of the U.S. Navy. After delivering critical parts for the first atomic bomb to the United States airbase at Tinian Island on July 26, 1945, it was in the Philippine Sea when attacked by a Japanese submarine. Most of the crew was lost to a combination of exposure, dehydration, and shark attacks while floating in the water for five days. Who was the captain of the ill-fated *Indianapolis*?

    a. Captain Husband Kimmel
    b. Captain Charles B. McVay
    c. Captain Joseph Hunt
    d. Captain Isadora Fish

94. In referring to the Royal Air Force and their heroic prevention of a Nazi invasion of Great Britain, who said, "Never has so much been owed by so many to so few"?

   a. Rommel
   b. Chamberlain
   c. Churchill
   d. Hitler

95. Hitler's invasion of the U.S.S.R. in June 1941 was called:

   a. Case Red (B)
   b. Operation Barbarossa
   c. Plan Lebensraum (English: "Living Space")
   d. Vorsehung (English: "Destiny" or "Providence")

96. Which Nazi leader cheated the gallows by taking cyanide the night before his execution?

   a. Goering
   b. Hess
   c. Ribbentrop
   d. Speer

97. Which was not a type of tank?

   a. Sheridan
   b. Tiger
   c. Sherman
   d. Pzkw IV H

98. Which of the following was not a bomber?

   a. P-51
   b. B-24
   c. B-29
   d. B-17

99. The four Japanese carriers sunk during the Battle of Midway were:

   a. *Akagi, Musashi, Tone,* and *Tsunami*
   b. *Akagi, Kaga, Soryu,* and *Hiryu*
   c. *Kaga, Hiryu, Soryu,* and *Fuso*
   d. *Akagi, Kato, Wasabi,* and *Sayonara-Maru*

100. Who designed the B-17?

   a. Northrop
   b. Boeing
   c. North American
   d. Lockheed

101. What aircraft was designated the Liberator?

   a. B-24
   b. HE 111
   c. B-29
   d. P-40

102. Who was the German general sent to Tripoli to stem Italian losses?

   a. Rommel
   b. Himmler
   c. Hess
   d. Goebbels

103. Each belligerent during World War II knew that the first country to develop a jet fighter (as opposed to slower aircraft that relied on a conventional reciprocating engine) would have a superweapon, if they could produce such aircraft in sufficient quantity. The first country to put operational units of jets into combat during World War II was:

   a. United States
   b. Germany
   c. Russia
   d. Japan

104. Which aircraft was designed by Reginald Mitchell?

   a. Lancaster
   b. Hurricane
   c. Spitfire
   d. Wellington

105. The battle that saved Britain from the hands of Hitler was:

   a. Battle of Britain
   b. Battle of Midway
   c. Battle of the Bulge
   d. Battle of English Channel

106. What general, fleeing from the Philippines, said, "I shall return"?

   a. Douglas MacArthur
   b. George Patton
   c. Dwight Eisenhower
   d. Mark Clark

107. The director of the Manhattan Project was:

   a. Leo Szilard
   b. J. Robert Oppenheimer
   c. Edward Teller
   d. Enrico Fermi

108. Japanese reinforcements had to run a gauntlet on their way to Guadalcanal from Rabaul and New Ireland, a narrow stretch of water between two parallel island chains, known as the:

   a. Slot
   b. Channel
   c. Trench
   d. Gut

109. Why was the invasion of Malaya critical to the Japanese war plan?

    a. Gain combat experience

    b. Land gateway into Singapore

    c. Natural resources of tin and rubber

    d. Lure the Commonwealth Army into the jungle

110. The overall commander of U.S. personnel in the Philippines during the Japanese invasion was:

    a. General Jonathan Wainwright

    b. General Dwight Eisenhower

    c. Admiral Chester Nimitz

    d. General Douglas MacArthur

111. The biggest tank produced during the war was introduced too late to have an impact. What was it called?

    a. Comet tank

    b. T-34

    c. Panzer IV

    d. Tiger II

112. On May 24, 1941, this warship scored one hit on the HMS *Hood* and four hits on the HMS *Prince of Wales*, but was forced to leave the KMS *Bismarck* to her fate:

    a. *Admiral Hipper*

    b. *Prinz Eugen*

    c. *Admiral Scheer*

    d. *Graf Spee*

113. The Battle of Narvik was fought off the coast of which country?

    a. Germany

    b. Iceland

    c. Norway

    d. Sweden

114. What made high-altitude bombing possible?

    a. Superchargers

    b. Powerful radial engines

    c. Oxygen tanks for the crew

    d. All of the above

115. What was the standard military handgun for the U.S. Army?

    a. Smith and Wesson 0.38/200

    b. M1917 revolver

    c. Colt M1911A1

    d. M1942 Liberator

116. The U.S. Army's standard-issue infantry rifle during the war was the:

    a. M1903 Springfield

    b. SMLE Lee-Enfield

    c. M1941 Johnson

    d. M1 Garand

117. The port on the English Channel that was the site of the evacuation of the British Expeditionary Force in 1940 was:

    a. Calais

    b. Omaha Beach

    c. Dunkirk

    d. Cherbourg

118. Which country flew the Zero?

    a. Russia

    b. Germany

    c. Japan

    d. Italy

119. The Japanese claimed they killed a million people in Nanjing because Chinese combatants had disguised themselves as civilians and were acting as insurgents. How do we know they were lying?

- **a.** Men who were killed were already tied up
- **b.** Japanese newspapers reported uniformed POWs marched in columns to the Yangtze River and executed
- **c.** The dead included women and children
- **d.** All of the above

120. What type of aircraft dropped the two atomic bombs?

- **a.** B-29
- **b.** P-80
- **c.** B-17
- **d.** F4F

121. What innovation greatly enhanced the T-34 tank's defensive posture?

- **a.** FM radio sets
- **b.** Self-sealing fuel tank
- **c.** Sloped armor
- **d.** Coaxial machine gun

122. What country had the T-80 light tank?

- **a.** Finland
- **b.** United States
- **c.** Russia
- **d.** Japan

123. What fate befell the HMS *Ark Royal* in November 1941?

- **a.** Sunk by Italian midget submarines
- **b.** Sunk by Japanese kamikaze attack
- **c.** Sunk by German fighter bombers
- **d.** Sunk by the German submarine U-81

124. What Japanese battleship was sunk by aircraft off Okinawa on April 7, 1945?

    a. *Yamato*
    b. *Korasi Mur*
    c. *Musashi*
    d. *Kagi*

125. The King George V–class battleship sunk by Navy aircraft torpedoes on December 10, 1941, off Kuantan, Malaya, in the South China Sea was:

    a. HMS *Duke of Kent*
    b. HMS *King George V*
    c. HMS *Prince of Wales*
    d. HMS *Duke of York*

126. Which aircraft is known as the P-38?

    a. Corsair
    b. Thunderbolt
    c. Mustang
    d. Lightning

127. Admiral Yamamoto was the Japanese leader blamed by U.S. leaders for the attack on Pearl Harbor. Thus military intelligence specifically tracked his travel plans in the Solomon Islands area and tasked aircraft operating out of Henderson Field on Guadalcanal to shoot him down on April 18, 1943. The death of Yamamoto greatly damaged the morale of Japanese naval personnel. What aircraft shot down Admiral Yamamoto?

    a. Lightning
    b. P-47 Thunderbolt
    c. De Havilland Mosquito
    d. P-51 Mustang

128. The British 9 millimeter submachine gun was the:

    a. Austen

    b. Owen Gun

    c. Lancaster

    d. Sten

129. Operation Torch referred to which operation?

    a. Trap set for the Japanese at Midway

    b. Building of the Burma Road

    c. Invasion of North Africa

    d. Return to the Philippines

130. Which countries were prosecutors at Nuremberg?

    a. France, Britain, United States, and Poland

    b. France, Holland, Ukraine, and Austria

    c. Britain, Italy, United States, and Germany

    d. France, Britain, U.S.S.R., and United States

131. Which is not a German aircraft?

    a. Bf 109

    b. Typhoon

    c. FW 190

    d. Ju 88

132. Hitler became chancellor of Germany in:

    a. 1934

    b. 1933

    c. 1932

    d. 1935

133. What was the name of the five brothers who died when the cruiser *Juneau* was torpedoed and sunk by a Japanese submarine?

    a. Anderson

    b. Donovan

    c. Sullivan

    d. Peterson

134. What aircraft was used to carry out the Doolittle Raid on Tokyo?
    a. B-17 Flying Fortress
    b. B-29 Stratofortress
    c. B-25 Mitchell
    d. B-26 Marauder

135. What pivotal event in the war in the South Pacific took place in early August 1942?
    a. U.S. Army invaded New Britain
    b. U.S. Marines landed in Guadalcanal
    c. U.S. Navy aircraft attacked Japanese bases on Guam
    d. U.S. Navy aircraft sank the battleship *Yamato*

136. The conference at which Truman, Stalin, and Churchill decided postwar strategy was:
    a. Berlin Conference
    b. 1945 Conference
    c. Potsdam Conference
    d. New York Conference

137. What was the most likely cause of the sinking of the HMS *Hood*?
    a. Sacrificed speed for armored protection
    b. Running low on fuel
    c. Not enough armament
    d. Sacrificed armored protection for speed

138. What warship was torpedoed in Scapa Flow harbor by a U-boat?
    a. *Resolution*
    b. *Royal Oak*
    c. *Sergeant York*
    d. *Royal Sovereign*

139. What sea battle, involving the carriers *Enterprise*, *Yorktown*, and *Hornet*, was the turning point in the carrier war in the Pacific?

   a. Battle of Savo Island
   b. Battle of the Coral Sea
   c. Battle of Midway
   d. Naval Battle of Guadalcanal

140. The battle between a German pocket battleship, two British light cruisers, and a British heavy cruiser was:

   a. Battle of Coronel
   b. Battle of San Jacinto
   c. Battle of the Denmark Straits
   d. Battle of the River Plate

141. Admiral Karl Doenitz was convicted at Nuremburg and sentenced to ten years in prison for what controversial order to the U-boats under his command?

   a. Sink shipping in Hudson Bay
   b. Do not rescue survivors
   c. Continue fighting after the war ended
   d. Gun down survivors in the water

142. The U.S. general who oversaw the plan to rebuild war-torn Western Europe was:

   a. Bradley
   b. Eisenhower
   c. Patton
   d. Marshall

143. The mass required to sustain fission in a nuclear weapon is called:

   a. Available mass
   b. Critical mass
   c. Self-sustaining mass
   d. Fissile mass

144. Who was the admiral in overall command of the Imperial Japanese Navy?

    a. Isoruku Yamamoto

    b. Kiyohide Shima

    c. Shoji Nishimura

    d. Admiral Tojo

145. Who uttered the words, "I am become Death, the shatterer of worlds"?

    a. Heinrich Himmler, who created the death camps

    b. Arthur Harris, who authorized the firebombing of Dresden

    c. Harry S Truman, who authorized the dropping of the first atomic bomb

    d. Robert Oppenheimer, who developed the first atomic bomb

146. Although Britain and the United States wanted to take Berlin, this Russian general got there first:

    a. Vasily Zaitsev

    b. Georgi Zhukov

    c. Alexey Gamelin

    d. Sergei Nemchinov

147. Who was the commander of the Luftwaffe?

    a. Warner Baumbach

    b. Rudolph Hess

    c. Hermann Goering

    d. Albert Speer

148. What was the primary reason given for the internment of Japanese Americans?

    a. The bombing of Pearl Harbor

    b. They were infected with a deadly virus

    c. They hated the United States

    d. They were spies for Japan

149. One Japanese American relocation camp was most comparable to a Nazi concentration camp because of its unsanitary, squalid living conditions, inadequate medical care, poor food, and unsafe working conditions. In November 1943 a series of meetings and protests by the inmates over poor living conditions prompted the Army to impose martial law over this camp:

   a. Tule Lake
   b. Topaz
   c. Manzanar
   d. Heart Mountain

150. The army of which nation reached Berlin on May 1, 1945?

   a. United States
   b. France
   c. England
   d. Soviet Union

151. Which country had the greatest number of civilian casualties?

   a. Germany
   b. Russia
   c. France
   d. Japan

152. Germany invaded Poland on:

   a. September 3, 1939
   b. September 2, 1939
   c. September 9, 1939
   d. September 1, 1939

153. The Battle of the Philippine Sea, in which Japanese carrier air power was destroyed, is also known as:

   a. Saipan Slaughter
   b. Battle of Samar
   c. Marianas Massacre
   d. Great Marianas Turkey Shoot

154. What was the first aircraft carrier in the U.S. Navy?

  a. *Enterprise*
  b. *Lexington*
  c. *Langley*
  d. *Saratoga*

155. The first pressurized U.S. heavy bomber used in the war was the:

  a. Boeing B-17-G Flying Fortress
  b. North American B-25 Mitchell
  c. Consolidated B-24-F Liberator
  d. Boeing B-29 Superfortress

156. What was the nickname of the Messerschmitt Me 163?

  a. Meteor
  b. Flying Pencil
  c. Schnell
  d. Komet

157. What was the first aircraft designed by the United States specifically as a night fighter?

  a. P-38M
  b. P-61 Black Widow
  c. P-70 Nighthawk
  d. Havoc MKII

158. This firearm was designed to have the attributes of both a rifle and a machine gun:

  a. Browning M2
  b. Browning M1919
  c. Browning automatic rifle
  d. Type 11 light machine gun

159. What was the primary rifle issued to U.S. soldiers?

  a. M1 carbine
  b. M1 Garand
  c. Thompson
  d. Browning automatic rifle

160. What was the battle in 1943 that paved the way for the invasion of mainland Europe?

    a. Normandy

    b. Kokoda Trail

    c. Gieszl

    d. Sicily

161. What was the last great tank offensive by the Germans on the Western Front? The film about this battle starred Henry Fonda and James MacArthur.

    a. Last Great Tank Battle

    b. Somme

    c. Operation Breakout

    d. Battle of the Bulge

162. What was the German code name for their summer invasion of Russia in 1941?

    a. Sealion

    b. Overlord

    c. Torch

    d. Barbarossa

163. This aircraft played a vital role in winning the Battle of Britain:

    a. P-51

    b. Spitfire

    c. Hellcat

    d. Zero

164. What happened to Mussolini, the leader of Italy?

    a. Shot by Americans

    b. Shot by Italians

    c. Shot by Germans

    d. Escaped to Argentina

165. Who was the greatest Soviet commander of the war?

    a. General Koniev
    b. General Yeremenko
    c. General Rokossovsky
    d. General Zhukov

166. What was the primary bomber of the Royal Air Force Bomber Command after 1943?

    a. Blenheim
    b. Stirling
    c. Lancaster
    d. Halifax

167. What island north of Guadalcanal was the backdrop for many of the surface naval battles?

    a. Santo
    b. Sago
    c. Savo
    d. Samar

168. Two admirals of the U.S. Navy died during the same night action on November 13, 1942, during the Battle of Guadalcanal, and both were awarded the Medal of Honor for their actions in defeating the Japanese. Who were they?

    a. Rear Admiral Scott and Rear Admiral Callaghan
    b. Vice Admiral Halsey and Admiral Nimitz
    c. Rear Admiral Turner and Rear Admiral Ghormley
    d. Vice Admiral Fletcher and Rear Admiral Spruance

169. What design drawback did the first T-34 tanks have?

    a. Crew arrangement
    b. Transmission
    c. Radios
    d. All of the above

170. How many Japanese carriers were sunk during the Battle of Midway?

    a. Four
    b. Twelve
    c. Three
    d. Nine

171. The *Graf Spee* was one of the most famous German commerce raiders of World War II. Although limited in size as a cruiser by the Treaty of Versailles, it was armed as a battleship. After sinking nine Allied merchant ships, it was finally caught by three British ships at the Battle of the River Plate. The *Graf Spee* went into a neutral port for repairs, but was forced to leave after seventy-two hours by international law. Faced with what he believed to be overwhelming odds, the captain scuttled his ship rather than risk the lives of his crew. What was this neutral port?

    a. San Carlos
    b. Buenos Aires
    c. Montevideo
    d. Narvik

172. What aircraft company built the F4U Corsair?

    a. Vought
    b. Lockheed
    c. Grumman
    d. Douglas

173. The British people were jubilant after the incredible evacuation of the British Army from Dunkirk. It prevented what would have been the largest surrender in British history, and would certainly have been followed by the immediate invasion of England by the Nazis. In response to this great victory, who said: "Wars are not won by evacuation"?

    a. Winston Churchill
    b. Lord Halifax
    c. Neville Chamberlain
    d. Clement Attlee

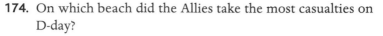
174. On which beach did the Allies take the most casualties on D-day?

    a. Utah
    b. Juno
    c. Gold
    d. Omaha

175. What country suffered the most military deaths in the war?

    a. U.S.S.R.
    b. United States
    c. Germany
    d. Great Britain

176. What caused the bad drop of airborne forces into Sicily?

    a. High winds
    b. Lack of radar pathfinders
    c. Badly trained aircrews
    d. All of the above

177. What was the antitank weapon whose name can be translated as "armor fist"?

    a. Bazooka M9
    b. Panzershreck
    c. Panzerfaust
    d. PIAT

178. What country gave the English language the word *quisling* (traitor) during the war?

    a. Denmark
    b. France
    c. Norway
    d. Soviet Union

179. The German 88 was a:

    a. Dive-bomber
    b. Antiaircraft and antitank weapon
    c. Flamethrower
    d. Rail gun

180. In what year did Adolf Hitler come to power in Germany?

    a. 1933

    b. 1939

    c. 1929

    d. 1934

181. What was the allegiance of Bulgaria during the war?

    a. Allies, then Axis

    b. Axis, then Allies

    c. Axis

    d. Allies

182. What was the official name for the internment camps for Japanese Americans?

    a. Moving centers

    b. Concentration camps

    c. Relocation centers

    d. Living centers

183. During which battle did a photographer take the picture of Marines raising the flag on Mount Suribachi?

    a. Okinawa

    b. Guadalcanal

    c. Midway

    d. Iwo Jima

184. Who was the Russian general who commanded the Sixty-second Army at the Battle of Stalingrad, and then later accepted the surrender of Berlin?

    a. Ivan Chernyakhovsky

    b. Vasily Chuikov

    c. Alexander Klubov

    d. Pavel Rybalko

185. What was the nickname for the P-51 aircraft?

   a. Liberator
   b. Mustang
   c. Thunderbolt
   d. Typhoon

186. Who was the officer in charge of the aircraft that dropped the atomic bomb on Hiroshima, and was later the subject of a movie starring Robert Taylor?

   a. Nick Heiser
   b. George Charter
   c. Paul Tibbets
   d. Ben Lang

187. After General MacArthur fled the Philippines, who did he leave in charge, who ultimately had to surrender his troops on Corregidor to the Japanese?

   a. General Blankenship
   b. General Wainwright
   c. General Sharp
   d. General Sutherland

188. What was the official designation of the Japanese fighter nicknamed the Zeke?

   a. Mitsubishi A6M Zero-Sen
   b. Kawasaki Ki-102
   c. Mitsubishi A5M
   d. Aichi D3A

189. What aircraft is better known as the Mitchell, named after General Billy Mitchell, who was court-martialed for advocating air power, and whose biopic starred Gary Cooper?

   a. B-24
   b. B-26
   c. B-25
   d. P-51

190. Which aircraft is also known as the Marauder?

    a. B-17
    b. B-26
    c. P-35
    d. P-47

191. This was a "trench gun" version of a shotgun that had been developed for clearing trenches during World War I, and that proved effective for the U.S. Marines in clearing the caves and trenches of Japanese-occupied islands in the Pacific during World War II:

    a. Winchester model 1912
    b. DeLisle shotgun
    c. Winchester model 1897
    d. Berthier 1916

192. Before the invasion of Poland and the start of the European war in 1939, which two countries were already at war?

    a. Japan and China
    b. Japan and Malaya
    c. Poland and the Soviet Union
    d. North Korea and South Korea

193. The Battle of the Bulge was a massive spearhead counterattack by 1 million German troops that occurred in which part of France?

    a. Hurtgen Forest
    b. Ardennes
    c. Champagne
    d. Monts Foucille

194. Which troops were the first to enter Berchtesgaden, Hitler's retreat in Austria?

    a. 101st Airborne
    b. Fifth Rangers
    c. Seventy-first Airborne
    d. Second Rangers

195. What did the Navy do to honor the Sullivan brothers after all five of them were killed in action when their warship was sunk?

  a. Buried them in Arlington National Cemetery
  b. Set up a fund for their family
  c. Gave their mother a plaque
  d. Named a ship after them

196. Churchill pushed the idea of attacking the "soft underbelly" of the Axis powers. Why anyone listened to him, after his similar campaign in the Dardanelles in World War I turned into a monumental disaster, is a puzzle. What was the country that Churchill considered the "soft underbelly"?

  a. Greece
  b. Austria
  c. Yugoslavia
  d. Italy

197. The largest tank battle of the war took place where?

  a. Stalingrad
  b. Leningrad
  c. Iwo Jima
  d. Kursk

198. What German-speaking region of Czechoslovakia did the Allies allow Hitler to annex to the Third Reich, after which Chamberlain announced that we had achieved "peace in our time"?

  a. Bavaria
  b. Alsace
  c. Sudetenland
  d. Lorraine

199. What was the main Soviet battle tank of the war?

  a. T62
  b. T51
  c. T72
  d. T34

200. The nickname given by the U.S. Marines to the nightly bombardment by Japanese warships of Henderson Field on Guadalcanal in October 1942 was:

    a. Tojo's Parade
    b. Death on Parade
    c. Yamato Express
    d. Tokyo Express

201. What was the date on which Japan formally signed the surrender documents?

    a. April 8, 1945
    b. December 15, 1945
    c. October 14, 1945
    d. September 2, 1945

202. The only nation that did not produce tank destroyers during the war was:

    a. United Kingdom
    b. Germany
    c. United States
    d. Japan

203. In what battle did the U.S. Navy lose the carrier *Yorktown*?

    a. Battle of the Coral Sea
    b. Key Atoll
    c. Battle of the Denmark Strait
    d. Battle of Midway

204. What type of vessel was successfully used to neutralize the *Tirpitz*, making it possible to sink it eventually?

    a. B-Craft
    b. X-Craft
    c. U-Craft
    d. Z-Craft

205. Who designed the P-51 aircraft?

    a. Northrop

    b. North American Aviation

    c. Boeing

    d. Douglas

206. Which two crewmen had battle stations in the nose of the B-17?

    a. Flight engineer and navigator

    b. Bombardier and navigator

    c. Radio operator and bombardier

    d. Radio operator and navigator

207. What was different about the Bell P-39 Airacobra fighter plane?

    a. Engine was located behind the cockpit

    b. Its gun fired through the propeller shaft

    c. It had a nose wheel

    d. All of the above

208. The term *doodlebugs* was used by the English to describe:

    a. German buzz bombs

    b. Small deadly land mines dropped by German aircraft

    c. Enemy aircraft burning as they fell

    d. The Horsley Hawker Bomber

209. Which hand grenade was popularly known as the potato masher?

    a. Mk 1

    b. RDG-33

    c. Stielhandgranate

    d. M2

210. The most feared German tank of the war was capable of destroying the American Sherman or British Churchill IV at ranges exceeding 1,600 meters, and the Soviet T-34 equipped with the 76.2 millimeter gun could not penetrate this tank in a face-to-face confrontation at any range. What was it called?

   a. Panzer Mk V Panther
   b. Panzer Mk VI Tiger
   c. Panzer Mk IV
   d. Panzer Mk VII Jaguar

211. Which type of aircraft saw military use for the first time during the war?

   a. Helicopter
   b. Harrier
   c. Biplane
   d. Osprey

212. What British warship was sunk while at anchor at Scapa Flow on October 14, 1939?

   a. *Hood*
   b. *Ark Royal*
   c. *Royal Oak*
   d. *Barham*

213. The greatest air raid of the war occurred on February 13–15, 1945, as part of Operation Thunderclap, in which bombers from the Royal Air Force and U.S. Air Force completely destroyed a German city with firebombs. The U.S. Army War College regularly assigns a paper in which students debate whether this raid should be considered a war crime. The city attacked was:

   a. Berlin
   b. Munich
   c. Hamburg
   d. Dresden

214. What event, orchestrated by Hitler, ensured that he would be declared dictator of Germany?

  a. Battle of Britain
  b. Destruction of Jewish shops
  c. Anschluss with Austria
  d. Reichstag fire

215. What was the only U.S. Army airborne division that did not go into combat during the war?

  a. Eighty-second Airborne
  b. Eleventh Airborne
  c. Thirteenth Airborne
  d. Seventeenth Airborne

216. After the surrender of France, a new government controlled and dominated by the Germans was established in which French town?

  a. Paris
  b. Vichy
  c. Bordeaux
  d. Marseille

217. The German Wirbelwind antiaircraft vehicle was fitted with how many 20 millimeter cannons?

  a. Four
  b. Three
  c. Six
  d. One

218. The most well known of the six flag raisers on Iwo Jima, he was the subject of songs recorded by Johnny Cash and Bob Dylan. He was the only American Indian among the flag raisers, and his biopic starred Tony Curtis. Who was he?

  a. Ira Hayes
  b. Franklin Sousley
  c. Mike Strank
  d. Harlon Block

219. The Japanese landed in Malaya and Thailand on December 8, 1941. How long was it before they covered the 550 miles to Singapore?

   a. Eighteen months
   b. Six months
   c. Two months
   d. Fourteen months

220. Who was the commanding general in Hawaii on the day that the Japanese bombed Pearl Harbor?

   a. Sherman Miles
   b. Walter C. Short
   c. Charles D. Herron
   d. Leonard T. Gerow

221. North American designed this long-range, single-engine fighter that featured six machine guns:

   a. P-38L
   b. P-47
   c. F6F
   d. P-51D

222. Different variants of the P-38 Lightning included:

   a. F-5 reconnaissance
   b. XP-58 chain
   c. XP-49 high altitude
   d. All of the above

223. Who was the first Frenchman in the war to beat the record of seventy-five kills set by René Fonck in the First World War?

   a. Francois Morel
   b. No one topped Fonck
   c. Pierre LeGloan
   d. Pierre Clostermann

224. Which of the following performed an appendectomy while aboard a U.S. submarine?

   a. Thomas Moore on the U.S.S. *Silversides*
   b. Wheeler B. Lipes on the U.S.S. *Seadragon*
   c. Harry B. Roby on the U.S.S. *Grayback*
   d. All of the above

225. The Reverend John Weir Foote was awarded the Victoria Cross for his part in the Dieppe Raid in 1942. Captain Foote, during the eight hours of the battle, walked about collecting the wounded. His actions saved many lives and inspired those around him by his example. At the end of this gruelling battle he climbed from the landing craft that was to have taken him to safety and deliberately walked into the German position in order to be taken prisoner so that he could help those men who would be in captivity, where he remained for the rest of the war. What was his nationality?

   a. English
   b. Canadian
   c. Australian
   d. Irish

226. Which country was not allied with Germany in Operation Barbarossa?

   a. Romania
   b. Soviet Union
   c. Slovakia
   d. Italy

227. What was the nickname the Allies gave to a German propaganda broadcaster?

   a. Munich Gertie
   b. Wartburg Wilma
   c. Berlin Barbie
   d. Axis Sally

228. On which river was the battle of Stalingrad fought?

   a. Don
   b. Donets
   c. Ural
   d. Volga

229. What was the date on which France and Britain declared war on Germany?

   a. October 6, 1939
   b. September 4, 1940
   c. September 3, 1939
   d. September 9, 1938

230. Why were the Solomon Islands important to the Allied strategy for winning the war against the Japanese in the Pacific?

   a. Protect the lifeline to Australia and New Zealand
   b. Stop the construction of an airfield on Guadalcanal
   c. The victory at Midway made it possible to go on the offensive
   d. All of these reasons

231. Which of the flag raisers on Iwo Jima was not a member of the U.S. Marine Corps?

   a. John Bradley
   b. Rene Gagnon
   c. Ira Hayes
   d. Mike Strank

232. Who was in command of the Pacific Fleet when the Japanese launched their sneak attack on Pearl Harbor, and who was played by Martin Balsam in the film *Tora! Tora! Tora!*

   a. Richmond Kelly Turner
   b. William F. Halsey
   c. Husband E. Kimmel
   d. Chester W. Nimitz

233. How long was the training given to crews on the Italian M13/40 and M14/41 tanks?

   a. Six months
   b. Twenty-five days
   c. One hundred twenty days
   d. One year

234. Which of the following was an armored car?

   a. M8 Greyhound
   b. P-38
   c. M22 Locust
   d. M4 Sherman

235. Which tank used during the war was not equipped with a cannon?

   a. Churchill
   b. Panzer I
   c. Panzer II
   d. M4 Sherman

236. Who was the captain of the *Bismarck*?

   a. Erich Forste
   b. Karl Topp
   c. Kurt Hoffmann
   d. Ernst Lindemann

237. Which German admiral was given the nickname Father of the U-Boat Weapon?

   a. Erich Raeder
   b. Wilhelm Marschall
   c. Otto Schultze
   d. Karl Donitz

238. Which torpedo problem was not experienced by U.S. submarines during the war?

   a. Inaccurate depth control
   b. Premature explosion
   c. Crushed firing pin
   d. Explosion too large

239. Who was the admiral in charge of the *Bismarck*?

   a. Luetjens
   b. Wattenburg
   c. Scheer
   d. Wolff

240. Torpedo bombers performed which ancillary task?

   a. Strafing
   b. Kamikaze runs
   c. Signaling
   d. Reconnaissance

241. Which U.S. fighter was unstable and had a tendency to spin, because its engine was located in the middle of the fuselage?

   a. Republic P-47 Thunderbolt
   b. Curtis P-40 Tomahawk
   c. Bell P-39 Airacobra
   d. Lockheed P-38 Lightning

242. The men under General Claire Chennault in the AVG in China, before the United States entered the war against Japan, were flying which aircraft?

   a. Chance-Vought F4U Corsair
   b. Brewster F2A-2 Buffalo
   c. Grumman F4F Wildcat
   d. Curtis P-40 Warhawk

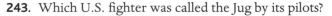

243. Which U.S. fighter was called the Jug by its pilots?

    a. P-47 Thunderbolt

    b. P-35 Buffalo

    c. P-51 Mustang

    d. P-38 Lightning

244. The unsuccessful twin engine medium bomber that was re-engineered and became the Lancaster was the:

    a. Whitley

    b. Manchester

    c. Hampden

    d. Wellington

245. Which combat rifle made a unique ping sound when the last round was ejected?

    a. Lee-Enfield

    b. Mosin-Nagant

    c. M1 Garand

    d. Gewehr 98

246. What was the name of the prison in which Rudolf Hess was held?

    a. Andersonville

    b. Alcatraz

    c. Spandau

    d. Libby

247. What action resulted in the sinking of the Sullivan brothers' ship?

    a. Collision with an enemy ship

    b. Torpedo

    c. Collision with an Allied ship

    d. Aircraft bombing

PRIVATE FIRST CLASS ANSWERS

1. a.	36. b.	71. d	106. a.	141. b.
2. c.	37. c.	72. c.	107. b.	142. d.
3. c.	38. c.	73. c.	108. a.	143. b.
4. c.	39. c.	74. c.	109. c.	144. a.
5. d.	40. b.	75. b.	110. d.	145. d.
6. b.	41. a.	76. a.	111. d.	146. b.
7. d.	42. a.	77. a.	112. b.	147. c.
8. a.	43. d.	78. b.	113. c.	148. d.
9. a.	44. c.	79. c.	114. d.	149. a.
10. a.	45. d.	80. c.	115. c.	150. d.
11. a.	46. b.	81. d.	116. d.	151. b.
12. d.	47. d.	82. a.	117. c.	152. d.
13. c.	48. b.	83. c.	118. c.	153. d.
14. b.	49. c.	84. d.	119. d.	154. c.
15. b.	50. a.	85. d.	120. a.	155. d.
16. d.	51. d.	86. c.	121. c.	156. d.
17. b.	52. d.	87. c.	122. c.	157. b.
18. b.	53. a.	88. b.	123. d.	158. c.
19. b.	54. c.	89. b.	124. a.	159. b.
20. a.	55. c.	90. c.	125. c.	160. d.
21. d.	56. d.	91. a.	126. d.	161. d.
22. c.	57. c.	92. c.	127. a.	162. d.
23. a.	58. c.	93. b.	128. d.	163. b.
24. c.	59. b.	94. c.	129. c.	164. b.
25. a.	60. c.	95. b.	130. d.	165. d.
26. c.	61. b.	96. a.	131. b.	166. c.
27. c.	62. d.	97. a.	132. b.	167. c.
28. a.	63. d.	98. a.	133. c.	168. a.
29. a.	64. b.	99. b	134. c.	169. d.
30. c.	65. d.	100. b.	135. b.	170. a.
31. b.	66. c.	101. a.	136. c.	171. c
32. c.	67. b.	102. a.	137. d.	172. a.
33. a.	68. c.	103. b	138. b.	173. a.
34. d.	69. d.	104. c.	139. c.	174. d.
35. b.	70. c.	105. a.	140. d.	175. a.

176. d.	191. a.	206. b.	221. d.	236. d.
177. c.	192. a.	207. d.	222. d.	237. d.
178. c.	193. b.	208. a.	223. b.	238. d.
179. b.	194. a.	209. c.	224. d.	239. a.
180. a.	195. d.	210. b.	225. b.	240. d.
181. b.	196. d.	211. a.	226. b.	241. c.
182. c.	197. d.	212. c.	227. d.	242. d.
183. d.	198. c.	213. d.	228. d.	243. a.
184. b.	199. d.	214. d.	229. c.	244. b.
185. b.	200. d.	215. c.	230. d.	245. c.
186. c.	201. d.	216. b.	231. a.	246. c.
187. b.	202. d.	217. a.	232. c.	247. b.
188. a.	203. d.	218. a.	233. b.	
189. c.	204. b.	219. c.	234. a.	
190. b.	205. b.	220. b.	235. b.	

SERGEANT

If you got this far, and have been successful in answering most of the questions, then it's time to pump up the volume. The questions just keep getting harder!

1. What type of aircraft was the German Stuka?
   a. Fighter
   b. Transport
   c. Bomber
   d. Dive-bomber

2. Which doctor became infamous for his experiments on prisoners at Auschwitz and fled to Argentina after the war?
   a. Josef Goebbels
   b. Horst Heinz Stramm
   c. Josef Bechel
   d. Josef Mengele

3. In what month and year did the Allies invade Sicily?
   a. August 1942
   b. July 1943
   c. May 1944
   d. September 1945

4. The first tank battle involving the United States in North Africa, in which an inferior number of battle-hardened Afrika Korps tankers inflicted a crushing defeat on a superior U.S. force, was the:

    a. Battle of Alam Halfa
    b. Battle of Kasserine Pass
    c. Battle of Bir Hacheim
    d. Battle of Halfaya Pass

5. Which Royal Navy aircraft carrier launched biplane Fairey Swordfish to attack the Italian naval base at Taranto in November 1940, sinking or disabling three Italian battleships and a cruiser?

    a. HMS *Courageous*
    b. HMS *Invincible*
    c. HMS *Glorious*
    d. HMS *Illustrious*

6. The reconnaissance pilot who found the survivors of the *Indianapolis* in the water, being eaten by sharks, was on a patrol searching for Japanese:

    a. Aircraft carriers
    b. Destroyers
    c. Cruisers
    d. Submarines

7. With the Army falling back on Manila, the warship *Canopus* sailed to Mariveles Bay at the tip of Bataan on Christmas Day. It received direct bomb hits that resulted in substantial damage to the ship. Working at a fevered pace, its crew continued to care for other ships while keeping their own afloat and in operation. To prevent further Japanese attack, smoke pots were placed around the ship, presenting the appearance of an abandoned hulk by day, while the ship hummed with activity by night. Upon the surrender of Bataan, *Canopus* was ordered scuttled and sunk, and on April 10, it was backed off into deep water under its own power, and the ship that the Japanese could not sink ended a lifetime of service to the Navy when it was laid to rest by its own men. What type of warship or support ship was the U.S.S. *Canopus*?

   a. Electric submarine
   b. Fleet oiler
   c. Destroyer
   d. Submarine tender

8. What enemy aircraft led to the design and production of the A-24 dive-bomber for the U.S. Army Air Corps?

   a. Ju 87 Stuka
   b. Blackburn Skua
   c. B6M
   d. Aichi D3A

9. What Army aircraft were loaded onto an aircraft carrier and launched on the Doolittle Raid to bomb Japan?

   a. B-25 Mitchell
   b. B-26 Marauder
   c. B-17 Flying Fortress
   d. B-24 Liberator

10. Which aircraft did the Germans call the fork-tailed devil?

    a. P-51 Mustang
    b. de Havilland Mosquito
    c. P-61 Blackwidow
    d. P-38 Lightning

11. Which of these Japanese war crimes was not widely reported during the Nanjing Massacre?

    a. Arson
    b. Corpse mutilation
    c. Grave desecration
    d. Theft

12. What was notable about the U.S.S. *Argonaut*?

    a. Originally designed as a minelayer
    b. Delivered Edson's Raiders onto Makin Island
    c. Too big for use as a submarine
    d. All of the above

13. Which of these men had at least one artificial limb?

    a. Artur Axmann, head of the Hitler Youth
    b. Douglas Bader, British ace
    c. Hans Rudel, German Stuka pilot
    d. All of the above

14. The U.S. government was looking for a remote location at which to build the camp to develop the atomic bomb. Robert Oppenheimer had hiked and camped in New Mexico before the war, and suggested that they take over a former boys' school, located at:

    a. Dugway
    b. White Sands
    c. Alamogordo
    d. Los Alamos

15. There were only three operational jet fighters in use during the war; the HE-162, the Meteor, and the:

    a. Messerschmitt Me 262
    b. Supermarine Spitfire
    c. P51 Mustang
    d. Messerschmitt Me 110

16. The most widely used bomber in the European and Pacific theaters was the:

    a. Boeing B-17
    b. Tupolev Tu2
    c. Lancaster
    d. Hienkel He 111

17. Who was the designer of the TT-33 pistol?

    a. Tokarev
    b. Mauser
    c. Luger
    d. Walther

18. The supply ship of the pocket battleship *Graf Spee* tried to return to Germany after the *Graf Spee* was scuttled near Montevideo, with 300 British merchant seamen aboard as prisoners of war. What was the supply ship's name?

    a. *Cossack*
    b. *Altmark*
    c. *Emden*
    d. *Lutzow*

19. On September 3, 1939, just hours after Britain declared war on Germany, U-boat 30 sank a passenger liner, mistaking it for an armed merchant cruiser. As this was an unarmed passenger ship, the attack was in violation of the prize rules under which U-boats were then operating, which obliged them to stop and search potential civilian targets and allow passengers and crew to abandon ship before sinking their vessel. A total of 118 passengers and crew were killed, including twenty-eight Americans, which led to German fears that the incident would bring the United States into the war. Having realized their error after the torpedoes hit, U-30 immediately disengaged, left the scene, and did not report its attack until it reached port. Since the torpedoing violated the rules of war then in force, Hitler ordered evidence of it suppressed, and Lemp's log was rewritten. What was the name of the ship?

    a. *Lusitania*
    b. *Athenia*
    c. *Imo*
    d. *Mont Blanc*

20. In what country is El Alamein, location of one of the major battles in North Africa?

    a. Libya
    b. Egypt
    c. Tunisia
    d. Algeria

21. The size of the main gun of the Sherman tank was:

    a. 75 millimeter
    b. 90 millimeter
    c. 37 millimeter
    d. 105 millimeter

22. Why wasn't Admiral Halsey present at the Battle of Midway?

    a. He was directing the battle from Guam
    b. His force was steaming in the wrong direction
    c. He was in the hospital
    d. He was in Washington meeting with the Joint Chiefs

23. Why was the capture of Corregidor so vital strategically to the Japanese?

    a. Contained a number of airstrips
    b. Gave them control of Manila Bay
    c. Shelter for submarines
    d. Housed a large stockpile of ammunition

24. What tank first saw action at the Battle of Kursk, was a direct response to the T-34, and came to be regarded as the best tank of the war?

    a. Tiger II
    b. Panzer IV
    c. Maus
    d. Panther

25. Which postwar tank was first used in action at the end of the war?

    a. M41 Walker Bulldog
    b. M26 Pershing
    c. Conqueror
    d. AMX-30

26. Which U-boat, commanded by Günther Prien, made a daring raid into Scapa Flow and sank the *Royal Oak*?

    a. U-331
    b. U-2501
    c. U-39
    d. U-47

27. The Japanese nickname for the Corsair was:

    a. Angel of Death
    b. Whistling Death
    c. Grim Reaper
    d. Fork-Tailed Devil

28. Which of the following was not the nickname of a British aircraft?

   a. Cyclone
   b. Hurricane
   c. Tempest
   d. Typhoon

29. The OSS used a single-shot .22 caliber weapon called the:

   a. Stinger
   b. Model 38
   c. Sleever
   d. Gnat

30. Germany's invasion of which country brought Britain and France into the war?

   a. Austria
   b. Poland
   c. Italy
   d. Belgium

31. What was the flower on the sleeve of the German mountain trooper uniform?

   a. Nord
   b. Totenkopf
   c. Das Reich
   d. Edelweiss

32. What South American country declared war on Germany, but was known for being pro-Nazi and gave refuge to Nazis after the war?

   a. Peru
   b. Brazil
   c. Colombia
   d. Argentina

33. Hitler's theory that it was the destiny of the German people to conquer and settle the vast lands of Russia was called:

    a. Untermensch
    b. Einsatzgruppe
    c. Lebensraum
    d. Verdunkeln

34. Which country flew the Mosquito?

    a. Great Britain
    b. United States
    c. Italy
    d. Russia

35. What is the geographical location of Singapore?

    a. Off the southern tip of the Malaysian Peninsula
    b. Between Vietnam and Thailand
    c. Off the eastern tip of Borneo
    d. Between Sumatra and Borneo

36. A Mogami class light cruiser was built in 1935 at Nagasaki and refitted in 1939 to become a heavy cruiser. It fought at the battle of Sunda Strait and was sunk at the Battle of Midway in 1942. What was the ship's name?

    a. *Noraski*
    b. *Ishima*
    c. *Mikuma*
    d. *Airuiki*

37. Which nation's army fielded the Autoblinda Lince scout car?

    a. Germany
    b. France
    c. Italy
    d. Poland

38. What German heavy cruiser sank on its maiden voyage in World War II?

   a. *Luetzow*
   b. *Hipper*
   c. *Prinz Eugen*
   d. *Bluecher*

39. U-boat is an English nickname for:

   a. Untersteuerbooten
   b. Unterseeboot
   c. Unter Hinweghelfen
   d. Unter Gezeiten

40. At noon on August 15, 1945, a speech was delivered over the radio in Japan, signifying the end of World War II. The speaker said, "The war situation has developed not necessarily to Japan's advantage. We have resolved to pave the way for a grand peace for all generations to come by enduring the unendurable and suffering what is unsufferable." Who made this speech?

   a. Yoshimichi Hara
   b. Hideki Tojo
   c. Kantaro Suzuki
   d. Emperor Hirohito

41. Which weapon was designed and built in Australia?

   a. Sten
   b. Owen Machine Carbine
   c. Thompson
   d. PPs 43

42. Awarded the Victoria Cross for aerial operations, after the war he founded a chain of homes for the incurably sick. Who was he?

   a. Willie Tait
   b. Guy Gibson
   c. Leonard Cheshire
   d. Johnnie Fauquier

43. What German battleship spent much of the war seeking refuge in a Norwegian fjord, where it posed a threat to Allied shipping?

   a. *Tirpitz*
   b. *Graf Spee*
   c. *Bismarck*
   d. *Scharnhorst*

44. Which field marshal commanded the German forces fighting the Allies in Italy?

   a. Albert Kesselring
   b. Erich Von Manstein
   c. Friedrich Paulus
   d. Gunther Von Kluge

45. What was the code name for the evacuation of the British Expeditionary Force at Dunkirk, which rescued over 300,000 men?

   a. Chromite
   b. Cobra
   c. Tiger
   d. Dynamo

46. The Navy admiral known as Bull for his aggressive tactics in battle was:

   a. William Halsey
   b. Raymond Spraunce
   c. Chester Nimitz
   d. Jackie Fisher

47. Which D-day landing went so badly that the Allies considered pulling the troops off the beach?

   a. Gold
   b. Utah
   c. Omaha
   d. Sword

48. Which was the first jet aircraft to see combat action?

   a. Bf 109

   b. P-47

   c. FW 190

   d. Me 262

49. Which Nazi Party member flew to Scotland in 1941?

   a. Hermann Goering

   b. Josef Goebbels

   c. Oskar Schindler

   d. Rudolf Hess

50. What was the primary fighter aircraft of the U.S. Army Air Force at the beginning of the war?

   a. P-38 Lightning

   b. P-51 Mustang

   c. P-47 Thunderbolt

   d. P-40 Warhawk

51. What does the letter L stand for in the acronym LVT?

   a. Landing

   b. Lightly

   c. Light

   d. Large

52. Two prototypes of this 188 ton tank were produced before the end of the war. One broke down and the other was captured by opposing forces. What was the tank?

   a. Tiger II

   b. Maus

   c. Panther II

   d. T-54

53. What U.S. carrier was nicknamed the Decrepid by the crews of other Navy ships?

   a. U.S.S. *Intrepid*

   b. U.S.S. *Franklin*

   c. U.S.S. *Saratoga*

   d. U.S.S. *Yorktown*

54. The body of water where the *Bismarck* was first sighted.

    a. Hudson Strait

    b. North Sea

    c. Denmark Strait

    d. Norwegian Sea

55. What was the engine and propeller configuration of the B-17?

    a. Two engines, with three blades per propeller

    b. Two engines, with four blades per propeller

    c. Four engines, with three blades per propeller

    d. Four engines, with four blades per propeller

56. The largest bomb of the war (other than the atomic bomb) was developed specifically to destroy the dams of Germany, in the hopes of flooding the industrial centers of the Ruhr Valley and shortening the war. It was first dropped by the Dam Busters from a Lancaster bomber on March 14, 1945, and was called:

    a. Tall Boy

    b. King Hit

    c. Sucker Punch

    d. Grand Slam

57. On February 22, 1944, the Eighth Air Force mistakenly bombed the following town(s):

    a. Nijmegen

    b. Deventer

    c. Arnhem

    d. All of the above

58. Who said, "The atom bomb was no 'great decision.' It was merely another powerful weapon in the arsenal of righteousness"?

    a. Winston Churchill

    b. Douglas MacArthur

    c. Harry S Truman

    d. Franklin Delano Roosevelt

59. What weapon was nicknamed Hitler's Buzzsaw?

    a. MG-34

    b. Gweher 43

    c. MG-42

    d. Fg-42

60. How did the first Special Forces crack the German fortifications during the Italian campaign?

    a. Heavy infantry attack with artillery support

    b. Nighttime stealth attack

    c. Attacked the German rear defenses

    d. Scaled a mountain thought impassible

61. One military leader initially conceived the idea for the airborne drop into Holland to seize bridges so that the Allies could advance quickly to Eindhoven. This was filmed as *A Bridge Too Far*. Who was the leader?

    a. General George Patton

    b. General Matthew Ridgeway

    c. Field Marshal Bernard Montgomery

    d. General Omar Bradley

62. What was the code name for Germany's invasion of Crete?

    a. Gold

    b. Mercury

    c. Silver

    d. Lead

63. The Sullivan brothers' neighbor, Bill Ball, was serving on which ship when it was sunk at Pearl Harbor?

    a. U.S.S. *Juneau*

    b. U.S.S. *Oklahoma*

    c. U.S.S. *Indianapolis*

    d. U.S.S. *Arizona*

64. Which country did not commit troops to the British Commonwealth Forces?

   a. Irish Free State
   b. New Zealand
   c. South Africa
   d. India

65. What unique weapon was issued to Japanese officers as a symbol of their status?

   a. Samurai sword
   b. Nambu Type 14 pistol
   c. Type 100 SMG
   d. Samurai dagger for hara-kiri

66. Which airborne division was not dropped over Normandy?

   a. 101st Airborne
   b. Third Airborne
   c. Sixth British Airborne
   d. Eighty-second Airborne

67. Nazi units consisting primarily of police and SS committed atrocities when Germany invaded the Soviet Union in June 1941. What were they called?

   a. Gebirgsjager
   b. Etappendienst
   c. Einsatzgruppen
   d. Forschungsamt

68. Winston Churchill, the British prime minister, had served as a junior officer in the military, but he entered politics in 1900 from which profession?

   a. Accountancy
   b. Journalism
   c. Shipping business
   d. Commercial fishing

69. Which long-range fighter enabled U.S. pilots to fly deep into Germany during the final years of the war?

    a. P-38
    b. Spitfire
    c. P-40
    d. P-51

70. The British used which submachine gun?

    a. Sten
    b. PPSh
    c. Bren
    d. MP40

71. What treaty formed the basis for the Axis Coalition?

    a. Anti-Comintern Pact
    b. Treaty of Versailles
    c. Tripartite Pact
    d. Atlantic Charter

72. Begun as a battleship in the same class as the *Yamato* and *Musashi*, it was completed as an aircraft carrier. It was sunk by the U.S.S. *Archerfish* on November 29, 1944. What was the ship called?

    a. *Yashimrio*
    b. *Shinano*
    c. *Muskato*
    d. *Ishimira*

73. Who was the commander of the Japanese force that attacked Pearl Harbor?

    a. Admiral Nagumo
    b. Admiral Abe
    c. Admiral Togo
    d. Admiral Yusaka

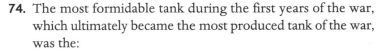
74. The most formidable tank during the first years of the war, which ultimately became the most produced tank of the war, was the:

   a. Panzer IV

   b. Panther

   c. T-34

   d. Cromwell tank

75. Which tank was nicknamed the Cigarette Lighter?

   a. Cromwell tank

   b. M4 Sherman

   c. Churchill tank

   d. T-34

76. After the fall of the Marianas, Imperial General Headquarters developed a plan to commit its entire navy to a decisive battle against the United States, known as:

   a. Go-Go Plan

   b. Tojo-Go Plan

   b. No-Go Plan

   d. Sho-Go Plan

77. The Germans began building only one aircraft carrier, but its construction was halted due to war shortages and it was never finished. What was it called?

   a. *Graf Spee*

   b. *Admiral Dönitz*

   c. *Hindenburg*

   d. *Graf Zeppelin*

78. The Royal Navy cruiser that was badly damaged in its fight with the *Graf Spee*:

   a. HMS *Norfolk*

   b. HMS *Fiji*

   c. HMS *Belfast*

   d. HMS *Exeter*

79. In 1942 the German Navy, in Operation Cerberus, attempted this maneuver in defiance of the Royal Navy:

    a. Shelling the Irish coast

    b. Passing through the English Channel

    c. Attacking Scapa Flow Naval Base

    d. Sinking three British carriers

80. What is the nickname given to the tail gun position?

    a. Thorn

    b. Stinger

    c. Peashooter

    d. Meat Grinder

81. What design feature, also incorporated in an Allied aircraft, made the TA 400 a unique German bomber?

    a. Quadruple vertical tail surfaces

    b. Six independent sets of landing gear

    c. Triple bomb bays

    d. Pressurized front and tail sections connected by a tunnel

82. During World War II, the sky was filled with Lancaster bombers, but few have survived to the present day, and even fewer are still flying. How many Lancasters were still operational at the start of the twenty-first century?

    a. None

    b. Two

    c. Five

    d. Fifteen

83. The P-38 was most successful in:

    a. Eastern Europe

    b. Southwestern Pacific

    c. Western Europe

    d. Northwestern Pacific

84. Which of the following is not a bolt-action rifle, but a semiautomatic rifle?

   a. Karabiner 98k

   b. Springfield 1903

   c. Moisin-Nagant 1891/30

   d. SVT-40

85. When and where was Adolf Hitler born?

   a. Hamburg, Germany; April 19, 1891

   b. Vienna, Austria; April 20, 1900

   c. Braunau am Inn, Austria; April 20, 1889

   d. Bonn, Germany; May 23, 1887

86. Who was the first general to command Chinese troops, who was not himself Chinese?

   a. Lieutenant General Joseph W. Stilwell

   b. General Albert C. Wedemeyer

   c. Lieutenant General Daniel I. Sultan

   d. Major General Patrick J. Hurley

87. The U.S. press christened this German commander in Italy "Smiling Albert":

   a. Guderain

   b. Kesselring

   c. Manstein

   d. Runsdedt

88. The commander of the U.S. Pacific Fleet at Pearl Harbor, who was relieved after the attack, was:

   a. Conrad Helfrich

   b. William Leahy

   c. Husband Kimmel

   d. Fred Sherman

89. The Puma was what type of combat vehicle?

   a. Heavy tank

   b. Heavy armored car

   c. Half-track

   d. Light tank

90. The largest aircraft carrier of the war was the:

   a. U.S.S. *Lexington*

   b. IJN *Shinano*

   c. HMS *Illustrious*

   d. SBK *Graf Zeppelin*

91. One of the worst aircraft for the United States was the Bell P-39. What country was successful in fielding the aircraft?

   a. United Kingdom

   b. Russia

   c. China

   d. France

92. The single-engine U.S. Navy fighter designed by Vought whose unique feature was an inverted gull wing was the:

   a. F4U

   b. F6F

   c. F4F

   d. AD-1

93. What did the "Bf" in Messerschmitt Bf 109 represent?

   a. Bomber-fighter

   b. Big fighter

   c. Bomben-Flugzeug

   d. Bayerische Flugzeugwerke

94. Where did the South African Air Force buy their aircraft at the beginning of the war?

   a. Black market

   b. German Air Force

   c. U.S. Air Force

   d. South African Airlines

95. What was the standard armament of the Republic P-47?

   a. Two 20 millimeter cannons

   b. Four .50 inch machine guns and two 20 millimeter cannons

   c. Four 20 millimeter cannons

   d. Six or eight .50 inch machine guns

96. What machine gun was called Hitler's Buzzsaw?

   a. MG42

   b. SG43

   c. MG34

   d. M2HB

97. In what year did the U.S. Army start their Airborne program?

   a. 1932

   b. 1915

   c. 1940

   d. 1955

98. On D-day, this town was taken by the Eighty-second Airborne, while the 101st Airborne held the surrounding causeways, preventing German reinforcements from reaching the Utah beachhead:

   a. Ste. Mere-Eglise

   b. Cherbourg

   c. Les Moullins

   d. Chef du Pont

99. On D-day, the Rangers had the tough job of taking the well-fortified guns in a position between the Omaha and Utah beachheads. They were shocked to discover, after heavy losses, that the guns had not been installed. What was the position called?

   a. Barfleur

   b. Valognes

   c. St. Lo

   d. Pointe du Hoc

100. What was the code name for the Allied campaign to take Arnhem in the fall of 1944 recounted in the feature film *A Bridge Too Far*?

   a. Operation Bridgehead
   b. Operation Flying Fox
   c. Operation Ulysses
   d. Operation Market Garden

101. In what year was Germany admitted to the League of Nations?

   a. 1926
   b. 1945
   c. 1933
   d. 1939

102. In what year did Chamberlain meet with Hitler at the Munich Conference?

   a. 1938
   b. 1941
   c. 1936
   d. 1933

103. Who was the most decorated soldier of World War II, whose decorations included the Congressional Medal of Honor?

   a. Captain Franklin Pierce
   b. Lieutenant Audie Leon Murphy
   c. Sergeant J. T. York
   d. Lieutenant Aaron Murray

104. What was the first jet-propelled fighter to see combat during the war?

   a. Me 336
   b. Fokker 265
   c. Junkers 47
   d. Me 262

105. What are the dates for the beginning and end of the war?

   a. September 1, 1939–August 14, 1945

   b. September 23, 1939–September 12, 1945

   c. August 31, 1938–August 23, 1945

   d. October 30, 1939–July 3, 1945

106. Which country, directly to the north of Germany, was taken over by the Nazis as part of their policy of Germanic unification?

   a. Sweden

   b. Britain

   c. Denmark

   d. Austria

107. What was the only part of British territory occupied by German forces during the war?

   a. Channel Islands

   b. Gibraltar

   c. Falkland Islands

   d. St. Helena

108. REMF is a military term still in common use. MF stood for "mother f**kers." What did RE stand for?

   a. Rear echelon

   b. Routine evacuee

   c. Restricted engagement

   d. Reserve enlisted

109. Between November 1944 and April 1945, Japan launched
over 9,000 fire balloons. Carried by the Pacific jet stream,
they were designed to float over the Pacific Ocean and land
in North America, where the Japanese hoped they would
start forest fires and cause other damage. About 300 were
reported as reaching North America, but little damage occurred. Six people (five children and a woman) became
the only deaths due to enemy action to occur in mainland
America during World War II, when one of the children
tampered with a bomb from a balloon and it exploded. In
what state did this occur?

   a. Washington
   b. Oregon
   c. Idaho
   d. California

110. What was the name by which Germany was known between the world wars?

   a. Weimar Republic
   b. German Republic
   c. Reichstag
   d. Federal Republic of Germany

111. What was the concrete-reinforced defensive position built
by the Germans along the French coast, which they thought
would prevent a successful invasion of the Continent?

   a. Atlantikwall
   b. Westwall
   c. Sudwall
   d. Ostwall

112. During the war, three short notes followed by one long
note became synonymous in the minds of the public with
the word *victory*. From what musical work did these notes
originate?

   a. Mozart's *Magic Flute*
   b. Beethoven's Fifth Symphony
   c. Haydn's "Surprise" Symphony
   d. Handel's *Music for the Royal Fireworks*

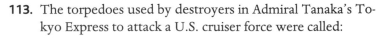
113. The torpedoes used by destroyers in Admiral Tanaka's Tokyo Express to attack a U.S. cruiser force were called:

    a. Long Lance
    b. Long Arrow
    c. Long Tom
    d. Long Harpoon

114. A Japanese submarine support ship named *Tsurugisaki* was converted into a light aircraft carrier and sunk during the Battle of the Coral Sea by dive-bombers and torpedo aircraft from the U.S.S. *Lexington* and U.S.S. *Yorktown*. What was the Japanese ship called?

    a. *Taiho*
    b. *Junyo*
    c. *Zuiho*
    d. *Shoho*

115. The method by which the brutal guards at the Cabanatuan camp killed prisoners for almost any offense was:

    a. Disembowling
    b. Firing squad
    c. Beheading
    d. Hanging

116. What was the island to which the U.S.S. *Indianapolis* delivered the atomic bomb?

    a. Guam
    b. Tinian
    c. Leyte
    d. Okinawa

117. The self propelled gun that used the T-34 tank chassis was the:

    a. SU-85
    b. SU-100
    c. SU-122
    d. All of the above

118. How many U.S. submarines were sunk during the war?

    a. 12

    b. 237

    c. 125

    d. 52

119. What was the largest German capital warship to survive the war?

    a. Heavy cruiser *Prinz Eugen*

    b. Destroyer Z-36

    c. Pocket battleship *Admiral Scheer*

    d. Battleship *Tirpitz*

120. Who designed the Spitfire?

    a. George de Havilland

    b. R. J. Mitchell

    c. H. Whitley Armstrong

    d. Jack Northrop

121. Which bomber was turned into the Havoc night fighter?

    a. Baltimore

    b. Boston

    c. Maryland

    d. Washington

122. The U.S. Liberty ship *Booker T. Washington* was the first U.S. merchant ship to be:

    a. Christened by an African American

    b. Named for an African American

    c. Commanded by an African American

    d. All of the above

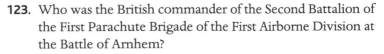
123. Who was the British commander of the Second Battalion of the First Parachute Brigade of the First Airborne Division at the Battle of Arnhem?

    a. Lieutenant Colonel Dobie
    b. Major Gough
    c. Brigadier Lathbury
    d. Lieutenant Colonel Frost

124. What American field commander was most respected by the German General Staff?

    a. General Dwight D. Eisenhower
    b. General Omar N. Bradley
    c. Field Marshal Bernard L. Montgomery
    d. General George S. Patton Jr.

125. The year that Japan invaded Manchuria was:

    a. 1939
    b. 1931
    c. 1941
    d. 1943

126. What was the heavy cruiser that was sunk with great loss of life two weeks before the end of the war?

    a. U.S.S. *New Jersey*
    b. U.S.S. *Indiana*
    c. U.S.S. *Chicago*
    d. U.S.S. *Indianapolis*

127. What future president was shot down as a U.S. Navy pilot over Iwo Jima and rescued by a submarine?

    a. Lyndon B. Johnson
    b. Gerald R. Ford
    c. Jimmy Carter
    d. George H. W. Bush

128. After Hitler absorbed Austria into the Third Reich, what was the next country on his list?

   a. Poland
   b. France
   c. Czechoslovakia
   d. Denmark

129. The Japanese general who with a much smaller force conquered Singapore, captured or killed 130,000 British, Australian, and Indian troops, and earned the nickname the Tiger of Malaya was:

   a. Iwabuchi
   b. Homma
   c. Yamashita
   d. Honda

130. General Patton, who commanded the U.S. Third Army in Europe, was under the direct operational control of:

   a. General Hodges
   b. Field Marshal Montgomery
   c. General Patch
   d. General Bradley

131. What was the nickname given to the seabed where many ships were sunk between Savo Island, Tulagi, and Guadalcanal?

   a. Ironbottom Sound
   b. Ironbottom Channel
   c. Ironbottom Strait
   d. None of the above

132. Of the six men who raised the flag on Iwo Jima, how many did not survive the battle?

   a. One
   b. Three
   c. Five
   d. None of them

133. The British officers charged with defending, and later surrendering, the fortress of Singapore believed that the Japanese soldiers were:

   a. Poor fighters with poor eyesight
   b. Battle hardened and disciplined
   c. Savage and ruthless
   d. Eager, but with poor command

134. Who was the Japanese commander of the island fortress of Iwo Jima?

   a. General Mitbishai
   b. General Mitubishi
   c. General Kuribayashi
   d. General Kuribashai

135. The U.S. Marines made a heroic stand in December 1941 on an island in the central Pacific. The event was made into a film named after the island, starring William Bendix. What island was it?

   a. Luzon
   b. Midway Island
   c. Wake Island
   d. Guadalcanal

136. How did the United States defeat the Japanese at Kiska during the campaign in the Aleutians?

   a. A critical Japanese supply ship was sunk
   b. The Japanese committed mass suicide
   c. Overwhelming superior force
   d. The Japanese evacuated before the landing

137. What was the first official designation of the Sherman tank?

   a. M4 medium tank
   b. Sherman
   c. M4 Sherman
   d. M4 light tank

138. At the Battle of Leyte Gulf, the Japanese divided their fleet into how many naval groups?
    a. Five
    b. Three
    b. Two
    d. Six

139. The caliber of the U.S.S. *Nevada*'s main armament was:
    a. 15 inch
    b. 13 inch
    c. 12 inch
    d. 14 inch

140. The prototype *panzerschiff* or pocket battleship took part in the Norwegian campaign in 1940, and in December 1942 fought at the Battle of the Barents Sea. On April 16, 1945, it was badly damaged by bombs at Swinemünde and subsequently scuttled. What was its name?
    a. *Tirpitz*
    b. *Deutschland*
    c. *Bismarck*
    d. *Hipper*

141. How many German submarines were lost in combat during the war?
    a. 59
    b. 125
    c. 781
    d. 1,203

142. What class of German cruisers did the *Hipper* belong to?
    a. Hipper
    b. Bismarck
    c. Dido
    d. Littorio

143. The Hawker Hurricane was built not only in Britain, but also in:

    a. United States
    b. Australia
    c. Sweden
    d. Canada

144. What bomber was used in the Doolittle Raid?

    a. B-29 Strofortress
    b. B-17 Flying Fortress
    c. B-25 Mitchell
    d. B-24 Liberator

145. What two-engine aircraft was Germany's multipurpose bomber?

    a. Ju 89
    b. He 111
    c. Ju 88
    d. Do 17

146. Since it was designed as a Navy fighter aircraft to be deployed on carriers, why were the first deliveries of the Corsair made to the U.S. Marine Corps?

    a. Insufficient numbers of aircraft
    b. Insufficient power at takeoff
    c. Initial problems with the rear landing gear
    d. Insufficient forward visibility for carrier operations

147. The B-17 G model had what new additional feature that distinguished it from previous models?

    a. Ball turret
    b. Bendix "chin" turret
    c. Flak radar
    d. Night vision bombsight

148. After the war, where were most of the B-17s scrapped?

   a. Provo, Utah
   b. Jacksonville, Florida
   c. Newark, New Jersey
   d. Kingman, Arizona

149. The aircraft designed to be the successor to Messerschmitt's Bf 110 Zerstörer fighter was such a disaster it was withdrawn from service, and almost ruined Messerschmitt's reputation. What model was it?

   a. Me 310
   b. Me 111
   c. Me 410
   d. Me 210

150. What did the prefix Ki on Japanese Army aircraft stand for?

   a. Kite
   b. Kippon
   c. Kit
   d. Kitai

151. What antiaircraft gun was adapted into an antitank gun?

   a. Flak-88
   b. 38 millimeter
   c. 105 millimeter
   d. 17lb QF

152. Of the following names, who was not one of the Sullivan brothers?

   a. Al
   b. Frank
   c. Peter
   d. George

153. What U.S. grocery product was usually available for purchase in English groceries?

a. MoonPies

b. Spam

c. Dinty Moore Beef Stew

d. Tootsie Rolls

154. What is the abbreviation for the Nazi Party?

a. NAZI

b. NPASD

c. NADPZ

d. NSDAP

155. The nickname of U.S. Marine Corps General Holland M. Smith, the pioneer of amphibious warfare, was:

a. He Man

b. Hoppin Mad

c. Howlin Mad

d. His Majesty

156. What was the nickname of the U.S. general who served on Chiang Kai-shek's staff and led Chinese troops in northern Burma?

a. Grim Joe

b. Vinegar Joe

c. Sour Face

d. Hard Ass

157. On the same day that they sank the HMS *Prince of Wales*, the Japanese also sank the:

a. HMS *Duke of York*

b. HMS *Ark Royal*

c. U.S.S. *Indianapolis*

d. HMS *Repulse*

158. What was the size of the artillery on the main battery on the Japanese battleship *Yamato*?

    a. 18 inch

    b. 14 inch

    c. 16 inch

    d. 12 inch

159. What were the primary shortcomings of the Sherman tank?

    a. Too heavy, engine unreliable

    b. Thin armor, low-velocity gun

    c. Armor too heavy, poor gun sights

    d. Engine unreliable, low-velocity gun

160. The Allied code name for the breakout at St. Lo, Normandy, was:

    a. Buffalo

    b. Cobra

    c. Crawdad

    d. Typhoon

161. What was the name of General George S. Patton's bull terrier, who traveled with him on missions in North Africa and in Europe?

    a. Scottie

    b. Willie

    c. Telek

    d. Jack

162. What was the caliber of the gun on the M36:

    a. 76 millimeter

    b. 90 millimeter

    c. 75 millimeter

    d. 125 millimeter

163. What was America's first heavy tank to see combat?

    a. M36 Jackson

    b. M4 Sherman

    c. M26 Pershing

    d. Tiger

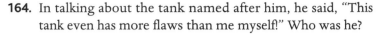
164. In talking about the tank named after him, he said, "This tank even has more flaws than me myself!" Who was he?

   a. Bernard Montgomery

   b. George Patton

   c. William Sherman

   d. Winston Churchill

165. What was the caliber of the main guns on the *Tirpitz*?

   a. 14 inch

   b. 15 inch

   c. 18 inch

   d. 17 inch

166. What warship earned twenty battle stars in the Pacific theater?

   a. U.S.S. *Missouri*

   b. U.S.S. *Washington*

   c. U.S.S. *Intrepid*

   d. U.S.S. *Enterprise*

167. Which U.S. ship was sunk by a Japanese submarine?

   a. U.S.S. *Langley*

   b. U.S.S. *Missouri*

   c. U.S.S. *Nevada*

   d. U.S.S. *Wasp*

168. Who was the commander of the Second Flotilla deployed against the German warships at Narvik?

   a. Nimitz

   b. Churchill

   c. Pound

   d. Warburton-Lee

169. Who was responsible for firing the chin turret in the B-17G during a head-on attack?

   a. Engineer

   b. Bombardier

   c. Radio operator

   d. Navigator

170. The inverted gull wing design of the Corsair resembled this German aircraft from earlier in the war:

    a. Junkers Ju 87
    b. Focke Wulf FW 152
    c. Focke Wulf FW 190
    d. Junkers Ju 88

171. What was the aircraft designation of the Japanese Zero?

    a. A6M
    b. A7M
    c. A5M
    d. A8M

172. The Baka aircraft, which came into operation late in the war, was designated the:

    a. Mitsubishi A5M
    b. Yokosuka D4Y Suisei
    c. Yokosuka MXY-7 Ohka
    d. Nakajima Ki-44 Shoki

173. The P-61 was also known as the:

    a. Mustang
    b. Aircobra
    c. Black Widow
    d. Kingcobra

174. What was the cherry blossom?

    a. Manned Japanese suicide flying bomb
    b. Nickname Japanese pilots had for tracer fire
    c. Personal suicide grenade carried by Japanese reconnaissance pilots
    d. German nickname for a distress flare

175. A German general said, in a letter to his wife in 1941 during his conquest of North Africa, "We've already reached our first objective, which we weren't supposed to do until the end of May. The British are falling over each other to get away. Our casualties small. Booty can't be estimated." Who was he?

    a. Hans Krebs

    b. Alfred Jodl

    c. Erwin Rommel

    d. Ludwig Beck

176. Which country bordered the Soviet Union and fought the Red Army?

    a. Sweden

    b. Denmark

    c. Finland

    d. Norway

177. The pivotal naval battle of the Pacific war was fought off the northeastern coast of Australia in May 1942. What was it called?

    a. Battle of Midway

    b. Battle of the Coral Sea

    c. Battle of Okinawa

    d. Battle of Guadalcanal

178. The Munich Agreement appeased Germany by granting them what piece of territory?

    a. Czechoslovakia

    b. Upper Silesia

    c. Sudetenland

    d. Alsace-Lorraine

179. Who was the German commando who rescued Mussolini from the Badglio Government on September 12, 1943?

    a. SS Colonel Otto Gunsche
    b. SS Major Otto Skorzeny
    c. Colonel Bernhard Ramcke
    d. Major Werner Pluskat

180. A key figure in the July 20, 1944, attempt on Hitler's life, later played by Tom Cruise in a film, was:

    a. Nikolaus von Below
    b. Heinrich Fraenkel
    c. Claus von Stauffenberg
    d. Erik von Amsberg

181. All of the following were sentenced to death at Nuremberg except:

    a. Wilhelm Keitel
    b. Alfred Jodl
    c. Hermann Goering
    d. Albert Speer

182. What is the date of death for President Franklin Roosevelt?

    a. May 12, 1944
    b. June 6, 1944
    c. April 12, 1945
    d. April 11, 1944

183. What French coastal city was the target of a disastrous commando raid by Canadian troops prior to the invasion of Normandy?

    a. Dieppe
    b. Cherbourg
    c. Brest
    d. Dunkirk

184. Who was the Luftwaffe general who had overall command of German ground troops in Italy during most of the fighting?

    a. Rommel
    b. Keitel
    c. Model
    d. Kesselring

185. What was the caliber of the cartridge on the Thompson?

    a. .45 caliber
    b. .30 caliber
    c. .40 caliber
    d. .223 caliber

186. What is a Horsa?

    a. Assault glider
    b. Landing craft
    c. Light tank
    d. British bomber

187. What did the Japanese capture on the island of Kiska during the invasion of the Aleutians?

    a. A very strategic mountain from which to battle
    b. U.S. military secrets
    c. A large treasure
    d. A weather station and ten soldiers

188. In the Pacific, what was the tactic used by American tanks when engaging enemy infantry in close quarters in the jungle?

    a. Retreat, to stay clear of the enemy
    b. Spray each other with machine gun fire, to kill the enemy soldiers dropping onto the tanks from the trees
    c. Spread out, to make it harder to hit the tanks
    d. Advance at full speed, so that the enemy could not catch them

189. Which German Army unit was the best equipped Panzer formation during the second half of the war?

    a. Seventh Panzer Division—the most famous division

    b. First Panzer Division—the senior formation

    c. Gross-Deutschland Division—elite division

    d. Brandenburg Division—elite formation

190. After the sinking of the *Hood*, aircraft from what British aircraft carrier were the first to attack the *Bismarck*?

    a. HMS *Duke of York*

    b. HMS *Renown*

    c. HMS *Indefatigable*

    d. HMS *Victorious*

191. Which was the flagship of the Combined Striking Force in the Battle of the Java Sea?

    a. *Soerabaja*

    b. *De Zeven Provinciën*

    c. *Soemba*

    d. *De Ruyter*

192. Which two battleships attacked the *Bismarck*?

    a. *Prince of Wales* and *Sheffield*

    b. *Zulu* and *Sikh*

    c. *Norfolk* and *Dorsetshire*

    d. *Rodney* and *King George V*

193. What Australian Navy heavy cruiser sank while covering U.S. Marine landings on Guadalcanal in August 1942?

    a. HMAS *Hobart*

    b. HMAS *Adelaide*

    c. HMAS *Canberra*

    d. HMAS *Brisbane*

194. The French battleship *Bretagne* was sunk by warships of which nation?

    a. Italy

    b. United States

    c. Great Britain

    d. Germany

195. Which tanker acted as supply ship for the pocket battleship *Graf Spee*?

    a. *Ostland*

    b. *Ostmark*

    c. *Altmark*

    d. *Reichsmark*

196. The Me 323 was one of the largest, slowest, and most vulnerable aircraft of the war. How many survived past 1944?

    a. Ten

    b. None

    c. Three

    d. One

197. The P-51 Mustang delivered to the Royal Air Force had one severe disadvantage:

    a. Decreasing performance above 15,000 feet

    b. Weak firepower

    c. Low top speed

    d. Low fuel capacity

198. The TV series *Black Sheep Squadron*, starring Robert Conrad, followed the experiences of which U.S. Marine Corps fighter squadron?

    a. VMF-44

    b. VMF-214

    c. VMF-311

    d. VF-17

199. Richard Bong was the United States' highest-scoring air ace during World War II, shooting down at least forty Japanese aircraft, and he was a recipient of the Medal of Honor. How did Richard Bong, the U.S. Ace of Aces, end his career?

   a. Killed in an accident while testing a P-80 jet
   b. Killed in combat trying to bring down fifteen Mitsubishi Zeros single-handedly
   c. Killed while dogfighting with Akira Sugimoto; he didn't jettison his drop tanks and the plane stalled
   d. General, chief of staff, Strategic Air Command

200. Three brothers, all of them aces, flew for the JG26 Schlageter, an elite Luftwaffe unit of the Western Front. What were their names?

   a. Vati, Adolf, and Werner Moelders
   b. Hans-Joachim, Manfred, and Siegfried Marseille
   c. Adolf, Paul, and Wilhelm-Ferdinand Galland
   d. Lothar, Manfred, and Wolfram-Freiherr Von Richthofen

201. What was the U. S. code name for the Aichi D3A naval dive-bomber?

   a. Kate
   b. Val
   c. Judy
   d. Frances

202. What nickname was given by the Japanese to the F4U Corsair?

   a. Wounded Gull
   b. Whistling Death
   c. Sun's Fire
   d. Black Rain

203. The Army general in charge of the Manhattan Project was:

   a. Leslie Groves
   b. Douglas MacArthur
   c. Vannevar Bush
   d. "Vinegar Joe" Stillwell

204. What was the hometown of the Sullivan brothers?

    a. French Lick, Indiana

    b. Mentor, Ohio

    c. Waterloo, Iowa

    d. Tempe, Arizona

205. What was the date of enlistment for the Sullivan brothers?

    a. November 13, 1942

    b. December 7, 1941

    c. September 1, 1939

    d. January 2, 1942

206. The first casualty of the German bombing of Leningrad was:

    a. Forward observer troops

    b. The only elephant in the zoo

    c. A Panzer tank

    d. Nothing; they missed everything

207. Audie Murphy, along with many other veterans, returned home with deep emotional scars known as:

    a. Combat exhaustion or shell shock

    b. Post-traumatic stress disorder (PTSD)

    c. Battle fatigue

    d. All are correct

208. What was the nickname of the Eighty-second U.S. Airborne Division?

    a. Thunderbolt

    b. Battle Axe

    c. All America

    d. Statue of Liberty

209. Five countries that did not exist previously were established on land that was carved out of Russian territory after World War I. They were Finland, Estonia, Latvia, Poland, and:

    a. Belarus

    b. Yugoslavia

    c. Czechoslovakia

    d. Lithuania

210. The biggest battleship ever built was:

   a. *Yamato*

   b. *Arizona*

   c. *Bismarck*

   d. *West Virginia*

211. The primary aircraft flown by the top aces of the Pacific Theater was the:

   a. P-40 Warhawk

   b. P-38 Lightning

   c. P-51 Mustang

   d. P-39 Airacobra

212. Who was the Japanese tactical mastermind who planned the attack on Pearl Harbor?

   a. Kyunosuke Kusaka

   b. Minoru Genda

   c. Shigeru Fukudome

   d. Shigekazu Shimada

213. What type of vehicle was the SdKfz 251?

   a. Half-track

   b. Self-propelled gun

   c. Tank

   d. Scout car

214. What was the name of the M3 Lee medium tank supplied to the British by the United States and used in North Africa?

   a. Grant

   b. Sherman

   c. Valentine

   d. Churchill

215. What ship dashed to the open seas through the English Channel with the *Scharnhorst* and the *Gneisenau*?

    a. *Admiral Hipper*
    b. *Prinz Eugen*
    c. *Lützow*
    d. *Admiral Scheer*

216. The U-boat that torpedoed the British battleship *Royal Oak* in Scapa Flow was:

    a. U-48
    b. U-99
    c. U-47
    d. U-46

217. The captain of the *Lancastria* had previously commanded another ship that had also been involved in a maritime disaster. What ship was it?

    a. *Titanic*
    b. *Glorious*
    c. *Hood*
    d. *Lusitania*

218. Which of these countries did not have any battleships with 16 inch guns?

    a. France
    b. Japan
    c. Britain
    d. United States

219. The Ju 88 Junker was what type of aircraft?

    a. No such craft
    b. Bomber only
    c. Multiple roles
    d. Fighter only

220. The B-17 flight engineer also had to operate the:

    a. Autopilot

    b. Radios

    c. Top turret

    d. Ball turret

221. How does one pronounce the squadron number of the 617 Squadron, the Dam Busters?

    a. Six, one, seven

    b. Six hundred and seventeen

    c. Six, seventeen

    d. Six hundred and seventeenth

222. German U-boat attacks threatened Britain's economy by concentrating on sinking tonnage along which vital supply route?

    a. Atlantic

    b. Mediterranean

    c. English Channel

    d. North Sea

223. What year was the Macy's Thanksgiving Day parade canceled and the rubber floats donated to the war effort?

    a. 1942

    b. 1939

    c. 1944

    d. 1941

224. The year that Hitler remilitarized the Rhineland was:

    a. 1938

    b. 1936

    c. 1932

    d. 1939

225. What was the code name for the evacuation of the British and French troops at Dunkirk?

    a. Operation Bertram
    b. Operation Acrobat
    c. Operation Nest Egg
    d. Operation Dynamo

226. The Allies wanted to hold the war crime trials in Berlin. Why did they have to settle for Nuremberg?

    a. Nazi leaders refused to return to Berlin as it was now in Russian control
    b. Nuremberg had not been bombed
    c. Nuremberg had an intact prison while Berlin did not
    d. Berlin had seen fierce fighting and was still not safe

227. All of the following are the names of carriers except:

    a. *Yorktown*
    b. *Saratoga*
    c. *Hornet*
    d. *Utah*

228. A few days after Pearl Harbor, these two ships, a British battleship and a battle cruiser, were sunk off the eastern coast of Malaya on their way to help Singapore:

    a. HMS *Royal Oak* and HMS *Curlew*
    b. HMS *Barham* and HMS *York*
    c. HMS *Hood* and HMS *Dunedin*
    d. HMS *Prince of Wales* and HMS *Repulse*

229. What was the historical significance of the Battle of Surigao Strait?

    a. Last Japanese victory of the war
    b. Worst Japanese losses of the war
    c. Worst U.S. battle losses of the war
    d. Last battleship engagement

230. The date on which the first Marines landed on Guadalcanal is:

a. August 7, 1942
b. November 20, 1943
c. April 1, 1945
d. September 15, 1944

231. The size of the main gun on the PzKw VI was:

a. 125 millimeter
b. 75 millimeter
c. 88 millimeter
d. 50 millimeter

232. What were the names of the two sister ships to the carrier *Enterprise*?

a. *Hornet* and *Wasp*
b. *Yorktown* and *Hornet*
c. *Lexington* and *Saratoga*
d. *Intrepid* and *Ranger*

233. What British warship was sunk by a Japanese carrier while returning to Trincomalee on April 9, 1942?

a. HMS *Ajax*
b. HMS *Hermes*
c. HMS *Thor*
d. HMS *Mercury*

234. What was the winning design for the German Air Ministry's requirement for a *Volksjager* (people's fighter) in September 1944?

a. Go 229
b. He 162
c. Ju 248
d. He 178

235. Which of the following weapons did not have the designation M1?

   a. Thompson
   b. Garand
   c. Springfield
   d. Carbine

236. What was the code name for the plan to fool the Germans into believing that the Allies were going to invade France through the French port of Calais?

   a. Operation Forthright
   b. Operation Phoney
   c. Operation Fortitude
   d. Operation France

237. What was the occupation of Tom Sullivan, the father of the Sullivan brothers?

   a. Railroad engineer
   b. Stock broker
   c. Meat packer
   d. Shop owner

238. The Japanese invasion of the Aleutian Islands was a diversion to draw the United States away from:

   a. Truk
   b. Midway
   c. Wake Island
   d. Pearl Harbor

239. Who was present at the Munich Conference?

   a. Chamberlain, Daladier, Mussolini, and Hitler
   b. Baldwin, Orlando, Stalin, and Hitler
   c. Chamberlain, Blum, Mussolini, and Hitler
   d. Lenin, Franco, Mussolini, and Hitler

240. What was the British Commando service knife?

   a. Fairbain-Sykes
   b. Knife model 41
   c. Knuckle Duster
   d. MODEL PARA

241. Who was the general who commanded the U.S. Third Army in the Battle of the Bulge?

   a. Omar Bradley
   b. George Patton
   c. Bernard Montgomery
   d. Mark Clark

242. Who met at the Yalta Conference in February 1945?

   a. Truman, de Gaulle, Churchill, and Stalin
   b. Roosevelt, Churchill, and Stalin
   c. Truman, Churchill, and Stalin
   d. Roosevelt, Churchill, Chiang Kai-shek, and Stalin

243. What German fighter ace had 352 confirmed kills?

   a. Gerhard Barkhorn
   b. Werner Molders
   c. Gunther Rall
   d. Erich Hartmann

244. Who was the British general who had to put up with constant political interference while conducting military operations in the Desert War, and who was relieved of command after the fall of Tobruk in June 1942?

   a. Harold Alexander
   b. Bernard Montgomery
   c. Archibald Wavell
   d. Claude Auchinleck

245. The number of Japanese Americans who were convicted of espionage in the United States during the war was:

    a. Eleven

    b. Three

    c. Zero

    d. Eight

246. The plan for the invasion of France in 1940 was named for its originator, who was:

    a. Heinz Guderian

    b. Franz Halder

    c. Gunther von Kluge

    d. Erich von Manstein

247. When did Germany attack Russia?

    a. June 1941

    b. December 1941

    c. September 1941

    d. March 1941

248. Which word was not part of the phonetic alphabet during the war?

    a. Able

    b. Brandy

    c. Charlie

    d. Dog

249. Who was the U.S. Navy commander in chief of the Pacific Fleet during the attack on Pearl Harbor?

    a. Admiral Mitscher

    b. Admiral Halsey

    c. Admiral Kimmel

    d. Admiral Fletcher

250. Which of the following words is not part of the word *Panzerkampfwagen*?

   a. Vehicle / car
   b. Fighting
   c. War
   d. Armored

251. Which of these British tanks had the slowest top speed?

   a. Crusader
   b. Cromwell
   c. Matilda
   d. Tetrarch

252. Who was rhe rear admiral in command of the Dutch Navy in the East Indies?

   a. Speyck
   b. De Ruyter
   c. Doorman
   d. Balkenende

253. Which engine powered the Corsair?

   a. Wright R2600 double cyclone fourteen cylinder
   b. Wright R1820 cyclone nine cylinder
   c. Pratt and Whitney R1830 twin wasp fourteen cylinder
   d. Pratt and Whitney R2800 double wasp eighteen cylinder

254. What does M.S. stand for in the designation M.S. 406 fighter of the French Air Force?

   a. Morane Simon
   b. Melrot Etampe
   c. Mercier Sud
   d. Morane Saulnier

255. Which weapon is considered the world's first assault rifle?

   a. MP-44
   b. Armalite AR-10
   c. CETME Mod. B
   d. M1 Carbine

256. What British battle cruiser was sunk in action with the British battleship HMS *Prince of Wales*?

   a. HMS *Ramilles*
   b. HMS *Repulse*
   c. HMS *Rodney*
   d. HMS *Warspite*

257. Lord Haw-Haw was the nickname of an announcer on the English-language propaganda radio program *Germany Calling*, broadcast by the Nazis to audiences in Great Britain and the United States. The program started on September 18, 1939, and continued until April 30, 1945, when Hamburg was overrun by the British Army. He was tried after the war and hanged. What was his real name?

   a. David Low
   b. Johnny Walker
   c. William Joyce
   d. Emil Fuchs

258. Who said, "Where Napoleon failed, I shall succeed. I shall land on the shores of Britain"?

   a. Himmler
   b. Goebbels
   c. Rommel
   d. Hitler

259. What was the standard Russian infantry rifle?

   a. Kar98k
   b. M1A1 Carbine
   c. Lee-Enfield
   d. Mosin-Nagant

260. Hitler committed suicide on:

   a. April 30, 1945
   b. April 25, 1945
   c. April 20, 1945
   d. April 15, 1945

261. Where were the guns located on the P-38 Lightning?

    a. On the wings
    b. In the nose
    c. In the nose and the wings
    d. In the rear

262. Who was the commander in chief of U.S. forces in the Central Pacific Theater of Operations?

    a. Admiral Chester Nimitz
    b. Admiral Raymond Spruance
    c. Admiral William "Bull" Halsey
    d. General Douglas MacArthur

263. What U.S. admiral was tricked into leaving the San Bernadino Strait unguarded while he raced north to engage a decoy force of Japanese carriers during the Battle of Leyte Gulf?

    a. Admiral Raymond Spruance
    b. Admiral Jack Fletcher
    c. Admiral William "Bull" Halsey
    d. Admiral Marc Michner

264. The unit sent to rescue the soldiers in the prison camp at Cabanatuan, to save them from being killed by the Japanese, was the:

    a. Sixth Coast Artillery
    b. Eighth Ranger Division
    c. Sixth Ranger Battalion
    d. 101st Airborne

265. The problem-plagued tank destroyer created by Ferdinand Porsche to fight in Operation Zitadelle was the:

    a. Nashorn
    b. Jagdpanzer IV
    c. Hummel
    d. Elefant

266. Which country designed and built the Semovente M41 self-propelled gun?

    a. Russia

    b. United States

    c. Germany

    d. Italy

267. What was the size of the gun on the Panzerjäger I?

    a. 47 millimeter

    b. 76 millimeter

    c. 75 millimeter

    d. 45 millimeter

268. A specialized type of A.F.V. called Scorpion or Crab (Matilda Scorpion, Grant Scorpion, Sherman Crab, etc.) was:

    a. Flamethrower tanks with armored fuel trailer

    b. Minesweeper flail tanks

    c. Soft-beach landing carpet layer tanks

    d. Bridge layer and tank recovery vehicles

269. What was the caliber of the main armament on the U.S.S. *Houston*?

    a. 15

    b. 8

    c. 12

    d. 16

SERGEANT ANSWERS

1. d.	**8.** a.	**15.** a.	**22.** c.	**29.** a.
2. d.	**9.** a.	**16.** a.	**23.** b.	**30.** b.
3. b.	**10.** d.	**17.** a.	**24.** d.	**31.** d.
4. b.	**11.** c.	**18.** b.	**25.** b.	**32.** d.
5. d.	**12.** d.	**19.** b.	**26.** d.	**33.** c.
6. d.	**13.** d.	**20.** b.	**27.** b.	**34.** a.
7. d.	**14.** d.	**21.** a.	**28.** a.	**35.** a.

36. c.	73. a.	110. a.	147. b.	184. d.
37. c.	74. c.	111. a.	148. d.	185. a.
38. c.	75. b.	112. b.	149. d.	186. a.
39. b.	76. d.	113. a.	150. d.	187. d.
40. d.	77. d.	114. d.	151. a.	188. b.
41. b.	78. d.	115. c.	152. c.	189. c.
42. c.	79. b.	116. b.	153. b.	190. d.
43. a.	80. b.	117. d.	154. d.	191. d.
44. a.	81. d.	118. d.	155. c.	192. d.
45. d.	82. b.	119. a.	156. b.	193. c.
46. a.	83. b.	120. b.	157. d.	194. c.
47. c.	84. d.	121. b.	158. a.	195. c.
48. d.	85. c.	122. d.	159. b.	196. b.
49. d.	86. a.	123. d.	160. b.	197. a.
50. d.	87. b.	124. d.	161. b.	198. b.
51. a.	88. c.	125. b.	162. b.	199. a.
52. b.	89. b.	126. d.	163. c.	200. c.
53. a.	90. b.	127. d.	164. d.	201. b.
54. c.	91. b.	128. c.	165. b.	202. b.
55. c.	92. a.	129. c.	166. d.	203. a.
56. d.	93. d.	130. d.	167. d.	204. c.
57. d.	94. d.	131. a.	168. d.	205. a.
58. c.	95. d.	132. b.	169. b.	206. b.
59. c.	96. a.	133. a.	170. a.	207. c.
60. d.	97. c.	134. c.	171. a.	208. c.
61. c.	98. a.	135. c.	172. c.	209. d.
62. b.	99. d.	136. d.	173. c.	210. a.
63. d.	100. d.	137. a.	174. a.	211. b.
64. a.	101. a.	138. b.	175. c.	212. b.
65. a.	102. a.	139. d.	176. c.	213. a.
66. b.	103. b.	140. b.	177. b.	214. a.
67. c.	104. d.	141. c.	178. c.	215. b.
68. b.	105. a.	142. a.	179. b.	216. c.
69. d.	106. c.	143. d.	180. c.	217. d.
70. a.	107. a.	144. c.	181. d.	218. a.
71. c.	108. a.	145. c.	182. c.	219. c.
72. b.	109. b.	146. d.	183. a.	220. c.

221. a.	**231.** c.	**241.** b.	**251.** c.	**261.** b.
222. a.	**232.** b.	**242.** b.	**252.** c.	**262.** a.
223. a.	**233.** b.	**243.** d.	**253.** d.	**263.** c.
224. b.	**234.** b.	**244.** d.	**254.** d.	**264.** c.
225. d.	**235.** c.	**245.** c.	**255.** a.	**265.** d.
226. c.	**236.** c.	**246.** d.	**256.** b.	**266.** d.
227. d.	**237.** a.	**247.** a.	**257.** c.	**267.** a.
228. d.	**238.** b.	**248.** b.	**258.** d.	**268.** b.
229. d.	**239.** a.	**249.** c.	**259.** d.	**269.** b.
230. a.	**240.** a.	**250.** c.	**260.** a.	

LIEUTENANT

1. What Belgian troopship was torpedoed by the U-486 on December 24, 1944?

   a. *Baudoinville*
   b. *Belgique*
   c. *Gandia*
   d. *Leopoldsville*

2. Who was the captain of the *Bismarck*?

   a. Captain Langsdorff
   b. Captain Raeder
   c. Captain Lindemann
   d. Captain Barkmann

3. The only biplane still in operation in German front-line attack squadrons in 1940 was the:

   a. Avia BK-534
   b. Henschel 123
   c. Arado 66
   d. Junkers Cl. 1

4. Who was the commanding officer of the 509th Composite Group, the air combat group created to drop the atomic bombs on Japan?

  a. Charles Sweeney

  b. Charles Schultz

  c. James Hopkins

  d. Paul Tibbets

5. What U.S. division was tasked with capturing Hitler's Eagle's Nest headquarters in the Alps?

  a. Twenty-ninth Infantry

  b. First Infantry

  c. 101st Airborne

  d. Eighty-second Airborne

6. How many times was Audie Murphy wounded during his two years of combat service?

  a. One

  b. Five

  c. None

  d. Three

7. Who was the chief of the German counterintelligence agency?

  a. Wilhelm Frick

  b. Kurt Daluege

  c. Admiral Canaris

  d. Franz Papen

8. The 442nd Regimental Combat Team included what soldiers?

  a. Japanese American soldiers recruited from American internment camps

  b. Norwegian demolition divers who escaped to the United States after the fall of Norway

  c. Italian special forces who switched sides

  d. British desert raiders, separated from their own army, who were incorporated into the American Army in North Africa

9. What was the code name for the U.S. air and ground operation that led to the breakout from the Normandy beachhead?

    a. Operation Cobra
    b. Operation Diadem
    c. Operation Goodwood
    d. Operation Pointblank

10. When Japanese soldiers were captured, they were asked for their names so that, in accordance with the Geneva Convention, their status could be reported to Japan. They often responded, "Naichi e namae wo shirasetakunai," which meant:

    a. I do not follow those rules
    b. Please say I was captured while wounded
    c. I am not required to say anything
    d. I do not want my name sent to the homeland

11. The highest scoring U.S. ace in the war was:

    a. Richard Bong
    b. Chuck Yeager
    c. James Doolittle
    d. "Pappy" Boyington

12. What was the major factor that led to the collapse of General Homma's humane plan for American POWs in the Philippines?

    a. They had nowhere to keep the prisoners
    b. His plan was not humane at all
    c. Men simply disobeyed his orders to be kind to POWs
    d. His men underestimated the number of prisoners

13. What was Admiral Nagumo's flagship for the Pearl Harbor attack?

    a. *Soryu*
    b. *Kaga*
    c. *Hiryu*
    d. *Akagi*

14. What Italian officer was nicknamed the Butcher?

   a. Marshal Rodolfo Graziani

   b. Field Marshal Phillip Tusung

   c. Marshal Domenici Olegro

   d. Major General Paolo Faldoni

15. Which German tank was initially designated the Panzer VI?

   a. Maus

   b. Tiger

   c. Panther

   d. Tiger II

16. When did the *Bismarck* depart for its only operational cruise?

   a. May 1940

   b. May 1942

   c. May 1941

   d. June 1941

17. The German shipyard responsible for producing over one-third of all U-boats commissioned during World War II was in:

   a. Hamburg

   b. Hannover

   c. Frankfurt

   d. Stuttgart

18. How many sailors died on the *Bismarck*?

   a. 110

   b. 1,000

   c. 2,100

   d. 1,500

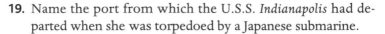
19. Name the port from which the U.S.S. *Indianapolis* had departed when she was torpedoed by a Japanese submarine.

    a. Leyte
    b. Guam
    c. Pearl Harbor
    d. Guadalcanal

20. What was the size of the deck gun on the U.S.S. *Argonaut*?

    a. 18 inch
    b. 6 inch
    c. 4 inch
    d. 40 millimeter

21. The original engine on the P-51, which suffered from being underpowered at high altitudes, was the:

    a. Curtis-Allison Straight 12
    b. Republic V-12
    c. Rolls-Royce Merlin
    d. Rolls-Royce Victor

22. The U.S. Navy's Brewster SB2A dive-bomber had a lot of operational problems. What was its name?

    a. Brigand
    b. Bull
    c. Buck
    d. Buccaneer

23. What was the name of the aircraft known as the P-39?

    a. Kingcobra
    b. Warhawk
    c. Black Widow
    d. Airacobra

24. What did the name Volksjager mean?

   a. People's revenge
   b. People's fighter
   c. People's airline
   d. People's unmanned flying bombs

25. How many rounds were in the standard magazine for the Browning BAR M1918A2?

   a. Eighteen
   b. Thirty
   c. Twenty-five
   d. Twenty

26. The last great battle of the war, one of the most fiercely fought battles in the Pacific theater, was:

   a. Iwo Jima
   b. Battle for Ulithi Atoll
   c. Peleliu
   d. Battle of Okinawa

27. In what Pacific battle did the Sullivans die?

   a. Battle of Midway
   b. Battle at Henderson Field
   c. Battle of the Bulge
   d. Battle of Guadalcanal

28. Which country did not issue scabbards with their bayonets?

   a. Italy
   b. Russia
   c. France
   d. Yugoslavia

29. Which leader proclaimed "peace in our time"?

   a. Stalin
   b. Churchill
   c. Chamberlain
   d. Roosevelt

30. On the night of November 11, 1940, the Royal Navy launched the first all-aircraft naval attack in history, flying from an aircraft carrier in the Mediterranean Sea and attacking the Italian fleet at anchor in port. This attack signaled the end of the battleship and the rise of the aircraft carrier. Air-launched torpedo experts in all navies had previously thought that torpedo attacks against ships required water at least 100 feet deep, and this harbor had a water depth of only 40 feet. However, the Royal Navy used modified torpedoes dropped from a very low height. Japanese planning staff studied this attack intensively when planning their successful attack on Pearl Harbor in 1941. In which Italian port did this attack occur?

    a. Taranto
    b. Napoli
    c. Anzio
    d. Sicily

31. The number of U.S. carriers sunk at Pearl Harbor is:

    a. One
    b. Three
    c. Two
    d. Zero

32. Who was Franklin D. Roosevelt's U.S. Army chief of staff?

    a. Dwight David Eisenhower
    b. Henry Harley Arnold
    c. Omar Nelson Bradley
    d. George Catlett Marshall

33. The inspector general of fighters in the Luftwaffe, and the youngest general in the German Armed Forces, was:

    a. Werner Molders
    b. Adolf Galland
    c. Hans Rudel
    d. Erich Hartmann

34. The year of the Munich Conference, at which the Allies attempted to appease Hitler, was:

   a. 1935
   b. 1938
   c. 1937
   d. 1936

35. Which general did not receive his fifth star?

   a. Patton
   b. Eisenhower
   c. MacArthur
   d. Marshall

36. What was the name of the monastery that was the focus of the battle of Monte Cassino?

   a. St. George's
   b. St. William's
   c. St. Benedict's
   d. St. Luke's

37. The final letter of Iwo Jima's commanding officer, General Kuribayashi, to his family included these words:

   a. Future generations will read of our valor with pride
   b. Americans will die like dogs
   c. Do not expect my return
   d. Gods are with us, so there is hope

38. When did Japan capture Singapore?

   a. February 19, 1942
   b. May 8, 1943
   c. June 9, 1941
   d. January 1945

39. What was the initial caliber of the main gun of the T-34 tank?

   a. 37 millimeter
   b. 76.2 millimeter
   c. 57 millimeter
   d. 85 millimeter

40. Which of the following was not a tank destroyer?

   a. M26 Pershing
   b. M18 Hellcat
   c. M10 Wolverine
   d. M36 Jackson

41. What was the caliber of HMS *Warspite*'s main armament?

   a. 12
   b. 15
   c. 12.5
   d. 16

42. What was the force identifier for the pursuit and sinking of the German battleship *Bismarck*?

   a. H
   b. G
   c. Z
   d. X

43. How many battle stars were earned by the *Enterprise*?

   a. Two
   b. Twenty
   c. Thirty-eight
   d. Five

44. On June 8, 1989, an expedition discovered the remains of the German battleship *Bismarck*. What was unusual about the wreck?

   a. All the main gun turrets fell off when the ship capsized as it sank (they were held in by gravity)
   b. Battleship was completely upside down
   c. Battleship was split in two like HMS *Hood*
   d. Battleship was almost buried in sand

45. How was the U.S.S. *Tang* sunk in October 1944?

   a. Friendly fire from a U.S. destroyer
   b. Depth charged by a Siamese destroyer
   c. By its own torpedo
   d. Bombed by Japanese aircraft

46. Which vessel intercepted the supply vessel *Altmark*?

    a. HMS *Hood*

    b. HMS *Repulse*

    c. HMS *Victorious*

    d. HMS *Cossack*

47. The Germans had two types of coastal craft—the R-Boot and the:

    a. Q-Boot

    b. Z-Boot

    c. S-Boot

    d. X-Boot

48. What was the number of crew members on the B-17?

    a. Eleven

    b. Thirteen

    c. Twelve

    d. Ten

49. What was unusual about Germany's BV 141 aircraft, designed by Blohm und Voss?

    a. Unusual coupled engines

    b. Asymmetric layout

    c. Odd armament

    d. Completely glazed centerline nacelle

50. What Soviet aircraft did Stalin say was more important than bread?

    a. Ilyushin Il-2

    b. Mikoyan-Gurevich MiG-3

    c. Yakovlev Yak-3

    d. Petleyakov Pe-2

51. What was the first jet aircraft to enter operational service and fly operational sorties?

    a. Me 263
    b. He 162
    c. Ar 234
    d. Me 163

52. Who designed the Manchester?

    a. Camm
    b. Chadwick
    c. Mitchell
    d. Smith

53. How did the pilot open the canopy on the Bell P-39?

    a. There was no canopy; it had an open cockpit
    b. Hinged sideways
    c. Canopy was fixed; the pilot entered the cockpit through a side door on the fuselage
    d. Slid it back

54. Someone said, "Germany is not a warlike nation. It is a soldierly one, which means it does not want a war, but does not fear it. It loves peace, but also loves its honor and freedom." Who was it?

    a. Neville Chamberlain
    b. Joseph Stalin
    c. Franklin D. Roosevelt
    d. Adolf Hitler

55. What was the ship on which the Sullivan brothers died?

    a. U.S.S. *Indianapolis*
    b. U.S.S. *San Francisco*
    c. U.S.S. *Juneau*
    d. U.S.S. *Des Moines*

56. What was the only country besides Germany to field jet aircraft in the European theater?

a. Britain
b. Soviet Union
c. United States
d. Italy

57. The founder of the Nazi Party was a member of the *völkisch* agitators who, together with journalist Karl Harrer, founded the German Workers' Party (DAP) in Munich with Gottfried Feder and Dietrich Eckart in 1919. Hitler later joined this party and suggested that they change the name to the National Socialist German Workers' Party early in 1920. By 1921, Hitler was rapidly becoming the undisputed leader of the party. In the summer of that year he traveled to Berlin to address a meeting of German nationalists from northern Germany. While he was away, the other members of the party committee, led by the party's founder, circulated a pamphlet that accused Hitler of seeking personal power without regard to other considerations. Hitler brought a libel suit and the founder was forced to repudiate at a public meeting. He was thereafter moved to the purely symbolic position of honorary president and left the party in 1923. Who was he?

a. Albert Speer
b. Wolfgang Puck
c. Anton Drexler
d. Heinrich Himmler

58. What connection did cosmetic manufacturer Elizabeth Arden have with the war?

a. She produced black face cream for use as camouflage
b. She personally paid for the construction of a B-29 bomber that was then nicknamed for her
c. She donated all of the profits of her company for the year 1944 to the war effort
d. No connection

59. When Colonel Yahara arrived at Okinawa, he said the relaxed atmosphere on the island reminded him of:

   a. Prewar Berlin

   b. Prewar suburbs of New York City

   c. Prewar Rome

   d. Small towns in the southern United States

60. What was the last Japanese capital ship to be built outside of Japan?

   a. *Fuso*

   b. *Kunyo*

   c. *Hirashiro*

   d. *Kongo*

61. Who was nicknamed the Father of Modern Amphibious Warfare?

   a. General Holland Smith

   b. Captain Michael Williams

   c. Coporal Cory Barnes

   d. Lieutenant General Keith Wilder

62. What designer's suspension system was used in the T-34 tank?

   a. J. F. C. Fuller

   b. John Walter Christie

   c. Basil Liddell Hart

   d. Vyacheslav Malyshev

63. Which tank was produced from the beginning right through to the end of the war?

   a. PzKw IV

   b. PzKw V

   c. PzKw III

   d. PzKw (38)ts

64. What was the armament on the Panzer I?

   a. Twin MG13 machine guns

   b. One MG34 machine gun and one 20 millimeter cannon

   c. One 37 millimeter cannon

   d. Twin 37 millimeter cannon

65. At the Battle of Leyte Gulf, which was the first carrier to be sunk by shell fire from the Japanese battleships?

   a. *Kitkun Bay*

   b. *Gambier Bay*

   c. *Fanshaw Bay*

   d. *Kalinin Bay*

66. July 1941 saw a decrease in Allied shipping losses from 300,000+ GRT to around 100,000 GRT. Which of the following did not play a factor?

   a. Effective intelligence from "Ultra"

   b. Introduction of continuous escort and more convoy routes

   c. Introduction of radar and "Huff-Duff"

   d. Heavy losses of German aircraft due to the CAM ships

67. On June 8, 1940, this battleship was steaming alone west of the Lofoten Islands in the Norwegian Sea when it was sunk by the KMS *Scharnhorst* and *Gneisenau*.

   a. HMS *Illustrious*

   b. HMS *Glorious*

   c. HMS *Invincible*

   d. HMS *Splendid*

68. During the Norwegian Campaign in April–June of 1940, the Germans lost this cruiser:

   a. *Oscarbourg*

   b. *Prinz Eugen*

   c. *Blücher*

   d. *Hipper*

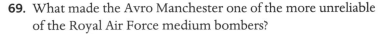

69. What made the Avro Manchester one of the more unreliable of the Royal Air Force medium bombers?

    a. Weak armor
    b. Little defensive weaponry
    c. Low offensive weaponry
    d. Bad engines

70. What was the Belgians' biplane fighter from Britain?

    a. Hawker Fury II
    b. Gloster Gauntlet Mk II
    c. Gloster Gladiator Mk I
    d. Fairey Fulmar Mk I

71. A Russian aircraft in the early part of the conflict on the Eastern Front was the Polikarpov I-16. The I- prefix stood for *Istrebetl*, which translates as:

    a. Bomber
    b. Fighter
    c. Reconnaissance
    d. Liaison

72. The first 1,000-bomber raid by the RAF took place on the night of May 30, 1942, and the target was Cologne. It was hoped that the devastation from such a raid might be enough to knock Germany out of the war or at least severely damage German morale. The raids were useful propaganda for the Allies, particularly for the concept of a strategic bombing offensive. Bomber Command's poor performance in bombing accuracy during 1941 had led to calls for the force to be split up and diverted to other urgent requirements. A headline-grabbing heavy raid on Germany was a way for Bomber Command to demonstrate to the War Cabinet that, given the investment in numbers and technology, Bomber Command could make a vital contribution to victory. The code name for this operation was:

    a. Operation Devastation
    b. Operation Millennium
    c. Operation Cologne
    d. Operation Bombossa

73. Mussolini, Daladier, and Chamberlain agreed that Germany could have the Sudetenland, and in return Hitler promised not to make any further territorial demands in Europe. When and where did this agreement take place?

    a. September 29, 1938, in Munich
    b. May 29, 1938, in Berlin
    c. April 29, 1938, in Stuttgart
    d. July 29, 1938, in Nuremberg

74. What was the name of the Allied operation to break out at St. Lo in Normandy?

    a. Supercharge
    b. Goodwood
    c. Lightfoot
    d. Cobra

75. The code name for the German invasion of Crete was:

    a. Sun
    b. Mercury
    c. Eagle
    d. Barbarossa

76. The code name for the Allied invasion of Sicily was:

    a. Fox
    b. Market Garden
    c. Husky
    d. Fortitude

77. What was the Anzio Express?

    a. First train to exceed 100 mph
    b. Nickname for a German train
    c. First train blown up by the enemy
    d. Nickname given to a German railway gun

78. After all of its modificiations, how many bullets did the Thompson hold in a magazine?

a. Twenty

b. Thirty

c. Forty

d. Ten

79. Where did Adolf Hitler meet Austrian Chancellor Kurt von Schuschnigg in February 1938?

a. Munich

b. Berchtesgaden

c. Konstanz

d. Nuremberg

80. The months following the German invasion of Poland in September 1939 and preceding the Battle of France in May 1940 were marked by a lack of major military operations in Continental Europe. The great powers of Europe had declared war on one another, yet neither side committed to launching a significant attack. While most of the German army was engaged in Poland, a much smaller German force manned the Siegfried Line, their fortified defensive line along the French border. At the Maginot Line on the other side of the border, British and French troops stood facing them, but there were only some local, minor skirmishes. Winston Churchill called it the Twilight War. It was also called the Phony War, or by this German word:

a. Sitzkrieg

b. Blitzkrieg

c. Langweilkrieg

d. Wartekrieg

81. Which German U-boat commander sank the most ships?

a. Otto Kretschmer

b. Herbert Schultze

c. Wolfgang Luth

d. Werner Henke

82. Field Marshal Gerd von Rundstedt was relieved as commander in chief in the West because:

   a. He told Hitler that the military situation was disastrous
   b. He lost the Twenty-first Panzer Division
   c. He failed to hold the Allies
   d. He was not relieved

83. Which of the following was not a commander of the Japanese forces in the Nanjing campaign?

   a. General Iwane Matsui
   b. Prince Asaka Yasuhiko
   c. Admiral Isoroku Yamamoto
   d. Lieutenant General Kesago Nakajima

84. After the fall of Singapore, 100,000 troops were placed in this infamous POW camp:

   a. Batavia
   b. Bilibid
   c. Changi
   d. Fukuoka

85. What was the only battleship to get underway and try to escape the attack on Pearl Harbor?

   a. U.S.S. *Nevada*
   b. U.S.S. *California*
   c. U.S.S. *Pennsylvania*
   d. U.S.S. *Oklahoma*

86. The Battle of Leyte Gulf is generally considered to be the largest naval battle of World War II. It was fought in waters near the Philippine island of Leyte, October 23–26, 1944, between naval and naval-air forces of the Allies and those of the Empire of Japan. The Battle of Leyte Gulf included four major naval battles: the Battle of the Sibuyan Sea, the Battle of the Surigao Strait, the Battle of Cape Engaño, and the Battle off Samar, as well as other actions. For the Japanese, it was a:

   a. Strategic victory
   b. Tactical victory
   c. Stalemate
   d. Defeat

87. What two U.S. aircraft carriers left Pearl Harbor prior to the Japanese attack?

   a. *Hornet* and *Lexington*
   b. *Lexington* and *Enterprise*
   c. *Saratoga* and *Enterprise*
   d. *Hornet* and *Saratoga*

88. What type of vehicle was the SdKfz 7 (Sonderkraftfahrzeug 7)?

   a. Scout car
   b. Armored car
   c. Truck
   d. Half-track

89. Which country created the Ram tank?

   a. United Kingdom
   b. United States
   c. France
   d. Canada

90. Which of these self-propelled guns mounted the 155 millimeter Long Tom gun?

   a. ISU-152
   b. Hummel
   c. M40
   d. Sexton

91. During the battle off Iceland, which was the first British ship to score a hit on the *Bismarck*?

   a. *Hood*
   b. *Prince of Wales*
   c. Both
   d. Neither

92. In what state was the *Yorktown* constructed?

   a. Pennsylvania
   b. Virginia
   c. New Jersey
   d. North Carolina

93. What caliber were the main armaments of the four combat-ants who fought off the coast of South America in 1939?

a. 6 inch, 9 inch, 11 inch
b. 5 inch, 9 inch, 15 inch
c. 6 inch, 8 inch, 11 inch
d. 4 inch, 7 inch, 12 inch

94. The most effective surface ammunition for use against a bat-tleship is called?

a. AP
b. MC
c. SAP
d. HC

95. On the B-17G, who were the only crew members who did not fire a defensive weapon?

a. Pilot, copilot, engineer
b. Pilot, copilot, radio operator
c. Navigator, pilot, engineer
d. Radio operator, engineer, navigator

96. Who designed the Defiant, one of the worst fighters to fly in the Royal Air Force?

a. Boulton Paul
b. Hawker
c. Vickers
d. Supermarine

97. Chuck Yeager became the first U.S. pilot to accomplish this while flying a P-51D:

a. Fly over Berlin
b. Down a rocket fighter
c. Down a jet fighter
d. Down a V-1 rocket bomb

98. The top-scoring Lightning ace had how many kills?

    a. Forty

    b. Twenty-six

    c. Fifty-two

    d. Thirty

99. Which aircraft was known as the flying panhandle?

    a. Wellington

    b. Hampden

    c. Blenheim

    d. Bombay

100. What was the first nickname of the Hawker Hurricane?

    a. Twister

    b. Fury Monoplane

    c. Tsunami

    d. Wave

101. What aircraft was called the Tankbuster?

    a. P-51

    b. P-40

    c. P-38

    d. P-47

102. President George H. W. Bush flew what aircraft in the Navy?

    a. TBF Avenger

    b. Hellcat

    c. Corsair

    d. Wildcat

103. What was the most common German submachine gun of the war?

    a. MP-44

    b. MP-40

    c. MP-38

    d. MP-18

104. Which naval battle thwarted Japanese attempts to land troops in New Guinea?

   a. Battle of Midway
   b. Battle of the Coral Sea
   c. Battle of Santa Cruz
   d. Battle of Truk

105. How many Luftwaffe pilots were put in the air to stop Allied troops during the Normandy invasion on D-day?

   a. 1,000
   b. Zero
   c. Two
   d. 100

106. What was the code name for the Allied invasion of the Italian mainland on September 8, 1943, under General Mark Clark?

   a. Operation Alpine
   b. Operation Avalanche
   c. Operation Austral
   d. Operation Kestral

107. The German expeditionary air force during the Spanish Civil War was known as:

   a. Storm Squadron
   b. Condor Legion
   c. Black Watch
   d. Luftspainaire

108. The alliance that France made in 1921 with Czechoslovakia, Romania, and Yugoslavia was called the:

   a. Quadruple-Edged Sword
   b. Le Secure
   c. Axis Alliance
   d. Little Entente

109. Who was the top flying ace of the Second World War?

    a. Gerhard Barkhorn
    b. Otto Kittel
    c. Gunther Rall
    d. Erich Hartmann

110. This general took over command of the First U.S. Army from Bradley on August 1, 1944, and directed their drive eastward until VE day:

    a. Leonard T. Gerow
    b. William H. Simpson
    c. Courtney R. Hodges
    d. Orlando Ward

111. What was the German objective of the 1942 summer offensive?

    a. Rostov
    b. Leningrad
    c. Stalingrad
    d. Moscow

112. What the world would call the Stalingrad Cauldron was no laughing matter. The German Army was dying from starvation, disease, and exposure, trapped inside a ring of Soviet armor. Shortages of fuel, ammunition, clothing, and all materiel needed to sustain an army in the field were building to a crisis. Morale remained fairly high among the Germans, and they nicknamed their position Der Kessel—the Kettle. The approximate number of troops surrounded by the Russians in Der Kessel was:

    a. 40,000
    b. 290,000
    c. 1,000,000
    d. 100,000

113. What was the name of the B-17 in which Clark Gable flew over Europe?

    a. Rhett 2

    b. Air 21

    c. 8-Ball

    d. Big Flier

114. Who was the U.S. Army commander in Hawaii during the attack on Pearl Harbor?

    a. General Small

    b. General Short

    c. General Long

    d. General Meek

115. Where was Alaska bombed prior to the invasion of the Aleutians?

    a. Unimak Island

    b. Anchorage

    c. Prince William Sound

    d. Dutch Harbor

116. When did the Japanese attack Timor?

    a. February 1942

    b. December 1941

    c. February 1944

    d. June 1943

117. What did the Japanese do with their healthy prisoners as the Allies closed in on Japan?

    a. Sent them to Japan

    b. Freed them

    c. Murdered them

    d. Nothing; they just left them in the camps

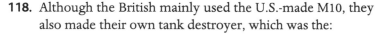
118. Although the British mainly used the U.S.-made M10, they also made their own tank destroyer, which was the:

    a. AEC Matador Deacon Tank Destroyer
    b. Archer Tank Destroyer
    c. A30 Avenger Tank Destroyer
    d. Charioteer Tank Destroyer

119. The Jagdpanther was based on the chassis of which tank, and featured what size gun?

    a. Tiger, 88 millimeter
    b. Panther, 75 millimeter
    c. Panther, 88 millimeter
    d. Panther, 122 millimeter

120. Which tank carried the largest gun?

    a. Char B1
    b. King Tiger
    c. IS-2 Josef Stalin
    d. M26 Pershing

121. During the Battle of Leyte Gulf, the Japanese Centre Force was ambushed by these two U.S. submarines:

    a. *Hake* and *Harder*
    b. *Tautog* and *Tunny*
    d. *Barb* and *Bonita*
    d. *Dace* and *Darter*

122. When was the keel laid for the *Bismarck*?

    a. May 27, 1941
    b. February 14, 1939
    c. July 1, 1936
    d. November 16, 1935

123. What was the first U.S. warship to be sunk during the war?

    a. U.S.S. *Arizona*
    b. U.S.S. *Gearing*
    c. U.S.S. *Ward*
    d. U.S.S. *Reuben James*

124. What British warship took part in the Battle of the River Plate, and then, on March 1, 1942, while northwest of Surabaya in the Java Sea, was attacked by a Japanese cruiser force and sunk?

  a. HMS *Exeter*
  b. HMS *Achilles*
  c. HMS *Cumberland*
  d. HMS *Ajax*

125. The P-63 Kingcobra was used by:

  a. Soviet Union
  b. Poland
  c. United Kingdom
  d. New Zealand

126. Which aircraft was the only bomber in the war to have a top speed of over 460 mph?

  a. Arado 234
  b. Heinkel 111P
  c. Arado 232
  d. Junkers 388K

127. Which of the following was the first four-engine jet to fly?

  a. Ba 349
  b. Ju 287
  c. Ar 234
  d. Hs 132

128. Name the Royal Air Force fighter which, after a failed daylight career, was successfully employed as a night fighter or night intruder in 1940–1941.

  a. Bristol Blenheim
  b. Boulton Paul Defiant
  c. Westland Whirlwind
  d. Hawker Hurricane

129. Guadalcanal, the scene of deadly fighting in the Pacific, is found in which group of islands?

    a. Solomon Islands
    b. Philippines
    c. New Guinea
    d. Indonesia

130. Who were the commanders of the Allied Airborne divisions at the Battle of Arnhem?

    a. Urquhart, Taylor, Gale, and Sosabowski
    b. Urquhart, Taylor, Gavin, and Sosabowski
    c. Taylor, Gavin, Gale, and Urquhart
    d. Horrocks, Gavin, Taylor, and Gale

131. After the ship had sunk, what was the leading cause of death among the sailors on the Sullivan brothers' ship?

    a. Enemy fire
    b. Burn wounds
    c. Shark attacks
    d. Blood loss

132. The Ploesti oil fields were vital to the German war effort and were the target of Allied bombing raids. In which country were they located?

    a. Hungary
    b. Romania
    c. Poland
    d. Ukraine

133. Where did Audie Murphy receive his basic training?

    a. Camp Blanding, Florida
    b. Camp Wolters, Texas
    c. Camp Funston, Kansas
    d. Camp Shelby, Mississippi

134. Who was the U.S. secretary of war during the war?

    a. Frank Knox

    b. Edward Stettinus

    c. James Forrestal

    d. Henry Stimson

135. What country was invaded on the day after the attack on Pearl Harbor?

    a. France

    b. Thailand

    c. Poland

    d. Laos

136. Lake Ladoga was the supply lifeline for what besieged Russian city?

    a. Leningrad

    b. Sevastopol

    c. Stalingrad

    d. Moscow

137. What German battleship fought against the Allied warships HMS *Exeter*, HMS *Ajax*, and HMS *Achilles* in the Battle of the River Plate?

    a. *Bismarck*

    b. *Prinz Eugen*

    c. *Scharnhorst*

    d. *Graf Spee*

138. Complete the following quote. "I would say to the House, as I said to those who have joined this government: I have nothing to offer but":

    a. Blood, toil, tears and laughter

    b. Blood, tears, sweat and toil

    c. Blood, blood, and more blood

    d. Blood, toil, tears and sweat

139. Who said, "All that the great Lenin created, we have lost forever!"

   a. Winston Churchill
   b. General Rokossovski
   c. Josef Stalin
   d. Adolf Hitler

140. When was Dwight D. Eisenhower promoted to the rank of five-star general?

   a. January 1945
   b. November 1945
   c. May 1945
   d. December 1944

141. Which of the following did not portray General George Patton in the movies?

   a. George C. Scott
   b. John Wayne
   c. George Kennedy
   d. Kirk Douglas

142. Who was the king of Belgium during Germany's invasion?

   a. William II
   b. Albert I
   c. Leopold I
   d. Leopold III

143. What date was originally designated as D-day?

   a. June 7, 1944
   b. June 8, 1944
   c. June 4, 1944
   d. June 5, 1944

144. What U.S. aircraft was unique in its use of a 37 millimeter cannon mounted directly in the nose?

   a. P-47 Thunderbolt
   b. P-38 Lightning
   c. P-39 Airacobra
   d. Seversky P-35

145. Medicine was almost nonexistent in Cabanatuan and men died by the thousands of disease. What disease caused limbs to swell to many times their normal size?

   a. Beriberi
   b. Diphtheria
   c. Malaria
   d. Cholera

146. The T34 Calliope rocket launcher was mounted on which vehicle?

   a. M4 Sherman
   b. M16 multiple gun motor carriage
   c. M4 mortar carrier
   d. T-34

147. What was the designation of the M24 Chaffee?

   a. Light Tank M24
   b. M42 Chaffee
   c. Light Tank M24 Chaffee
   d. Chaffee

148. Designed originally as a battle cruiser, this aircraft carrier survived the war only to be blown up in the Bikini atomic tests:

   a. *Graf Zeppelin*
   b. IJN *Kaga*
   c. U.S.S. *Saratoga*
   d. HMS *Furious*

149. What ship was torpedoed by the U-30 under the command of Lemp on September 3, 1939?

   a. *Athenia*
   b. *Ark Royal*
   c. *Alexandria*
   d. *Barham*

150. What was the S-J type radar used for?

    a. Mine detection

    b. Air search

    c. Surface search

    d. Underwater search

151. Japanese aircraft engineers designed the MXY-7 Ohka piloted missile, which the U.S. troops called:

    a. Fire Blossom

    b. Rita

    c. Baka

    d. Toa

152. German engineers designed the Fi-103R, a piloted version of the V-1. What was the pilot expected to do?

    a. Bail out and make his way back to German lines

    b. Stay in the aircraft

    c. Bail out and be picked up by experimental helicopters

    d. Commit suicide using a small pistol

153. During the Battle of Britain the Spitfire and Bf 109 were almost equally matched, but the Bf 109 had what advantage?

    a. Armament was more evenly spaced, creating a bigger firing pattern

    b. None; the two aircraft were evenly matched

    c. Engine of the Bf 109 was less susceptible to battle damage

    d. It could dive without having to half-roll first

154. What was the P-51's Achilles heel in combat?

    a. Its radiator was located in the belly

    b. Aircraft had only four 50 caliber machine guns

    c. Pilot's seat was unarmored

    d. P-51 did not have self-sealing gas tanks

155. Who was the commanding general of the bomber squadrons operating out of Saipan and Tinian?
   a. Arthur "Bomber" Harris
   b. Carl "Tooey" Spatz
   c. Curtis LeMay
   d. "Hap" Arnold

156. What tactical change did the U.S. bomber command make in the Pacific in the spring of 1945?
   a. Stripped the guns from the B-29s so that they could carry more bombs
   b. Switched to low-level carpet bombing, using incendiaries
   c. Had the formations fly lower and slower to improve accuracy
   d. None of these

157. The last variant of the Lancaster was the Avro:
   a. Shackleton
   b. Sentry
   c. Lincoln
   d. Nimrod

158. The British admiralty threw every available ship and plane into the hunt for the *Bismarck*, which promptly sank which Royal Navy capital ship?
   a. HMS *King George V*
   b. HMS *Rodney*
   c. HMS *Royal Oak*
   d. HMS *Hood*

159. Which German officer rescued Mussolini from Gran Sasso after he was imprisoned by his own countrymen?
   a. Fritz Witt
   b. Otto Skorzeny
   c. Joachim Peiper
   d. Max Wünsche

160. Who were known as the Desert Rats?

    a. British SAS
    b. British Seventh Armored Division
    c. British No. 2 Commandos
    d. German Afrika Korps

161. On what day did Britain and France declare war on Germany?

    a. September 9, 1940
    b. September 1, 1940
    c. September 3, 1939
    d. September 6, 1939

162. What finally stopped the rape of Nanking?

    a. Emperor Hirohito's tour of the city
    b. There was no definitive end; the massacre gradually trailed off
    c. Diversion of troops back to the siege of Shanghai
    d. Declaration of war by the United States

163. How many men raised the U.S. flag on Iwo Jima?

    a. Three
    b. Six
    c. Four
    d. Five

164. Which Japanese general was in charge of the invasion of the Aleutians?

    a. Hideichiro Higuda
    b. Hirohito
    c. Isoroku Yamamoto
    d. Hideki Tojo

165. In Palemband, what was the objective of the paratroopers?

    a. Capture airfield
    b. Capture government offices
    c. Capture oil refineries
    d. Seize airfield and oil refineries

166. The United States called the tank destroyer the M10. What did the British call it?

    a. Priest

    b. Chieftain

    c. Humber

    d. Wolverine

167. How many T-34 tanks were produced?

    a. 84,000

    b. 26,385

    c. 34,760

    d. 34,085

168. In the 1970 film *Patton*, the German panzer forces are anachronistically shown using what postwar tank?

    a. T54

    b. Centurion

    c. Leopard

    d. M48

169. What was the caliber of the main armament on the U.S.S. *Texas*?

    a. 14

    b. 12

    c. 13

    d. 8

170. In October 1941, the Germans sank the first U.S. Navy ship lost in World War II. What was it?

    a. U.S.S. *Niblack*

    b. U.S.S. *Kearney*

    c. U.S.S. *Reuben James*

    d. U.S.S. *Ward*

171. How many sailors served on the *Bismarck*?

    a. 4,500

    b. 3,000

    c. 2,200

    d. 5,500

172. Name the first nuclear-powered warship to see combat, which was named after a famous World War II carrier.
    a. U.S.S. *Nautilus*
    b. U.S.S. *Enterprise*
    c. U.S.S. *Long Beach*
    d. U.S.S. *Kentucky*

173. How was the *Georg Thiele* disengaged during the Battle of Narvik?
    a. Sunk
    b. Scuttled
    c. Blown up
    d. Beached

174. What single-engine fighter proved to be a complete failure for the Royal Air Force during the Battle of Britain?
    a. Defiant
    b. Gladiator
    c. Battle
    d. Roc

175. What was the first four-engine bomber to enter service with the Royal Air Force?
    a. Stirling
    b. Lancaster
    c. Halifax
    d. Liberator

176. How many beaches were designated by the Allied troops for D-day?
    a. Three
    b. Four
    c. Five
    d. Six

177. The 1943 invasion of Sicily by British and U.S. troops was known as Operation:

   a. Cricket

   b. Bulldog

   c. Husky

   d. Rugby

178. What was the name of General Patton's dog?

   a. Franklin

   b. Montgomery

   c. Charlie

   d. Willie

179. Which Allied aircraft did bomber crews nickname Little Friend?

   a. Mustang

   b. Hellcat

   c. Spitfire

   d. Thunderbolt

180. Who was the commander of the Japanese Thirty-second Army on Okinawa?

   a. Major General Isamu Cho

   b. Major General Kitagawa

   c. Lieutenant General Watanabi

   d. Lieutenant General Mitsuru Ushijima

181. What was the most heavily armed fighter used by the U.S. Army Air Force in the Pacific?

   a. P-61 Black Widow

   b. P-47 Thunderbolt

   c. P-51 Mustang

   d. P-40 Warhawk

182. Erwin Rommel commanded what unit during the 1940 French campaign, before he became the commander of the Afrika Korps?

    a. Sixth Panzer Division
    b. First Panzer Korps
    c. Fourth Light Division
    d. Seventh Panzer Division

183. What was the caliber of the main guns on the HMS *Rodney*?

    a. 16
    b. 6
    c. 12
    d. 15

184. On its Atlantic cruise, which German warship was disguised to deceive the enemy?

    a. *Bismarck*
    b. *Admiral Graf Spee*
    c. *Deutschland*
    d. *Admiral Scheer*

185. How was the carrier HMS *Hermes* sunk in April 1942?

    a. Sunk by Japanese carrier bomber attacks
    b. Torpedoed by Japanese midget submarines
    c. Torpedoed by the German submarine U-501
    d. Sunk by Japanese kamikaze attack

186. On January 30, 1945, this steamer was torpedoed by Russian submarine S-13, drowning an estimated 10,000 people during the evacuation of German troops from Baltic ports:

    a. *Karl Gustav*
    b. *Wilhelm Gustloff*
    c. *Prinz Eugen*
    d. *Blücher*

187. What percentage of German U-boats were lost?

   a. 90 percent

   b. 50 percent

   c. 70 percent

   d. 30 percent

188. How many sailors from the *Indianapolis* were rescued?

   a. 100

   b. 432

   c. 250

   d. 316

189. What was the most novel defense feature of the Ju 390 bomber?

   a. Gasoline-powered flamethrower-like turrets

   b. Carrying an Me 328 parasite fighter

   c. Speed

   d. Defensive rockets fired from the wings

190. Sir Robert MacLean coined the name Spitfire based on:

   a. An in-house contest

   b. A newspaper contest

   c. The name of a very successful Vickers transport

   d. His daughter's nickname

191. Which aircraft was an operational failure for the German Luftwaffe but was a success with the Hungarian Air Force?

   a. Fieseler Fi 156

   b. Junkers Ju 87

   c. Messerschmitt Me 210

   d. Blohm und Voss Bv 138

192. The B-17 bomber was built by:

   a. Boeing

   b. Lockheed-Vega

   c. Douglas

   d. All of the above

193. The Belgians were integrated with which section of the Royal Air Force?

    a. Bomber Command
    b. Coastal Command
    c. Fleet Air Arm
    d. Volunteer Reserve

194. In U.S. Navy nomenclature, what letter was used to identify Grumman as the aircraft's manufacturer?

    a. F
    b. N
    c. G
    d. R

195. What was the most important target for the Allied air forces over Holland from the end of 1944 until April 1945?

    a. V-1 rocket sites
    b. Airfields
    c. Troop concentrations
    d. V-2 rocket sites

196. The South African Air Force was the only Commonwealth air force:

    a. Which flew the Hurricane
    b. Not to fly under the Royal Air Force insignia
    c. Which took part in the desert battles
    d. Not to see action over Europe

197. The Republic P-43 fighter was the:

    a. Apache
    b. Thunderbolt
    c. Warhawk
    d. Lancer

198. What machine gun was used as an LMG and as a general-purpose machine gun?

   a. Breda M37

   b. MG34

   c. SG-43

   d. Vickers Machine Gun

199. Which aircraft dropped the atomic bomb on Nagasaki?

   a. Great Artiste

   b. Bocks Car

   c. Big Stink

   d. Necessary Evil

200. Which British battleship and battle cruiser were sent to Singapore to help prevent the Japanese invasion of Malaya?

   a. HMS *Prince of Wales* and HMS *Azalea*

   b. HMS *Prince of Wales* and HMS *Repulse*

   c. HMS *Repulse* and HMS *King George V*

   d. HMS *King George V* and HMS *Churchill*

201. Which unit was the leading force in the advance at the Battle of Arnhem?

   a. Guards' Division

   b. Forty-third Wessex Division

   c. Guards' Armored Division

   d. Seventh Armored Division

202. Why was XXX Corps forced to stop after they reached Eindhoven during the Battle of Arnhem?

   a. A German counterattack stopped the British advance

   b. A bridge had been destroyed

   c. The British advance did not stop at Eindhoven

   d. Because of roadblocks

203. A study of U.S. pilots who became aces (shot down more than five enemy planes) during World War II revealed that the most prevalent eye color among them was:

  a. Brown
  b. Bloodshot
  c. Chestnut
  d. Blue or green

204. What was the purpose of the Comintern?

  a. To outlaw communism in Germany
  b. To promote Soviet interests abroad and "spread the revolution"
  c. To create a broad-left alliance against fascism
  d. To set up a Soviet bloc in Eastern Europe

205. The pact that Germany, Italy, and Japan signed on September 27, 1940, was called the:

  a. Axis Pact
  b. Berlin Pact
  c. Third Reich Pact
  d. Tripartite Pact

206. What was the longest battle of the war?

  a. Midway
  b. Battle of the Atlantic
  c. Battle of the Bulge
  d. Kursk

207. The invasion of Normandy had two operation code names. Overlord was one; the second code name was:

  a. Operation Advance
  b. Operation Avalanche
  c. Operation Dragon
  d. Operation Neptune

208. On October 31, 1941, weeks before a declaration of war, this U.S. Navy destroyer was torpedoed and sunk by a German U-boat.

   a. U.S.S. *Reuben James*
   b. U.S.S. *Breckinridge*
   c. U.S.S. *Greer*
   d. U.S.S. *Lawrence*

209. What is the nickname of the U.S. Eighth Infantry division?

   a. Cactus Division
   b. Pathfinder
   c. Angels
   d. Viking

210. To mislead the Germans about Allied plans and unit strengths as preparations were made to invade Europe, an intricate deception plan was undertaken that involved fake radio traffic and inflatable tanks, and was commanded by General Patton. This was called:

   a. Operation Pogo
   b. Operation Thrust
   c. Operation Fortitude
   d. Operation Valiant

211. In what year did Japanese Americans receive an apology for their internment?

   a. 1948
   b. 1992
   c. 1976
   d. 1988

212. What was the fictitious unit commanded by General Patton as part of the deception plan executed prior to the invasion of Normandy?

   a. First U.S. Army Group (FUSAG)
   b. American Expeditionary Force (AEF)
   c. Tenth U.S. Fleet
   d. Allied Liberation Force (ALF)

213. What was the nickname for the parachute dummies used on D-day?

    a. Oscars
    b. Ruperts
    c. Steves
    d. Toms

214. How many Chinese were murdered by the Japanese army in the Nanjing Massacre?

    a. 3,000,000
    b. 20,000
    c. 1,000,000
    d. 300,000

215. The date of the U.S. invasion of the island of Okinawa was:

    a. April 1, 1945
    b. February 19, 1945
    c. June 6, 1944
    d. August 7, 1942

216. Name the Japanese warship that was built in 1920 and blew up at anchor near Hiroshima on June 6, 1943, possibly as the result of faulty ammunition:

    a. *Ise*
    b. *Mutsu*
    c. *Fuso*
    d. *Yamashira*

217. What are the dates of the Battle of Midway?

    a. April 14–16, 1942
    b. May 26–28, 1942
    c. June 4–6, 1942
    d. December 7–9, 1941

218. What was the original purpose of the Panzer I (Panzerkampfwagen I)?

   a. Cruiser tank
   b. Main battle tank
   c. Training tank
   d. Infantry tank

219. The largest gun on the M4 was:

   a. 150 millimeter
   b. 75 millimeter
   c. 105 millimeter
   d. 55 millimeter

220. Which German tank was in production throughout the entire war?

   a. Panzer IV
   b. Tiger
   c. Panzer III
   d. Nashorn

221. Over 58,000 of this tank were built during the war:

   a. T-34
   b. M4 (Sherman)
   c. Panzerkampfwagen IV
   d. Churchill

222. In its last battle, the *Bismarck* was up against the battleship HMS *King George V* and the HMS:

   a. *Renown*
   b. *Duke of York*
   c. *Repulse*
   d. *Rodney*

223. What British ship was the first to locate the *Bismarck* as it passed Greenland and Iceland?

   a. HMS *Suffolk*
   b. HMS *Maori*
   c. HMS *Norfolk*
   d. HMS *Neptune*

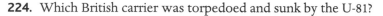
224. Which British carrier was torpedoed and sunk by the U-81?

    a. HMS *Victorious*
    b. HMS *Ark Royal*
    c. HMS *Eagle*
    d. HMS *Courageous*

225. When was the *Bismarck* launched?

    a. July 1, 1936
    b. May 27, 1941
    c. August 24, 1940
    d. February 14, 1939

226. Which German bomber used in the Battle of Britain could carry the most tonnage, and which could carry the least?

    a. Junkers 88; Junkers 87
    b. Junkers 87; Junkers 88
    c. Heinkel 111; Dornier 17
    d. Dornier 215; Heinkel 111

227. The Messerschmitt Komet was uncatchable except during what time?

    a. Attacking
    b. Climbing
    c. Gliding
    d. Takeoff

228. The first two atomic weapons utilized which elemental isotope of uranium?

    a. U-233
    b. U-238
    c. U-235
    d. U-234

229. What was the main German machine gun issued to infantry troops at the start of the war?

    a. MG-42
    b. MG-34
    c. FG-42
    d. MG-15

230. In what year did the U.S. Army establish the Paratrooper Division?

   a. 1943
   b. 1938
   c. 1941
   d. 1942

231. Name the dates on which the atomic bombs were dropped on Hiroshima and Nagasaki:

   a. August 6 and August 10, 1945
   b. August 8 and August 10, 1945
   c. August 7 and August 10, 1945
   d. August 6 and August 9, 1945

232. During the war, what was the first foodstuff rationed in the United States?

   a. Soft cheese
   b. Canned milk
   c. Coffee
   d. Sugar

233. Which fighter was flown by U.S. Navy and Marine pilots throughout 1942?

   a. Grumman F6F Hellcat
   b. Grumman F4F Wildcat
   c. Chance-Vought F4U Corsair
   d. Lockheed P-38 Lightning

234. Who was the Japanese ambassador to the United States at the time of the sneak attack on Pearl Harbor on December 7, 1941?

   a. Saburo Kurusu
   b. Kichisaburo Nomura
   c. Takeo Yoshikawa
   d. Ryunosuke Kusaka

235. What was the code name for the invasion of the Gilbert Islands?

  a. Operation Super Gymnast
  b. Operation Galvanic
  c. Operation Helina
  d. Operation Pominan

236. What was the size of the *Bismarck*'s main armament?

  a. 457 millimeter (18 inch)
  b. 406 millimeter (16 inch)
  c. 380 millimeter (15 inch)
  d. 355 millimeter (14 inch)

237. What was the deciding factor for the Japanese in the Battle of the Java Sea?

  a. Long Lance torpedo
  b. Battleships
  c. Aircraft
  d. Submarines

238. Which Japanese carrier sent aircraft that crippled the *York-town*?

  a. *Akagi*
  b. *Soryu*
  c. *Kaga*
  d. *Hiryu*

239. Which nation produced the oxygen torpedo?

  a. United States
  b. Japan
  c. Germany
  d. United Kingdom

240. What German U-boat commander was captured by the British on the high seas after his submarine went down?

a. Prien
b. Kretschmer
c. Schepke
d. Endrass

241. How many U.S. airmen were rescued by the U.S.S. *Tang* off the shores of Truk during U.S. bombing missions in August 1944?

a. Twenty-two
b. Six
c. Three
d. Eleven

242. Which aircraft, initially flown by Marine pilots, was the first that could match the Japanese Zero in almost every regard, but was more heavily armed and armored?

a. Grumman F4F Wildcat
b. Lockheed P-38 Lightning
c. Grumman F6F Hellcat
d. Chance-Vought F4U Corsair

243. Because of the demand for the Corsair, two additional companies were contracted to produce the aircraft under license. Which companies were they?

a. Boeing and Republic
b. Lockheed and Douglas
c. Brewster and Goodyear
d. North American and Curtis

244. What percentage of the isotope needed for an atomic weapon is found in uranium ore?

a. 0.71 percent
b. 6.03 percent
c. 14.26 percent
d. 3.73 percent

245. The main rifle issued to the German troops during the war was the:

   a. Karabiner 98 Kurz
   b. Gewehr 43
   c. Gewehr 98
   d. MP 40

246. What craft could land troops on virtually any stretch of land?

   a. Higgins boat
   b. LCT
   c. LCI
   d. Motor torpedo boat

247. When did Germany launch the first V-2 bombs against Britain?

   a. December 15, 1942
   b. October 10, 1943
   c. September 8, 1944
   d. January 1, 1945

248. Who publicly spoke out in wartime Britain against carpet bombing?

   a Michael Foot
   b. Eleanor Rathbone
   c. Stafford Cripps
   d. George Bell, bishop of Chichester

249. What was the Bouncing Betty?

   a. A German mine that exploded above ground
   b. A Sicilian prostitute shot as a German spy
   c. A British bomb that skimmed across water
   d. A female German American propaganda broadcaster

250. What was the code name for the Japanese attack on Pearl Harbor?

   a. Operation V
   b. Operation T
   c. Operation Z
   d. Operation J

251. Who was not a vice president under Franklin D. Roosevelt?

   a. John Garner
   b. Al Smith
   c. Harry Truman
   d. Henry Wallace

252. Which German general reached the Suez Canal and opened the way to the oil-rich Middle East?

   a. Erwin Rommel
   b. Archibald Wavell
   c. Albrecht Kesselring
   d. No German general did that in the war

253. What Japanese aircraft carrier was sunk at the Battle of the Coral Sea?

   a. *Shoho*
   b. *Hiyo*
   c. *Zuiho*
   d. *Ryujo*

254. Why was the Lee Enfield Mark 5 Jungle Carbine taken out of service?

   a. Desire for self-loading rifles; the Mark 5 had poor accuracy and hard recoil
   b. British bought the SLR
   c. Desire for self-loading weapons
   d. It was too inaccurate

255. The Panzerkampfwagen II was ultimately developed as a fast reconnaissance vehicle. What was its nickname?

   a. Luchs (Lynx)
   b. Maus (Mouse)
   c. Puma
   d. Hummel (Bumble Bee)

256. Why was there a congressional inquiry into the sinking of the *Indianapolis?*

    a. Henry Cabot Lodge had a son onboard

    b. President Truman's son was onboard

    c. A congressman's son died

    d. It was protocol at the time

257. Who came to the defense of the captain of the *Indianapolis* during his court-martial?

    a. President Truman

    b. Mochitsura Hashimoto

    c. Douglas MacArthur

    d. Chester Nimitz

258. What was the first U.S. aircraft carrier sunk in action?

    a. U.S.S. *Wasp*

    b. U.S.S. *Yorktown*

    c. U.S.S. *Hornet*

    d. U.S.S. *Lexington*

259. What were the two Royal Air Force turret fighters that saw service?

    a. Blackburn Roc and Westland Pterodactyl

    b. Blackburn Botha and Curtis Buccaneer

    c. Boulton Paul Defiant and Blackburn Botha

    d. Boulton Paul Defiant and Blackburn Roc

260. What company designed the U.S. P-66 Vanguard used in combat by the Chinese Air Force?

    a. Vought

    b. Grumman

    c. Republic

    d. Vultee

261. What was the code name of the Luftwaffe attack on January 1, 1945, on the Allied airfields in the Netherlands, Belgium, and northern France?

   a. Bodenplatte
   b. Fall Gelb
   c. Eagle Day
   d. Wacht am Rhein

262. Although all the following Luftwaffe aircraft operated at night, one of them never had a radar installation. Which one was it?

   a. Fw 189
   b. Bf 109
   c. Fw 190
   d. Si 204

263. What year did the Germans start work on their first jet?

   a. 1942
   b. 1939
   c. 1938
   d. 1944

264. What admiral was blamed for heavy U.S. losses at the Battle of Leyte Gulf by his commander, Admiral Nimitz?

   a. Admiral William Halsey
   b. Admiral Ernest King
   c. Admiral Raymond A. Spruance
   d. Admiral Harold Rainsford Stark

265. What was Alois Schicklgruber's claim to infamy?

   a. He was Adolf Hitler, by his original name
   b. German master spy
   c. German army general
   d. He was Adolf Hitler's father

266. What French ocean liner was seized by the U.S. government after the fall of France and turned into a troop ship?

   a. SS *Liberté*

   b. SS *Île de France*

   c. SS *Normandie*

   d. SS *Champlain*

267. Operation Cobra was the code name for:

   a. Allied breakout from Normandy

   b. Building of the airfield on Tinian for the A-bomb

   c. British attempt at relieving Greece

   d. Failed attempt on Hitler's life in 1944

268. The tank produced in the greatest numbers was the:

   a. T-34

   b. Churchill

   c. Panther

   d. Sherman

269. What was the code name for the Allied invasion of southern France?

   a. Dragoon

   b. Plunder

   c. Sea Lion

   d. Dragon

270. The commander in chief of the German Army at the outbreak of the war was relieved after the army's failure to capture Moscow in 1941. Who was he?

   a. Wilhelm von Leeb

   b. Walter von Reichenau

   c. Walter von Brauchitsch

   d. Paul von Kleist

271. Which islands in the Pacific took U.S. forces the longest to
subdue?

    a. Iwo Jima
    b. Guadalcanal
    c. Eniwetok
    d. Saipan

272. Which two generals carried out a five-day assault that forced
the Italian army to retreat back to Libya?

    a. Thomkins and O'Connor
    b. Thomkins and Montgomery
    c. Wavell and O'Connor
    d. Montgomery and Wavell

273. During the Battle of Leyte Gulf, a Japanese kamikaze aircraft struck the Seventh Fleet and succeeded in sinking this
escort carrier:

    a. *St. Lo*
    b. *Fanshaw Bay*
    c. *Kitkun Bay*
    d. *Kalinin Bay*

274. On what date was the carrier *Yorktown* sunk?

    a. May 30, 1942
    b. May 27, 1941
    c. June 7, 1942
    d. June 4, 1942

275. What sank the HMS *Courageous* in September 1939?

    a. German midget submarine
    b. German submarine U-29
    c. German dive-bomber
    d. German KMS *Scharnhorst*

276. Who was the highest ranking officer killed during the Pearl Harbor attack on December 7, 1941?

   a. Admiral Arthur W. Radford
   b. Fleet Admiral Frank Knox
   c. Captain Franklin Van Valkenburgh
   d. Rear Admiral Isaac C. Kidd

277. In which state was the submarine manufacturing facility Manitowoc?

   a. California
   b. Rhode Island
   c. Wisconsin
   d. Virginia

278. What advantage did the Spitfire pilots use against the Japanese fighters in the Pacific?

   a. Turning radius
   b. They had no overall advantage; they were evenly matched
   c. Low-altitude performance
   d. Speed

279. What was unusual about the PZL P.11 fighter's wing?

   a. It was a triplane
   b. It was a sesquiplane
   c. It had an inverted gull wing design
   d. It had a marked dihedral

280. How many Japanese aircraft were shot down for every Corsair lost in combat?

   a. Six
   b. Four
   c. Fourteen
   d. Eleven

281. The Hungarian Weiss WM 21 Sólyom reconnaissance bi-plane was a refined version of the:

    a. Fokker C.V

    b. Aero A.100

    c. Bristol F2B

    d. Gotha Go.145

282. The He 112 fighter saw action in the air force of:

    a. Bulgaria

    b. Croatia

    c. Hungary

    d. Romania

LIEUTENANT ANSWERS

1. d.	**22.** d.	**43.** b.	**64.** a.	**85.** a.
2. c.	**23.** d.	**44.** a.	**65.** b.	**86.** d.
3. b.	**24.** b.	**45.** c.	**66.** d.	**87.** b.
4. d.	**25.** d.	**46.** d.	**67.** b.	**88.** d.
5. c.	**26.** d.	**47.** c.	**68.** c.	**89.** d.
6. d.	**27.** d.	**48.** d.	**69.** d.	**90.** c.
7. c.	**28.** b.	**49.** b.	**70.** c.	**91.** b.
8. a.	**29.** c.	**50.** a.	**71.** b.	**92.** b.
9. a.	**30.** a.	**51.** d.	**72.** b.	**93.** c.
10. d.	**31.** d.	**52.** b.	**73.** a.	**94.** a.
11. a.	**32.** d.	**53.** c.	**74.** d.	**95.** b.
12. d.	**33.** b.	**54.** d.	**75.** b.	**96.** a.
13. d.	**34.** b.	**55.** c.	**76.** c.	**97.** c.
14. a.	**35.** a.	**56.** a.	**77.** d.	**98.** a.
15. b.	**36.** c.	**57.** c.	**78.** b.	**99.** b.
16. c.	**37.** c.	**58.** a.	**79.** b.	**100.** b.
17. a.	**38.** a.	**59.** d.	**80.** a.	**101.** d.
18. c.	**39.** b.	**60.** d.	**81.** a.	**102.** a.
19. b.	**40.** a.	**61.** a.	**82.** a.	**103.** b.
20. b.	**41.** b.	**62.** b.	**83.** c.	**104.** b.
21. a.	**42.** a.	**63.** a.	**84.** c.	**105.** c.

106. b.	142. d.	178. d.	214. d.	250. c.
107. b.	143. d.	179. a.	215. a.	251. b.
108. d.	144. c.	180. d.	216. b.	252. d.
109. d.	145. a.	181. a.	217. c.	253. a.
110. c.	146. a.	182. d.	218. c.	254. a.
111. c.	147. a.	183. a.	219. c.	255. a.
112. b.	148. c.	184. b.	220. a.	256. c.
113. c.	149. a.	185. d.	221. b.	257. b.
114. b.	150. c.	186. b.	222. d.	258. d.
115. d.	151. c.	187. c.	223. a.	259. d.
116. a.	152. a.	188. d.	224. b.	260. d.
117. a.	153. d.	189. b.	225. d.	261. a.
118. b.	154. a.	190. d.	226. c.	262. b.
119. c.	155. c.	191. c.	227. c.	263. c.
120. c.	156. b.	192. d.	228. c	264. a.
121. d.	157. a.	193. d.	229. b.	265. d.
122. c.	158. d.	194. a.	230. d.	266. c.
123. d.	159. b.	195. d.	231. d.	267. a.
124. a.	160. b.	196. b.	232. d.	268. a.
125. a.	161. c.	197. d.	233. b.	269. a.
126. c.	162. b.	198. b.	234. b.	270. c.
127. b.	163. b.	199. b.	235. b.	271. b.
128. b.	164. a.	200. b.	236. c.	272. c.
129. a.	165. d.	201. c.	237. a.	273. a.
130. b.	166. d.	202. b.	238. d.	274. c.
131. c.	167. a.	203. d.	239. b.	275. b.
132. b.	168. d.	204. b.	240. b.	276. d.
133. b.	169. a.	205. d.	241. a.	277. c.
134. d.	170. c.	206. b.	242. d.	278. d.
135. b.	171. c.	207. d.	243. c.	279. c.
136. a.	172. b.	208. a.	244. a.	280. d.
137. d.	173. d.	209. b.	245. a.	281. a.
138. d.	174. a.	210. c.	246. a.	282. d.
139. c.	175. a.	211. b.	247. c.	
140. d.	176. c.	212. a.	248. d.	
141. b.	177. c.	213. b.	249. a.	

MAJOR

1. The first operational reconnaissance jet or rocket operation was flown by what aircraft?
   a. Hs 132
   b. He 178
   c. Ar 234
   d. Me 262

2. What was the first atomic weapon tested in New Mexico?
   a. Jumbo
   b. Gadget
   c. Little Boy
   d. Thin Man

3. What was the most common rifle used by the U.S. Marines at the beginning of the Pacific war?
   a. M1 Garand
   b. Lee-Enfield Mk III
   c. M1 Carbine
   d. Springfield 1903

4. Which country suffered the largest number of civilian deaths?

    a. Germany
    b. U.S.S.R.
    c. Poland
    d. Japan

5. What was unique about the Triple Nickels, the 555th Airborne, a detachment of the Eighty-second Airborne?

    a. They were the first African American paratroopers
    b. They specialized in amphibious assault methods
    c. They fought on every continent at war
    d. They were a mix of Australians and Canadians

6. At Stalingrad, the largest offensive and counteroffensive occurred at a small factory called:

    a. Red October Factory Complex
    b. May Day Factory Complex
    c. Lenin Factory Complex
    d. Great Stalin Factory Complex

7. From July 1942 to January 1943, Australian troops fought a battle against the Japanese along a jungle trail in the highlands of New Guinea called:

    a. Kodak Trail
    b. Konyoda Trail
    c. Kodiak Trail
    d. Kokoda Trail

8. To whom did Adolf Hitler dictate *Mein Kampf*?

    a. Hermann Goering
    b. Martin Bormann
    c. Rudolf Hess
    d. Ernst Röhm

9. On November 29, 1945, the prosecution at Nuremberg revealed the true horrors of Nazism by showing a film of:

   a. The conditions at Auschwitz
   b. The concentration camp at Belsen
   c. The German advance into Russia
   d. Nazi troops invading Poland

10. Who was Hitler's chief architect?

    a. Adam Speer
    b. Adalbert Spier
    c. Alfred Speer
    d. Albrecht Speer

11. Name two tanks that were very evenly matched:

    a. Pzkpf VI Tiger and the IS-2
    b. Pzkpf V Panther and the T-34
    c. Pzkpf IV and the M4 Sherman
    d. Pzkpf VII King Tiger and the Tetrach

12. Which Russian armored unit stopped the German advance on Kursk, at the village of Prokhorovka, on July 12, 1943?

    a. Second Guards tank army
    b. Fifth Guards tank army
    c. Fifth tank army
    d. Fourth Shock army

13. What was unique about the Japanese battleships *Ise* and *Hyuga*?

    a. Main guns were two different calibers
    b. All main guns were aft
    c. No pagoda masts
    d. They were hybrid battleships, that is, battleships converted into aircraft carriers

14. What was Rainbow Five?

    a. Basic U.S. Navy war plan
    b. Basic U.S. Army war plan
    c. Call sign for Japanese scout aircraft
    d. Name of Japanese midget submarine

15. What tank destroyer was nicknamed the Hellcat for its amazing speed and maneuverability?

   a. M50

   b. M18

   c. M36

   d. M56

16. Which SS unit, known as the Wiking Division, was made up of volunteers from the Scandinavian countries?

   a. Fifteenth Light Division

   b. Second SS Division

   c. Fifth SS Division

   d. Fourth SS Division

17. On what date was the wreck of the *Bismarck* found?

   a. September 1, 1985

   b. June 8, 1989

   c. February 1, 1983

   d. January 26, 1986

18. In which shipyard did the U.S. Navy build the *Enterprise*?

   a. Newport News

   b. Norfolk

   c. Philadelphia

   d. Bremerton

19. What kind of U-boat was the U-460?

   a. Electric drive

   b. Coastal

   c. Refueling

   d. Snorkel

20. During the later stages of the war, modified P-51B/Cs were used to counter:

   a. High-flying Luftwaffe bombers

   b. V-1s

   c. High-speed jet bombers

   d. V-2 rockets

21. Heinkel's heavy bomber He 177 was prone to catching fire, so its crews nicknamed it:

    a. Widow Maker
    b. Cigarette Lighter of the Reich
    c. Old Smokey
    d. Burninator

22. Designed for the northern waters near Russia, the KOR-1 was a failure as a:

    a. Catapult-launched flying boat
    b. ASW flying boat
    c. Patrol bomber
    d. Transport

23. Which was the heaviest U.S. bomber to fly in the European theater?

    a. Boeing B-17 Flying Fortess
    b. Consolidated B-24 Liberator
    c. North American B-25 Mitchell
    d. Martin B-26 Marauder

24. The Fiat G.55, the Macchi C.205, and this fighter were later-generation "5-series" Italian fighters based on the DB 605 engine:

    a. Reggiane Re.2005
    b. Fiat CR.25
    c. Caproni-Vizzola F.5
    d. IMAM Ro.55

25. Which part of the name "PBY Catalina" revealed its manufacturer?

    a. Y
    b. B
    c. P
    d. Catalina

26. The Sea Otter was designed as a replacement for which aircraft?

    a. Albacore
    b. Walrus
    c. Swordfish
    d. Barracuda

27. What was the main duty of the Armstrong Whitworth Albermarle?

    a. Bomber
    b. Glider tug
    c. Transport
    d. Covert operations

28. What Axis weapon was created to provide a shorter service rifle?

    a. Carcano M1891
    b. Gewehr 43
    c. Karabiner 98k
    d. Arisaka Type 38

29. What U.S. submachine gun that was designed and manufactured during the war was later used in Vietnam?

    a. Browning Automatic Rifle (BAR)
    b. M3 "Grease Gun"
    c. M1A1 Thompson
    d. Browning 1911

30. Who was the British commander of the Allied forces in Malaya and Singapore?

    a. General Percival
    b. Vice Admiral Phillips
    c. General Brett
    d. General Wavell

31. What occupied nation was the subject of the harshest rationing?

   a. Finland
   b. Russia
   c. Poland
   d. France

32. What admiral commanded the *Bismarck* and went down with the ship?

   a. Karl Doenitz
   b. Guenther Lutjens
   c. Heinrich Raeder
   d. Maximilian Graf von Spee

33. Who signed the Potsdam Agreement in August 1945?

   a. Stalin, Churchill, and de Gaulle
   b. Roosevelt, Attlee, and Churchill
   c. Truman, Roosevelt, and Churchill
   d. Stalin, Truman, and Attlee

34. Who were known during the war as the Brylcream Boys?

   a. Royal Air Force members
   b. A USO comedy troop
   c. General Eisenhower's staff
   d. FDR, Churchill, and Stalin

35. Anderson Shelter was:

   a. A British general captured in North Africa
   b. A British air raid shelter named after Sir John Anderson
   c. A spy for Germany
   d. A U.S. fighter ace serving with the Eagle Squadron

36. What name was given to Russian deserters working for the Germans?

   a. Russkies
   b. Traitors
   c. Tongues
   d. Hiwis

37. What percentage of recruits qualified as Airborne?

    a. 35 percent

    b. 67 percent

    c. 50 percent

    d. 10 percent

38. What is the most difficult part of jumping?

    a. Jumping out of the aircraft

    b. Carrying the supplies

    c. Jolt from the parachute

    d. Landing on the ground

39. Which aircraft was used for the delivery of Japanese parachutists?

    a. Lockheed Lodestar

    b. DC-2

    c. Topsey

    d. DC-3

40. In what year did the T-34 tank start production?

    a. 1935

    b. 1940

    c. 1938

    d. 1942

41. The heaviest tank was named the:

    a. King Tiger

    b. IS2

    c. M26

    d. Maus

42. What was special about the Sherman Rhino version tank?

    a. Hedge-cutter

    b. Bulldozer

    c. DD version

    d. Equipped with a flamethrower

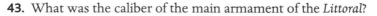

43. What was the caliber of the main armament of the *Littoral*?

   a. 5.25

   b. 16

   c. 15

   d. 12

44. At the outset of the war, the Royal Navy adopted a policy to counter German U-boats that was ahead of its time. What was it?

   a. Use of ASDIC

   b. Blockade of German ports

   c. Sowing minefields in coastal waters

   d. Formation of hunting groups to "take the fight to the enemy"

45. This was the worst British maritime disaster, with losses estimated up to 6,000 souls lost when it was sunk ten miles off St. Nazaire on June 17, 1940:

   a. *Devonshire*

   b. *York*

   c. *Lancastria*

   d. *Somerset*

46. Which Spitfire was equal to the Fw 190?

   a. Mk VII

   b. Mk VIII

   c. Mk IX

   d. F.Mk IV

47. Which U.S. Navy fighter was the first to match the Japanese Zero?

   a. Grumman F6F Hellcat

   b. Grumman F4F Wildcat

   c. Chance-Vought F4U Corsair

   d. Lockheed P-38 Lightning

48. Which way did the B-17's main landing gear retract?

   a. Outward and into the wings

   b. Inward and into the wings

   c. Backward and into the outboard engine nacelles

   d. Forward and into the inboard engine nacelles

49. What was the most modern fighter that Belgium fielded at the beginning of the war?

   a. Fokker D XXI (21)

   b. Supermarine Spitfire

   c. Hawker Hurricane

   d. Brewster F2A

50. What kind of Bell Airacobra fighters were rejected for Royal Air Force service and diverted to the U.S. Army Air Force?

   a. P-39RAF

   b. P-39R

   c. P-400

   d. P-100

51. What was the Vickers replacement for the Wellington?

   a. Wolsey

   b. Worcester

   c. Warwick

   d. Wendover

52. What was considered Germany's best night fighter?

   a. Ar 240

   b. Ju 188

   c. He 219

   d. Me 110H

53. Which of the following was not a Nazi concentration camp?

   a. Auschwitz in Poland

   b. Berchtesgaden in Germany

   c. Mauthausen Gusen in Austria

   d. Majdanek in Poland

54. On which two beaches did the British land on D-day?

    a. Gold and Juno

    b. Omaha and Utah

    c. Sword and Gold

    d. Utah and Juno

55. Operation Dragoon was the invasion of:

    a. Salerno Beachhead

    b. Guadalcanal

    c. Iwo Jima

    d. Southern France

56. The invasion of Japan, which would have cost millions of lives, was called Operation:

    a. Spectre

    b. Cave or Fire (Cave for the aerial assault; Fire for the landings)

    c. Olympic

    d. Pearl Necklace

57. A drug used for "battle fatigue" cases at convalescent hospitals was thought to get combat soldiers over their fear of battle by causing them to dream flashbacks of their combat experiences. What was it called?

    a. Panzer Poppers

    b. Blue .88s

    c. Stuka Shriekers

    d. Potato Skull Mashers

58. Who was the commander of the U.S. II Corps at the defeat at the Battle of Kasserine Pass?

    a. Mark W. Clark

    b. George S. Patton

    c. Lloyd R. Fredenhall

    d. Omar N. Bradley

59. What was the message sent by Admiral Halsey to Admiral Mitscher on Guadalcanal to proceed in the plan to shoot down the aircraft carrying Japanese Admiral Yamamoto on April 18, 1943?

   a. It appears the peacock will be on time. Fan his tail.
   b. It seems the lion has awoke. Strangle the beast.
   c. Golden Goose is on the loose. Get the hunters ready.
   d. Great White is among us. Harpoons on the ready.

60. Adolf Hitler's rise to power in Germany can be attributed to a series of events, one of them being the Reichstag fire. In which year did this occur?

   a. 1933
   b. 1936
   c. 1934
   d. 1932

61. Intrepid was the code name for this head of the British intelligence network:

   a. Sir Lawrence Olivier
   b. Sir Conan Doyle
   c. Sir Arthur Scott
   d. Sir William Stephenson

62. What class of battleship was the U.S.S. *Iowa*?

   a. Missouri class
   b. Outside any class
   c. North Carolina class
   d. Iowa class

63. Which U.S. submarine commander sank the most ships?

   a. Richard Donafrio
   b. Edward Shelby
   c. Richard O'Kane
   d. John Lee

64. What was the date of V-E day?

   a. May 10, 1945
   b. May 11, 1945
   c. May 8, 1945
   d. May 9, 1945

65. Which of the following was not *Time* Magazine's Man of the Year during the war?

   a. Truman
   b. Stalin
   c. Churchill
   d. FDR

66. What happened to Mussolini after he was dismissed by the Grand Fascist Council?

   a. He was kidnapped by the SS and made head of a new Nazi puppet state in northern Italy
   b. He was kidnapped by Italian antifascist guerrillas
   c. He was put on trial, but died before the trial ended
   b. He was held in custody until the end of the war, and then tried at Nuremberg

67. What size was the standard Japanese rifle round?

   a. 8 millimeter
   b. 7.92 millimeter
   c. 7.7 millimeter
   d. .30 cal

68. What was the death rate of U.S. POWs in Japanese camps?

   a. 15 percent
   b. 42 percent
   c. 7 percent
   d. 27 percent

69. What was the most powerful German tank destroyer?

    a. Marder III

    b. Wespe

    c. Jagdpanther

    d. Jagdtiger

70. The most common tank used by the Germans during the invasion of France and the Low Countries was the:

    a. Panther

    b. Panzer II

    c. Panzer IV

    d. Panzer III

71. What was the only tank designed and produced in Australia?

    a. Sentinel

    b. Priest

    c. Ram

    d. AMR 33

72. How many panzers were used by the German armed forces for the invasion of France and the Low Countries?

    a. 1,279

    b. 6,345

    c. 2,439

    d. 12,125

73. What type of Japanese warships were originally designed as light cruisers with 6 inch guns, but converted into heavy cruisers armed with 8 inch guns?

    a. Atago class

    b. Tone class

    c. Myoko class

    d. Mogami class

74. How many German U-boats were commissioned into active service with the Kriegsmarine between 1935 and 1945?

   a. 3,150

   b. 2,150

   c. 650

   d. 1,150

75. What battleship was preserved as a museum before being re-commissioned as IX-22 during the war?

   a. U.S.S. *Maine*

   b. U.S.S. *Virginia*

   c. U.S.S. *New Hampshire*

   d. U.S.S. *Oregon*

76. Name the Japanese submarine capable of launching aircraft.

   a. Ro-103

   b. I-400

   c. I-58

   d. I-571

77. How many long-range bomber types did the Germans propose that would be capable of crossing the Atlantic and bombing New York?

   a. Six

   b. Three

   c. Four

   d. Five

78. What about the Bachem 349 Natter's landing gear was unique? It took off:

   a. On a skid

   b. From a vertical platform

   c. On tricycle landing gear

   d. On a jettisonable trolley

79. Which air force had a mix of Messerschmitt Bf 109s, Hawker Hurricanes, Dornier Do 17s, and Bristol Blenheims in its inventory at the same time?

   a. Romania
   b. Yugoslavia
   c. Hungary
   d. Bulgaria

80. What was the Czech-designed reconnaissance biplane used by the wartime Slovakian Air Force?

   a. Aero A-204
   b. Letov S-528
   c. Letov S-328
   d. Aero A-304

81. With twelve air victories and four shared victories, Lily Litvak was one of only two female fighter aces in the world. This top Russian female ace, who died August 1, 1943, had a large flower painted on the side of her aircraft, which resulted in the nickname:

   a. The White Lily of Leningrad
   b. The Black Lily of Sevastopol
   c. The Jasmine of Kharkov
   d. The White Rose of Stalingrad

82. What did the initials SNCAO, SECM, SNCASCO, SNCAC, SNCAN, and SNCASO signify in relation to French military aircraft?

   a. Type designations
   b. Year of manufacture
   c. Armament configurations
   d. Regional manufacturing groups

83. Which aircraft went by the name Tabby?

   a. Douglas C-47 Dakota
   b. Mitsubishi Ki-67 Hiryu
   c. Mitsubishi Ki-49 Donryu
   d. Mitsubishi G3M

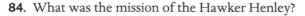

84. What was the mission of the Hawker Henley?

    a. Communications

    b. Covert missions

    c. Artillery spotting

    d. Target tug

85. The main Belgian sidearm was the:

    a. Colt M1911

    b. Walther PP

    c. Lahti L-35

    d. Browning Hi-Power

86. During Audie Murphy's combat service, approximately how many enemy soldiers was he credited with killing?

    a. 130

    b. 240

    c. 200

    d. 320

87. What was the nickname of the Thirty-sixth U.S. Infantry Division?

    a. Tiger

    b. Spearhead

    c. Texas

    d. Super Thirty-sixth

88. Which of these groups is generally accepted as having the highest casualties of the war?

    a. Allied civilians

    b. Allied soldiers

    c. Axis civilians

    d. Axis soldiers

89. Who was the commander of the U.S. Fifth Army in Italy?

    a. George S. Patton

    b. John P. Lucas

    c. Mark W. Clark

    d. Lucian P. Truscott Jr.

90. What was the nickname given to the Christmas cards sent out by King George VI of England in 1940?

    a. London Greetings

    b. Blitzmas Cards

    c. Peace Next Christmas

    d. Buckingham Greetings

91. Name the third major U.S. carrier to be lost in the Pacific theater.

    a. *Hornet*

    b. *Enterprise*

    c. *Saratoga*

    d. *Wasp*

92. What was the date of the first day of the battle of Iwo Jima?

    a. March 20

    b. March 19

    c. February 19

    d. February 20

93. What was the name of the fast Japanese destroyers armed with the long-lance torpedo?

    a. Kango

    b. Kirimushi

    c. Kushi

    d. Kagero

94. What day was the U.S.S. *Indianapolis* sunk?

    a. July 30, 1945

    b. July 30, 1944

    c. August 1, 1945

    d. August 1, 1944

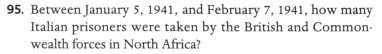

95. Between January 5, 1941, and February 7, 1941, how many Italian prisoners were taken by the British and Commonwealth forces in North Africa?

   a. 80,000

   b. 113,000

   c. 60,000

   d. 73,000

96. Which Polish tank was based on the Vickers six ton?

   a. Poland did not have tanks

   b. 10-TP

   c. 7-TP

   d. 14-TP

97. Where did the Twenty-first Panzer Division first serve?

   a. Yugoslavia

   b. Poland

   c. North Africa

   d. Russia

98. During the Battle of Leyte Gulf, Admiral Nishimura's Southern Force steamed through which strait?

   a. Torres

   b. Malacca

   c. Surigao

   d. San Bernadino

99. What was the last Japanese carrier sunk at the Battle of Midway?

   a. *Soryu*

   b. *Hiryu*

   c. *Akagi*

   d. *Kaga*

100. What auxiliary cruiser sacrificed itself to allow the convoy it was escorting to escape the German surface raider *Admiral Scheer*?

    a. *Rawalpindi*
    b. *Jervis Bay*
    c. *Empire Tide*
    d. *Audacity*

101. What happened to Captain-Lieutenant Gunther Prien's U-47 during March 1941?

    a. Went into Scapa Flow, Scotland, to sink the *Ark Royal*
    b. Captured on the high seas
    c. Sank the aircraft carrier HMS *Eagle*
    d. Sunk by the British

102. How was LST 289 damaged during a mock landing in Normandy?

    a. Torpedoed by a motorboat
    b. Hit by a cruiser
    c. Torpedoed by a U-boat
    d. Bombed by aircraft

103. The official German designation *Panzerschiff* translates into the English term:

    a. Pocket battleship
    b. Battleship
    c. Battle cruiser
    d. Light cruiser

104. The oddest transport aircraft was definitely the Antonov A-40, which was a:

    a. Human-powered aircraft
    b. Flying submarine
    c. Tank with wings attached
    d. Huge flying wing

105. Why was the Mustang the escort fighter of choice in Europe?

   a. It had two wing-mounted drop tanks
   b. It had the best dogfighting specs
   c. It was faster than any other fighter in the air until the Me 262 came online
   d. None of these reasons

106. German fighter pilots were skeptical of the Fw 190 D-9 because its engine was originally designed for bombers. What was the engine?

   a. Junkers Jumo 213
   b. DB 605
   c. BMW 801
   d. Argus 410

107. Flying a Corsair from the deck of HMS *Formidable*, this Canadian pilot single-handedly sank a Japanese destroyer:

   a. Johnny Johnstone
   b. Robert Hampton Gray
   c. Douglas Bader
   d. George Richardson

108. Which aircraft is known as the B-18?

   a. Avenger
   b. Bolo
   c. Lancaster
   d. Marauder

109. How did the Royal Air Force designate the Curtiss P-40 supplied to them by the United States?

   a. Mohawk
   b. Tomahawk and Kittyhawk
   c. Kittyhawk
   d. Tomahawk

110. Which Luftwaffe fighter made up more than half of Germany's night fighter strength from 1943 to 1945?

   a. Me 110F
   b. Me 110G
   c. Ju 88C
   d. Ju 88G

111. Special plants were built to separate and concentrate the required uranium isotope for the atomic bombs in:

   a. Wendover, Utah
   b. Hanford, Washington
   c. Oak Ridge, Tennessee
   d. Los Alamos, New Mexico

112. What Australian city was bombed more heavily than Pearl Harbor?

   a. Darwin
   b. Melbourne
   c. Sydney
   d. Perth

113. Where was the last major airborne operation carried out by the German Army?

   a. Crete
   b. Stalingrad
   c. Battle of the Bulge
   d. Anzio

114. When did the Anschluss take place?

   a. September 1939
   b. March 1939
   c. March 1938
   d. September 1936

115. Mustard gas, heavily used in World War I, also resulted in the loss of life during World War II. In which action was it used?

   a. Japanese used it against U.S. Marines in Okinawa
   b. German Luftwaffe blew up a U.S. supply ship that had the gas on board at Bari, Italy
   c. German Luftwaffe dropped gas bombs on Stalingrad
   d. Germans fired it in artillery shells at Warsaw, Poland

116. What was the fate of the aircraft carrier U.S.S. *Saratoga*?

   a. Sunk by Japanese aircraft in the Battle of Wake Island
   b. Decommisioned August 13, 1956
   c. Sunk at Guadalcanal
   d. Sunk in nuclear bomb test at Bikini Atoll

117. On what date was Mussolini killed?

   a. April 29, 1944
   b. April 28, 1945
   c. April 30, 1944
   d. April 31, 1945

118. Which air force had the worst bomber production-to-loss ratio during 1942?

   a. Royal Air Force
   b. Luftwaffe
   c. U.S. Army Air Force
   d. RAAF

119. On what date did the war officially end?

   a. October 3, 1990
   b. September 15, 1945
   c. September 2, 1945
   d. August 29, 1945

120. After his return home, what was John "Doc" Bradley's occupation?

    a. Dentist
    b. Undertaker
    c. Bank executive
    d. Electrician

121. Name the hybrid battleship carrier sunk July 24, 1945, in shallow water near Kure:

    a. *Hyuga*
    b. *Fuso*
    c. *Taiho*
    d. *Kongo*

122. Which Marine outfit served as the beach defense on Corregidor?

    a. Sixth Marine Regiment
    b. First Marine Raider Battalion
    c. Fourth Marine Regiment
    d. Third Marine Division

123. Who stated, "Help is on the way" in a report to the troops in the Philippines on January 15, 1942, when he knew it wasn't true?

    a. Franklin D. Roosevelt
    b. Harry S Truman
    c. General Krueger
    d. General MacArthur

124. What did the U.S. Navy call the Japanese Navy's operational code?

    a. JN19
    b. JN25
    c. JN12
    d. JN15

125. What was the Biscay Cross?

    a. German submariner slang for the Knight's Cross

    b. Primitive radar antenna

    c. Medal awarded for ten successful patrols

    d. Medal awarded to Coastal Command crews for sinking a U-boat

126. Where was the heavy cruiser *Blücher* sunk?

    a. Narvik

    b. Oslofjord

    c. Altenfjord

    d. Bergen

127. Which carrier accompanied the *Enterprise* in the Battle of Santa Cruz?

    a. *Saratoga*

    b. *Wasp*

    c. *Intrepid*

    d. *Hornet*

128. How long were the sailors of the *Indianapolis* in the water before being rescued?

    a. Three days

    b. Five days

    c. One day

    d. Six days

129. After many experiments, what engine was finally settled on, creating the P-51B Mustang?

    a. Allison V-1710

    b. Packard Merlin V 1650

    c. Pratt and Whitney R-2800

    d. Packard Merlin V-1630

130. What was the Mustang's Achilles heel?

   a. Vulnerable cooling system

   b. Tendency for engine to lock up at low altitudes

   c. Exposed radiator

   d. Weak underside armor

131. What fighter aircraft was used during the early part of 1942 by the U.S. Army Air Corps, Navy, and Marine pilots in the Pacific theater?

   a. Curtis P-40 Tomahawk

   b. Brewster F2A-2 Buffalo

   c. Bell P-39 Airacobra

   d. Grumman F4F Wildcat

132. What was the difference between an Me 321 and an Me 323?

   a. Me 323 used nonstrategic materials

   b. Me 321 had four engines; the Me 323 had six

   c. Me 321 was a glider

   d. There never was an Me 321

133. What was the name of the Curtiss P-36 fighter in the Royal Air Force?

   a. Skyhawk

   b. Warhawk

   c. Mohawk

   d. Blackhawk

134. France's primary fighter when the Germans invaded in May 1940 was the:

   a. Fokker D. XXI

   b. Hawk 75A

   c. M.S. 406

   d. D. 520

135. General Leslie Groves, military leader of the Manhattan Project, had previously overseen:

    a. Construction of the Pentagon

    b. Construction of the airfields in Honolulu

    c. Development of the Sherman tank

    d. Development of the B-17 bomber

136. What size ammunition was used in the MG-42?

    a. 7.62 millimeter

    b. .30 inch

    c. .303 inch

    d. 7.92 millimeter

137. Who was the first U.S. general to command four field armies?

    a. Mark Clark

    b. Dwight D. Eisenhower

    c. Omar N. Bradley

    d. Louis A. Craig

138. How many eggs per week did the German government allow each citizen in 1940?

    a. Two

    b. Five

    c. Twelve

    d. None

139. Audie Murphy was attached to which unit when he arrived in Casablanca, North Africa, in 1943?

    a. Twenty-fifth Infantry Division (Tropic Lightning)

    b. Second Armored Division (Hell on Wheels)

    c. First Infantry Division (Big Red One)

    d. Third Infantry Division (Rock of the Marne)

140. Where did Audie Murphy first see combat action?

   a. North Africa

   b. Southern Italy

   c. France

   d. Sicily

141. Audie Murphy received the medal of honor for action in which battle?

   a. St. Vith, Belgium

   b. Anzio, Italy

   c. Arnhem, Holland

   d. Holtzwihr, France

142. Which of the following is the operational code name for the Canadian raid on Dieppe?

   a. Operation Lightfoot

   b. Operation Totalize

   c. Operation Plunder

   d. Operation Jubilee

143. Which inhabited continent did not contribute troops to the war?

   a. None

   b. Oceania

   c. South America

   d. Africa

144. Name the U.S. general who directed the bombing of Japan:

   a. Curtis E. LeMay

   b. Carl A. Spaatz

   c. James H. Doolittle

   d. George C. Kenney

145. What was the code name of the German counteroffensive in the Ardennes forest (the Battle of the Bulge)?

    a. Winter Snow
    b. Restore Hope
    c. Autumn Mist
    d. Spring Awakening

146. Where did President Franklin Roosevelt sometimes go for medical treatment?

    a. Bridge Court
    b. Hot Springs
    c. Warm Springs
    d. Franklins Palace

147. Bella Russa was a:

    a. Soviet ship that was accidentally sunk by a U.S. submarine in May 1943
    b. Female officer in the Soviet Army who rose to the rank of general
    c. Female spy for Germany who was tried and hanged after being caught giving secrets to a Soviet double agent
    d. Female Soviet fighter ace who scored seventy-three kills

148. What aircraft was called the Jabo by German ground troops?

    a. P-47
    b. Me 262
    c. Bf 109
    d. Ju 87

149. What company first manufactured the Lee-Enfield used by the British?

    a. Colt
    b. Remington
    c. Kalashnikov
    d. Winchester

150. Paris was liberated on what date?

    a. July 25, 1944
    b. August 25, 1944
    c. June 25, 1944
    d. September 25, 1944

151. What was the main reason for the failure of Operation Market Garden? (If you saw *A Bridge Too Far*, you know the answer.)

    a. Eighty-second Airborne's failure to capture Nijmegen Bridge
    b. Lack of communication
    c. 101st's failure to capture Eindhoven Bridge
    d. Failure to update intelligence about the location of panzers

152. What are the approximate dates of the Nanjing Massacre?

    a. September–October 1937
    b. December 1936–March 1937
    c. December 1937–February 1938
    d. November 1941–January 1942

153. John Rabe pursued a career in business. Between 1908 and 1938, he worked for the Siemens AG China Corporation in Shenyang (Mukden), Beijing (Peiping), Tianjin (Tientsin), Shanghai, and finally Nanjing (Nanking). Rabe used his membership in a specific organization for humanitarian purposes, to create the Nanjing Safety Zone, which encompassed several foreign-owned properties and diplomatic missions, with the U.S. Embassy in the center. It ultimately sheltered some 200,000 Chinese from slaughter during the Nanjing Massacre. What organization did he belong to that gave him such pull with the Japanese military?

    a. U.S. Democratic National Committee
    b. Red Cross
    c. Nazi Party
    d. Freemasons

154. Which of the following was one of the six men who raised the flag on Iwo Jima?

    a. John Bradley
    b. Tim Block
    c. James Bradley
    d. Matt Block

155. General Douglas MacArthur fulfilled his pledge ("I shall return.") when he stepped ashore on which Philippine island in October 1944?

    a. Leyte
    b. Luzon
    c. Mindanao
    d. Quemoy

156. Where did the Japanese first use parachute troops?

    a. Philippines
    b. Battle of Midway
    c. Aleutian Islands
    d. Sumatra

157. What was the Allied designation for the Japanese DC-2?

    a. Zeke
    b. Pine
    c. Louise
    d. Tess

158. The Black Prince tank was based on the:

    a. Churchill
    b. Matilda II
    c. Sherman
    d. Mk VII Tetrarch

159. During the Battle of Leyte Gulf, a series of air strikes was launched against Admiral Kurita's Centre Force and this battleship was sunk:

a. *Yamato*

b. *Musashi*

d. *Haruna*

d. *Nagato*

160. What French battleship was forced to evacuate from Toulon to Dakar before completion, surrendered to the Allies, and was ultimately deployed to the East Indies with the British fleet?

a. *Jean Bart*

b. *Richelieu*

c. *Dunkerque*

d. *Strasbourg*

161. The type XXI U-boat was another superweapon that was too little and too late. How many were operational by the end of the war?

a. None

b. Two

c. Nine

d. Five

162. A Japanese steamer was torpedoed by the British submarine HMS *Tradewind* off the coast of Sumatra. The British did not know that the ship was carrying Dutch, British, American, and Australian POWs and Javanese slave laborers for work on a railway in Sumatra. What was the steamer called?

a. *Kobiashi Maru*

b. *Junyo Maru*

c. *Akagi*

d. *Soryu*

163. What battleship was severely damaged by the U.S.S. *Massachusetts* at the Battle of Casablanca?

  a. *Jean Bart*
  b. *Richelieu*
  c. *Roma*
  d. *Bretagne*

164. What was significant about the B-17s that arrived in the middle of the Pearl Harbor attack?

  a. Made first U.S. aircraft kill in the war
  b. There were no B-17s at Pearl Harbor
  c. Took pictures of the Japanese attack aircraft
  d. Were first U.S. aircraft shot down in the war

165. The Fairy Battle, a light attack aircraft of the Royal Air Force at the beginning of the war, first fought in what engagement?

  a. Battle of France
  b. Battle of Malta
  c. Battle of Dunkirk
  d. Battle of the Meuse

166. Which of the following pilots did not fly the P-51?

  a. Chuck Yeager
  b. Thomas McGuire
  c. Bud Anderson
  d. Robin Olds

167. What was the designation of the U.S. single-engine dive-bomber built to replace the Dauntless?

  a. TBM
  b. TBU
  c. TB2D
  d. SB2C

168. The JU-87 Stuka had a siren on its port landing gear, which was given this nickname:

    a. Horns of the Reich

    b. Trumpets of Jericho

    c. Sirens of Jericho

    d. Trumpets of Victory

169. Which of the following aircraft was not a British design?

    a. Master

    b. Wirraway

    c. Dominie

    d. Bolingbroke

170. During the invasion of what island did the South African Air Force support ground forces?

    a. Crete

    b. Mauritius

    c. Sardinia

    d. Madagascar

171. "Nick" is better known as the:

    a. Mitsubishi A6M

    b. Aichi B7A Ryusei

    c. Kawasaki Ki-45 Toryu

    d. Kawanishi N1K1-J

172. The base used by the 509th Group to launch aircraft over Japan was located on:

    a. Okinawa

    b. Kwajalein

    c. Midway

    d. Tinian

173. The most common German sidearm was the:

    a. Luger P08

    b. Browning 1911

    c. Walther PPK

    d. Walther P38

174. The average German received coupons to purchase this every two years:

   a. Winter boots

   b. Dress coat

   c. Winter coat

   d. Diapers

175. What did the Locarno Treaty guarantee?

   a. Germany's western borders as set out in the Versailles Treaty

   b. Germany's admission that it caused World War I

   c. Germany's eastern borders as set out in the Versailles Treaty

   d. France's willingness to allow German troops into the Rhineland

176. On June 15, 1944, B-29 bombers dropped the first bombs on Japan since Doolittle's raid. The code word for success was:

   a. Climb Mt. Fuji

   b. Betty, Betty, Betty

   c. Remember Bataan

   d. Enola Gay, all the way

177. What was the operational name for the Russian offensive to surround the Germans at Stalingrad?

   a. Ring

   b. Uranus

   c. Pluto

   d. Saturn

178. What German U-boat commander sank the greatest tonnage of Allied shipping?

   a. Wolfgang Luth

   b. Otto Kretschmer

   c. Gunther Prien

   d. Erich Topp

179. Name the French premier who accompanied British Prime Minister Chamberlain to the Munich Conference to appease Hitler:

　a. Foche
　b. Poetain
　c. de Gaulle
　d. Daladier

180. How many paratroopers took part in the D-day invasion?

　a. 15,100
　b. 10,000
　c. 13,400
　d. 12,300

181. At what speed did the aircraft go when they dropped parachuters?

　a. 150 kph
　b. 130 kph
　c. 130 mph
　d. 150 mph

182. Which of the following is not an aircraft carrier designation?

　a. CV
　b. CVE
　c. CVP
　d. CVA

183. Originally an Amagi Class battle cruiser, it was converted to a carrier and led the attack on Pearl Harbor, only to be sunk seven months later at the Battle of Midway. What was the ship's name?

　a. *Kaga*
　b. *Shoho*
　c. *Soryu*
　d. *Akagi*

184. What was the date of the Japanese invasion of the Philippines?

   a. December 7, 1941
   b. January 2, 1942
   c. December 10, 1941
   d. December 8, 1941

185. What was the name of the Philippine Scouts stationed in the barrio nearest to the Cabanatuan POW camp, who scouted the camp for intelligence vital to the rescue mission?

   a. Ranger
   b. Recon
   c. Liberty
   d. Alamo

186. Which Royal Navy carrier launched the raid on Taranto that disabled half the battleships of the Italian navy?

   a. *Illustrious*
   b. *Eagle*
   c. *Ark Royal*
   d. *Hermes*

187. What was the main feature that distinguished the *Scharnhorst* from its sister ship, the *Gneisenau*?

   a. Size of the aircraft hangar
   b. "Atlantic" bow
   c. Location of the mainmast
   d. Size of the funnel cap

188. The HMS *Barham* was sunk in the Mediterranean in 1941 by:

   a. U-47
   b. U-1943
   c. U-101
   d. U-331

189. Although the P-51D was the best version of the fighter, what claim to fame did the P-51B/C have that the later version lacked?

   a. Better armor
   b. Slightly better gun accuracy
   c. Slightly better fuel economy
   d. Greater speed

190. Reimar and Walter Horton designed which jet fighter-bomber?

   a. Fi 103
   b. Ar 234
   c. Go 229
   d. Ju 287

191. The Me 163 flew operationally with which Jagdgeschwader?

   a. JV44
   b. JG1
   c. JG400
   d. JG7

192. The "Lily" twin-engine bomber was better known as the:

   a. Kawasaki Ki-45 Toryu
   b. Mitsubishi G4M
   c. Kawasaki Ki-48
   d. Mitsubishi Ki-30

193. The "Sally" twin-engine bomber was officially designated the:

   a. Mitsubishi Ki-21
   b. Nakajima Ki-49 Donryu
   c. Mitsubishi Ki-67 Hiryu
   d. Nakajima Ki-44 Shoki

194. What was the first single-seat, twin-engine fighter to enter service with the Royal Air Force?

    a. Mosquito
    b. Lightning
    c. Whirlwind
    d. Beaufighter

195. Name the person who said, "If leaders are called to account and condemned, very well, but you cannot punish the German people at the same time. The German people are free of guilt."

    a. Wilhelm Keitel
    b. Alfred Rosenberg
    c. Hermann Goering
    d. Joachim von Ribbentrop

196. Which German SS tank divisions took part in the Battle of Arnhem?

    a. First SS Panzerdivision "Leibstandarte Adolf Hitler" and Third SS Panzerdivision "Totenkopf"
    b. Ninth SS Panzerdivision "Hohenstauffen" and Tenth SS Panzerdivision "Frundsberg"
    c. Twelfth SS Panzerdivision "Hitlerjugend" and Tenth SS Panzerdivision "Hohenstauffen"
    d. First SS Panzerdivision "Leibstandarte Adolf Hitler" and Second SS Panzerdivision "Das Reich"

197. Which weapon was originally developed in Czechoslovakia as the ZB-26?

    a. Sten
    b. M-3 "Grease Gun"
    c. Bren
    d. MP-38

198. Who was the first of the five Sullivan brothers to marry?

   a. George
   b. Joe
   c. Al
   d. Matt

199. Replacement depots in the European theater of operations were known as:

   a. Meat markets
   b. Repple-Depples
   c. New useless guy (NUG) factories
   d. Camp Disney

200. In early 1942, what general oversaw the retreat from Burma?

   a. Stilwell
   b. Bradley
   c. MacArthur
   d. Merrill

201. The Allied effort to capture Sardinia was called Operation:

   a. Husky
   b. Brimstone
   c. Chesterfield
   d. Gold

202. What model of the Thompson machine gun did the British acquire from the United States?

   a. M1a1
   b. M1
   c. M1928a1
   d. M1921

203. Which one of the six Japanese carriers that were part of the attack on Pearl Harbor was subsequently sunk during the Battle of Midway by dive-bombers from the U.S.S. *Yorktown*?

   a. *Hiryu*
   b. *Soryu*
   c. *Shoho*
   d. *Kagi*

204. What was the name of the atomic bomb dropped on Nagasaki?

   a. Fat Man
   b. Fat Boy
   c. Little Boy
   d. Little Man

205. Who was the U.S. ambassador to Japan on December 7, 1941, the date of the sneak attack on Pearl Harbor?

   a. Bertrand W. Gerhart
   b. Frank B. Keefe
   c. Harold L. Ickes
   d. Joseph C. Grew

206. What theme do the British traditionally follow when naming their self-propelled guns?

   a. Anglican saints
   b. Carnivorous animals
   c. Prime ministers
   d. Religious titles

207. The outset of war found two of the German Navy's heavy units at sea. Which ships were they?

   a. *Admiral Graf Spee* and *Deutschland*
   b. *Admiral Scheer* and *Deutschland*
   c. *Admiral Scheer* and *Admiral Graf Spee*
   d. *Admiral Graf Spee* and *Admiral Hipper*

208. Which of the following reasons was not a contributing factor to the Royal Navy's destroyer shortage in the summer and autumn of 1940?

   a. Destroyers held in reserve in case of invasion
   b. Destroyers lost in Norway
   c. Destroyers lost in Operation Dynamo
   d. Destroyers transferred for duties in the western Atlantic

209. The Messerschmitt Me 264 was abandoned as a candidate for the Amerika Bomber contest because:

   a. Messerschmitt needed to focus on the Me 262
   b. Its payload was too small
   c. It was too expensive
   d. It had weak armor and the engines were prone to failure

210. Where did Spitfires make their combat debut?

   a. Battle of Dunkirk
   b. Battle of Malta
   c. Defense of France
   d. Battle of Britain

211. The P-61 Black Widow was built by:

   a. Lockheed
   b. Republic
   c. North American
   d. Northrup

212. The Messerschmitt Bf 109T was:

   a. Designed as a carrier-borne fighter
   b. The fastest Bf 109
   c. An unarmed reconnaissance version
   d. A submarine

213. Name the German medium bomber converted into a night fighter that was unpopular with its crews:

   a. Junkers 88
   b. Dornier 217
   c. Messerschmitt 110
   d. Junkers 188

214. What was Stuka dive-bomber pilot Hans-Ulrich Rudel's final score?

    a. 132 tanks and 8 aircraft

    b. 300 tanks, 600 other vehicles, and 20 aircraft

    c. 519 tanks, 1,000 other vehicles, 150 artillery pieces, 11 aircraft, 1 battleship, 2 cruisers, and a destroyer

    d. 419 tanks, 623 other vehicles, 23 aircraft, and a destroyer

215. What was the P-400 fighter?

    a. Version of the P-40 fighter

    b. Version of the P-39 fighter

    c. Experimental fighter design

    d. 400th aircraft produced in the P-40 production line

216. On September 7, 1939, French Army forces invaded Germany from the west. The code name for this action was Operation:

    a. Saar

    b. Baytown

    c. Epsom

    d. Coronet

217. What was the starting date for the trial of the major Nazi war criminals?

    a. November 15, 1945

    b. November 20, 1945

    c. January 1, 1946

    d. January 25, 1946

218. What battleship was beached at Pearl Harbor, and later salvaged?

    a. *Utah*

    b. *Arizona*

    c. *Nevada*

    d. *Oklahoma*

219. The top American ace was:

   a. Jimmy Stewart
   b. Don Gentile
   c. Richard Bong
   d. Jay Robbins

220. The Japanese military hierarchy referred to their foot soldiers as *issen gorin*, which meant the soldiers were:

   a. Loyal to the emperor
   b. Expendable and easily replaced
   c. Bloodthirsty
   d. Divinely blessed

221. Name the battle at which the Japanese first deployed the kamikaze.

   a. Philippine Sea
   b. Okinawa
   c. Saipan
   d. Leyte Gulf

222. What U.S. submarine was credited with sinking the largest aircraft carrier in the Japanese fleet?

   a. U.S.S. *Archerfish* SS-311
   b. U.S.S. *Bonefish* SS-223
   c. U.S.S. *Guardfish* SS-217
   d. U.S.S. *Spearfish* SS-190

223. The Elefant tank was based on the chassis of the:

   a. King Tiger
   b. Sherman
   c. Tiger
   d. Panther

224. Which tank destroyer had a permanently rear-facing gun?

    a. M18 Hellcat
    b. Hetzer
    c. Jagdpanzer IV
    d. Archer

225. The U.S. concept for a tank destroyer during the war was:

    a. A tank with the main gun rechambered to take armor-piercing composite rigid (tungsten core) ammunition
    b. A lightly armored, long-barreled, self-propelled cannon, to be stationed at concealed defensive positions
    c. A tank with the same chassis as the tank on which it was based, but without the turret to allow a heavier gun
    d. A lightly armored vehicle with a powerful gun and great speed

226. How many Reichsmarks did it cost to produce one Tiger tank?

    a. 500,000
    b. 800,000
    c. 100,000
    d. 1,000,000

227. When were the first three panzer divisions formed?

    a. January 1933
    b. October 1935
    c. June 1937
    d. April 1939

228. The maximum speed of the *Bismarck* was:

    a. 28 knots
    b. 30 knots
    c. 24 knots
    d. 20 knots

229. The U.S. carrier *Yorktown* earned three battle stars for its World War II service, two of them for the significant part it played in stopping Japanese expansion and turning the tide of the war at the battles of Coral Sea and Midway, before being sunk in 1942. The wreck of the *Yorktown* was found and photographed by renowned oceanographer Dr. Robert D. Ballard, who also discovered the wreck of RMS *Titanic*. The *Yorktown*, three miles beneath the surface, was surprisingly intact, with much paint and equipment still visible after so many years underwater. In what year did he locate the wreck?

   a. 1995
   b. 2000
   c. 1999
   d. 1998

230. What was the caliber of the U.S.S. *Arkansas*'s main armament?

   a. 12 inch
   b. 16 inch
   c. 13 inch
   d. 15 inch

231. How many men were on the battleship *Bismarck* during its final battle in Operation Rheinübung, of which only 116 survived?

   a. 2,130
   b. 2,430
   c. 2,330
   d. 2,230

232. What was the first neutral ship to be sunk by a mine laid by a German U-boat?

   a. *Alexander van Opstal*
   b. *Suzon*
   c. *Solaas*
   d. *Hoegh Transport*

233. Name the British carrier torpedoed on September 17, 1939:

    a. HMS *Courageous*

    b. HMS *Furious*

    c. HMS *Ark Royal*

    d. HMS *Victory*

234. The carrier *Eagle* was torpedoed on August 11, 1942, by:

    a. U-148

    b. U-331

    c. U-73

    d. U-100

235. The captain of the *Lancastria*:

    a. Went down on the bridge of the *Lancastria*

    b. Was court-martialed and stripped of his rank

    c. Was never seen again

    d. Survived the disaster but was killed two years later

236. How many B-17 bombers did the super-interceptor Me 163 shoot down?

    a. Nine

    b. One

    c. None

    d. 116

237. What German fighter was the only aircraft that could keep pace with the Mustang?

    a. Fw 190

    b. Me 110

    c. Me 109

    d. Me 262 (Jet)

238. What was Romania's only fighter aircraft of native design during the war?

    a. IAR 80

    b. IAR 25

    c. PZL P.24

    d. PZL P.11

239. Generalmajor Adolf Galland took command of which fighter unit after being relieved of command of the post General der Jagdflieger in 1945?

    a. Kommando Nowotny
    b. JG7
    c. Erprobungskommando
    d. JV44

240. Which air force lost the most aircraft over the Netherlands?

    a. U.S. Army Air Force
    b. Royal Air Force
    c. Luftwaffe
    d. Dutch Air Force

241. How many Fokker D. XXIs did the Dutch Air Force have in May 1940?

    a. 28
    b. 76
    c. 70
    d. 100

242. How many Belgian pilots fought in the Battle of Britain?

    a. 107
    b. 16
    c. 29
    d. 14

243. What country used the PTRD-41, and what size ammunition did it use?

    a. Japan, 7.7 × 58 millimeter
    b. Germany, 7.92 × 94 millimeter
    c. Soviet Union, 14.5 × 114 millimeter
    d. Soviet Union, 7.92 × 45 millimeter

244. Which U.S. general captured Rome two days before D-day?

    a. George Patton
    b. Omar Bradley
    c. Bernard Montgomery
    d. Mark Clark

245. After the Nuremberg war crime trials, the convicted were hanged. Their bodies were photographed, and then:

    a. Were buried in a mass grave, whose location was kept secret

    b. Were given back to their families, for burial in their hometowns

    c. Were removed after the execution and were dumped at sea

    d. Were cremated in the death ovens at Dachau, to give them the same ultimate fate as their victims

246. How many countries signed the United Nations declaration during the war?

    a. Twenty-six

    b. Forty-seven

    c. Thirty-eight

    d. Twenty-nine

247. What women were called the "night witches"?

    a. Russian partisans

    b. U.S. workers on night shifts

    c. French Resistance

    d. Russian combat pilots

248. How many Purple Hearts were awarded to Audie Murphy?

    a. Four

    b. One

    c. Three

    d. Two

249. You would find a Biscay Cross on a:

    a. Destroyer

    b. Submarine

    c. Aircraft

    d. Tank

250. The Battle of Britain started on what date?

    a. July 13, 1940
    b. July 11, 1940
    c. July 10, 1940
    d. July 12, 1940

251. Where did Roosevelt, Churchill, and Stalin meet for the first time?

    a. Yalta
    b. Moscow
    d. Tehran
    c. London

252. What was the nickname given to the U.S.S. *Massachusetts*?

    a. Big Bertha
    b. Big Mamie
    c. Boston's Biggie
    d. Masses Fighter

253. What was the largest island in the Tarawa group, taken in 1943 by the U.S. Marines?

    a. Betio
    b. Moorea
    c. Saipan
    d. Tinian

254. How many carriers did the Japanese deploy in the attack on Pearl Harbor?

    a. Three
    b. Five
    c. Four
    d. Six

255. What was the name of the atomic bomb dropped on Hiroshima?

    a. Little Boy
    b. Little Man
    c. Fat Man
    d. Fat Boy

256. What was the required age range for paratroopers?

    a. 15–26

    b. 20–35

    c. 18–30

    d. 20–25

257. Name the first Japanese aircraft carrier sunk by the U.S. Navy:

    a. *Shoho*

    b. *Soryu*

    c. *Horyu*

    d. *Akagi*

258. Which U-boat sank the British battleship *Barham*?

    a. U-373

    b. U-100

    c. U-331

    d. U-101

259. What was HMS *Warspite*'s problem with its turrets at the Battle of Narvik?

    a. Crew accidentally fired with the muzzle closed

    b. Gun failed to turn

    c. Blast bags flew off and the turret filled with fumes

    d. Gun failed to elevate

260. How many times was the *Lancastria* hit by the thirty German Dornier Do 17 bombers that attacked?

    a. Four

    b. Seventeen

    c. One

    d. Twelve

261. The main disadvantage of the B-17 was:

    a. Weak armor

    b. Small payload

    c. Highly flammable engines

    d. A tendency to be unbalanced when loaded

262. Which one of the following countries never utilized the B-17?

   a. Soviet Union

   b. Brazil

   c. Nazi Germany

   d. Saudi Arabia

263. The biggest weakness of the Spitfire was:

   a. Single-stage supercharger

   b. None; the Spitfire really had no overall weakness

   c. A very temperamental radiator

   d. An exposed glycol system

264. The Polish aircraft LWS-4 Zubr was used to:

   a. Drop leaflets

   b. Undertake suicide raids

   c. Act as a bombing decoy

   d. Transport troops over distances of up to ninety miles

265. The Me 410 Hornisse (Hornet) fighter had a very heavy long-range gun that could literally obliterate a B-17 or B-24. This weapon was called:

   a. MG 81 7.92 millimeter

   b. BK5 50 millimeter

   c. MG 131 13 millimeter

   d. PaK 40 75 millimeter

266. The Blohm und Voss Bv 138 flying boat was nicknamed the:

   a. Widowmaker

   b. Flying Clog

   c. Flying Pancake

   d. One Way Trip

267. Name the twin-engine British night fighter, known to the Japanese as "whispering death":

   a. Beaufort

   b. Beaufighter

   c. Blenheim

   d. Mosquito

268. What obsolete German bomber was used for high-altitude reconnaissance for a short period of time after the Battle of Britain?

    a. Dornier 23R
    b. Junkers 88P
    c. Junkers 86R
    d. Dornier 217N

269. What was the first jet fighter developed by Germany?

    a. He 100
    b. He 178
    c. He 162
    d. He 280

270. On Dutch Fokker designs, what letter prefix indicated that it was a single-seat fighter?

    a. C
    b. T
    c. D
    d. G

271. What was the first monoplane to have retractable landing gear?

    a. Focke Wulf 190
    b. Polikarpov I-15ter
    c. Polikarpov I-16
    d. Curtiss P-36

272. What aircraft was known as the Stormbird?

    a. Me 262
    b. Me 109
    c. Me 111
    d. Fw 190

273. On what date was the first atomic weapon detonated in New Mexico?

    a. June 24, 1945
    b. August 1, 1945
    c. July 5, 1945
    d. July 16, 1945

274. Which machine gun was developed in Czechoslovakia?

   a. Sten

   b. PPSH-41

   c. BAR (Browning Automatic Rifle)

   d. Bren

275. Three miniature Japanese submarines sank the HMAS *Kuttabul* in the harbor of the city of:

   a. Hong Kong

   b. Pearl

   c. Bangkok

   d. Sydney

276. The Allies were concerned about pushing back the Germans in the Hurtgen Forest, despite large numbers of casualties, in order to:

   a. Find an alternative route around the Siegfried Line

   b. Give green troops combat experience

   c. Decimate the German Northern Army

   d. Take control of the dams on the Roer River

277. Who was the Führer's "Brown Eminence"?

   a. Rudolf Hess

   b. Hermann Goering

   c. Albert Speer

   d. Martin Bormann

278. Who was the officer in charge of German espionage during the war?

   a. Reichsleiter Robert Ley

   b. Admiral Wilhelm Canaris

   c. Gruppenführer Heinrich Muller

   d. Reichsführer-SS Heinrich Himmler

279. The Sullivan brothers' only sister was:

   a. Jennifer

   b. Genevieve

   c. Gwendolyn

   d. Gladys

280. The Treaty of Versailles was signed on:
   a. June 28, 1919
   b. July 28, 1919
   c. June 28, 1918
   d. November 28, 1918

281. Name the person who said of the Treaty of Versailles, "The economic clauses of the treaty were malignant and silly to the extent that made them obviously futile."
   a. Adolf Hitler
   b. Neville Chamberlain
   c. Benito Mussolini
   d. Winston Churchill

282. The captain of the U.S.S. *Indianapolis* was the only U.S. Navy officer to be court-martialed for losing a ship in the war. Fleet Admiral Chester Nimitz remitted his sentence and restored him to active duty. Many of the *Indianapolis* survivors said he was not to blame for the sinking, but the families of other sailors hounded him, until he committed suicide in 1968, using his Navy-issue revolver. He was discovered with a toy sailor in one of his hands on his front lawn. In October 2000, the U.S. Congress passed a resolution that his record should state that "he is exonerated for the loss of the USS *Indianapolis*." Who was the captain?
   a. Lieutenant Commander E. C. Burchett
   b. Lieutenant Commander H. P. Black
   c. Captain C. B. McVay
   d. Captain L. C. Ramsey

283. What was the date of the signing of the Japanese surrender treaty aboard the U.S.S. *Missouri*?
   a. September 1, 1945
   b. August 12, 1945
   c. September 2, 1945
   d. August 7, 1945

MAJOR ANSWERS

1. c.	36. d.	71. a.	106. a.	141. d.
2. b.	37. d.	72. c.	107. b.	142. d.
3. d.	38. d.	73. d.	108. b.	143. a.
4. b.	39. c.	74. d.	109. b.	144. a.
5. a.	40. b.	75. d.	110. b.	145. c.
6. a.	41. d.	76. b.	111. c.	146. c.
7. d.	42. a.	77. c.	112. a.	147. a.
8. c.	43. c.	78. b.	113. a.	148. a.
9. b.	44. d.	79. b.	114. c.	149. b.
10. d.	45. c.	80. c.	115. b.	150. b.
11. b.	46. c.	81. d.	116. d.	151. d.
12. b.	47. a.	82. d.	117. b.	152. c.
13. d.	48. d.	83. a.	118. b.	153. c.
14. a.	49. c.	84. d.	119. c.	154. a.
15. b.	50. c.	85. d.	120. b.	155. a.
16. c.	51. c.	86. b.	121. a.	156. d.
17. b.	52. c.	87. c.	122. c.	157. d.
18. a.	53. b.	88. a.	123. d.	158. a.
19. c.	54. c.	89. c.	124. b.	159. b.
20. b.	55. d.	90. b.	125. b.	160. b.
21. b.	56. c.	91. d.	126. b.	161. b.
22. a.	57. b.	92. c.	127. d.	162. b.
23. b.	58. c.	93. d.	128. b.	163. a.
24. a.	59. a.	94. a.	129. b.	164. d.
25. a.	60. a.	95. b.	130. a.	165. a.
26. b.	61. d.	96. c.	131. b.	166. b.
27. b.	62. d.	97. c.	132. c.	167. d.
28. c.	63. c.	98. c.	133. c.	168. b.
29. b.	64. c.	99. b.	134. c.	169. b.
30. a.	65. a.	100. b.	135. a.	170. d.
31. c.	66. a.	101. d.	136. a.	171. d.
32. b.	67. c.	102. a.	137. c.	172. d.
33. d.	68. d.	103. a.	138. a.	173. d.
34. a.	69. d.	104. c.	139. d.	174. a.
35. b.	70. b.	105. a.	140. d.	175. a.

176. b.	**198.** c.	**220.** b.	**242.** c.	**264.** c.
177. b.	**199.** b.	**221.** d.	**243.** c.	**265.** b.
178. b.	**200.** a.	**222.** a.	**244.** d.	**266.** b.
179. d.	**201.** b.	**223.** c.	**245.** d.	**267.** b.
180. c.	**202.** c.	**224.** d.	**246.** b.	**268.** c.
181. d.	**203.** b.	**225.** d.	**247.** d.	**269.** b.
182. c.	**204.** a.	**226.** b.	**248.** c.	**270.** c.
183. d.	**205.** d.	**227.** b.	**249.** b.	**271.** c.
184. d.	**206.** d.	**228.** b.	**250.** c.	**272.** a.
185. d.	**207.** a.	**229.** d.	**251.** d.	**273.** d.
186. a.	**208.** d.	**230.** a.	**252.** b.	**274.** d.
187. c.	**209.** a.	**231.** d.	**253.** a.	**275.** d.
188. d.	**210.** d.	**232.** a.	**254.** d.	**276.** d.
189. d.	**211.** d.	**233.** a.	**255.** a.	**277.** d.
190. c.	**212.** a.	**234.** c.	**256.** d.	**278.** b.
191. c.	**213.** b.	**235.** d.	**257.** a.	**279.** b.
192. a.	**214.** c.	**236.** a.	**258.** c.	**280.** a.
193. a.	**215.** b.	**237.** a.	**259.** c.	**281.** d.
194. c.	**216.** a.	**238.** a.	**260.** a.	**282.** c.
195. c.	**217.** b.	**239.** d.	**261.** b.	**283.** c.
196. b.	**218.** c.	**240.** b.	**262.** d.	
197. c.	**219.** c.	**241.** a.	**263.** d.	

COLONEL

1. Admiral Yamamoto, who had planned the invasion of Pearl Harbor, was intercepted and shot down less than a year and a half later. This action was made possible by the breaking of the Japanese naval code by Operation:

   a. Magic
   b. Red Piano
   c. Venona
   d. Setting Sun

2. A "G.I. party" is:

   a. An organized cleanup of a latrine area
   b. A roving band of inebriated soldiers looking for a fight with sailors or marines
   c. The beating of a soldier who brought collective punishment on the unit
   d. Surprise P.T.

3. Who scored the lowest marks on the IQ test administered to the soldiers at Nuremberg?

   a. Hess
   b. Kaltenbrunner
   c. Sauckel
   d. Streicher

4. On what date did Japan invade China?

   a. June 6, 1938
   b. November 6, 1937
   c. August 7, 1938
   d. July 7, 1937

5. Tadao Fuchikami, during the December 7, 1941, raid on Pearl Harbor, was the:

   a. First pilot shot down, who spent the war in a POW camp, married an American, and ran unsuccessfully for Congress
   b. Pilot who released the torpedo that sank the *Arizona*
   c. Messenger who delivered the belated "war warning" cable in Washington, DC, which was supposed to be delivered before the commencement of the attack, but which was not delivered in time
   d. Pilot who became lost, landed on an American carrier by mistake, and was so humiliated that he committed suicide the next day

6. Complete this quote: "The atom bomb was no great decision. It was merely another powerful weapon in the"

   a. Arsenal of war
   b. Arsenal of righteousness
   c. Arsenal of weapons
   d. Arsenal of toys

7. On what date did France and the U.S.S.R. sign a treaty of alliance?

   a. March 14, 1944
   b. July 22, 1943
   c. October 7, 1941
   d. December 10, 1944

8. What role did the troops of the Japanese First Infantry play in the defense of Okinawa?

   a. None; they had been posted to the island of Daitojima
   b. None; the ship carrying them was sunk
   c. They were the first line of defense on the beach
   d. They were annihilated in a "banzai" charge

9. What Japanese carrier was sunk by dive-bombers from the U.S.S. *Enterprise* at the battle of Midway?

   a. *Kiryu*
   b. *Akagi*
   c. *Kaga*
   d. *Kuashi*

10. Forty-eight civilians were killed during the attack on Pearl Harbor by:

    a. Japanese strafing runs
    b. Friendly fire
    c. Japanese bombs
    d. Panic

11. Where was a makeshift airbase built to facilitate an attack on Attu and Kiska in the invasion of the Aleutians?

    a. Unalaska
    b. Atka
    c. Amchitka
    d. Adak

12. Where did Japanese paratroops conduct an airborne operation on December 6, 1944?

    a. China
    b. Operation was scrapped
    c. India
    d. Philippines

13. How did the rescuers at Cabanatuan POW camp plan to transport those prisoners who could not walk back to safety?

    a. Carabao
    b. Carry them on stretchers
    c. Donkeys
    d. All of the prisoners could walk

14. What Japanese submarine torpedoed and sank the U.S.S. *Indianapolis*?

    a. I-57
    b. I-58
    c. I-48
    d. I-47

15. The gun on the M10 was how many millimeters wider than the gun on the M4 Sherman?

    a. 10 millimeters
    b. 1 millimeter
    c. 2 millimeters
    d. 6 millimeters

16. The more common name for the Panzerkampfwagen VIII is the:

    a. Tiger
    b. Maus
    c. King Tiger
    d. Panther

17. Which of the following was an amphibious tank?

    a. Type 3 Ka-Chi
    b. Panzerkampfwagen VIII
    c. Sherman Firefly
    d. Type 98 Ke-Ni

18. The greatest number of U-boats were sunk by:

    a. Aircraft
    b. Ramming
    c. Depth charges
    d. Scuttling

19. In what year was the carrier *Enterprise* commissioned?

    a. 1933
    b. 1936
    c. 1939
    d. 1938

20. Which carrier was a CV-2?

    a. *Saratoga*
    b. *Ranger*
    c. *Hornet*
    d. *Lexington*

21. What was the top speed of Germany's pocket battleships?

    a. 28 knots
    b. 26 knots
    c. 30 knots
    d. 27 knots

22. What was the mission of the Breda Ba. 88, perhaps one of the worst Italian aircraft?

    a. Bomber
    b. Ground attack
    c. Fighter
    d. Recon

23. What most hindered the B-29s from hitting their industrial targets in Japanese cities?

    a. Bad bombsights
    b. Heavy flak and fighter opposition
    c. Jet stream
    d. Constant cloud cover

24. What is the twin-engine German recon aircraft with a twin-boom design which proved useful over the Russian front?

    a. Bv 141
    b. He 219
    c. Hs 130
    d. Fw 189

25. In the Fleet Air Arm, the British tried to rename this aircraft the Avenger, but this U.S. name stuck:

    a. Vengeance
    b. Shark
    c. Spearfish
    d. Tarpon

26. What was the greatest cause of air losses for the Luftwaffe when they attacked the Netherlands in May 1940?

    a. Fighters

    b. Flak

    c. Landing incidents

    d. Mechanical problems

27. The Curtis Cleveland was the Royal Air Force version of which U.S. aircraft?

    a. Dauntless

    b. SBC-4 Helldiver

    c. Hellcat

    d. Buffalo

28. What was the main infantry rifle used by the Russian Army?

    a. Mosin-Nagant M1891/30

    b. Mosin-Nagant M1944 Carbine

    c. Mosin-Nagant M1938 Carbine

    d. Simonov AVS-36

29. Name the first naval battle where opposing fleets never actually came in contact with each other:

    a. Midway

    b. Vella Gulf

    c. Iwo Jima

    d. Coral Sea

30. In what year did the Soviet Union enter the League of Nations?

    a. 1922

    b. 1934

    c. 1926

    d. 1928

31. Which Hilfskreuzer was destroyed by a direct hit in the mine storage compartment?

    a. *Atlantis*
    b. *Kormoran*
    c. *Pinguin*
    d. *Stier*

32. What U.S. general was a pioneer of strategic bombing and is credited as being the father of the Superfortress?

    a. Curtis E. LeMay
    b. Carl A. Spaatz
    c. James H. Doolittle
    d. Henry H. "Hap" Arnold

33. When General Montgomery defeated the Afrika Korps at El Alamein in Egypt, Rommel was back in Germany on medical leave. Who was in command?

    a. General Georg von Stumme
    b. General Karl von Ludendorf
    c. General Lloyd Frenendall
    d. General Hermann Hoff

34. The Germans gave the nickname the Devil's Brigade to this Allied unit:

    a. U.S. Ninth Army
    b. First Special Service Force
    c. British Sixth Airborne
    d. Russian Third Army

35. Which military commander was nicknamed Bomber because of his advocacy of strategic area bombing?

    a. Curtis LeMay
    b. Arthur Harris
    c. Toohey Spaatz
    d. Hap Arnold

36. Name the commander of the British Expeditionary Forces in France in 1940, who was responsible for saving the Army at Dunkirk:

    a. Edmund Ironside
    b. John Gort
    c. John Dill
    d. Alan Brooke

37. What year was the Lee Enfield No.4 Mk1 .303 rifle created?

    a. 1936
    b. 1939
    c. 1934
    d. 1942

38. In which ocean is Iwo Jima located?

    a. South Pacific
    b. South Atlantic
    c. North Atlantic
    d. North Pacific

39. What type of weapon was used against the Japanese attacking Corregidor?

    a. 12 inch mortar
    b. 12 inch rifle
    c. 14 inch gun
    d. 105 millimeter field gun

40. What is considered the greatest naval battle in history?

    a. Midway
    b. Leyte Gulf
    c. Coral Sea
    d. Java Sea

41. Who were the secretary of war and the secretary of the navy at the outbreak of the war with Japan?

    a. Frank Knox and Henry L. Stimson
    b. Henry L. Stimson and Cordell Hull
    c. Cordell Hull and Frank Knox
    d. Henry L. Stimson and Frank Knox

42. How many parts were contained in the Japanese diplomatic message that severed diplomatic relations with the United States?

   a. Twelve
   b. Ten
   c. Fourteen
   d. Eight

43. At the Battle of Midway, the *Enterprise, Yorktown,* and *Hornet* sent forty-one torpedo aircraft to look for the Japanese carriers. How many returned?

   a. None
   b. Forty-one
   c. Six
   d. Twenty

44. Which of the following was a serious problem for the German Navy during the war?

   a. Faulty torpedoes
   b. Lack of mine-laying capacity
   c. Lack of mine-sweeping capacity
   d. Failure to prioritize their carrier, the *Graf Zeppelin*

45. The U-331 sank which British warship?

   a. HMS *Ark Royal*
   b. HMS *Hermes*
   c. HMS *Barham*
   d. HMS *Queen Elizabeth*

46. Which ammunition ship exploded in the South Pacific on July 1, 1944?

   a. U.S.S. *Nitro*
   b. U.S.S. *Rainier*
   c. U.S.S. *Mount Hood*
   d. U.S.S. *Pyro*

47. Which Luftwaffe fighter aircraft had greatly decreased performance above 25,000 feet?

   a. Messerschmitt Bf 109K
   b. Focke Wulf Fw 190A
   c. Junkers JU 88G-7b
   d. Fokker D. XXI

48. Which uprising was supplied with weapons and food by the South African Air Force?

   a. Yugoslav
   b. Paris
   c. Burma
   d. Warsaw

49. What was the official name of the single-engine bomber nicknamed Jill?

   a. Nakajima B6N Tenzan
   b. Nakajima Ki-84 Hayate
   c. Nakajima J1N1
   d. Yokosuka P1Y1 Ginga

50. The submarine U.S.S. *Archerfish* did the following:

   a. Sank the Japanese carrier *Shinano* four hours after it was launched
   b. Rescued future president George H. W. Bush after his aircraft was shot down
   c. Sank three Japanese submarines in four days
   d. Sank the German submarine U-171 in Tokyo Bay

51. Which submachine gun inspired the Soviet Army to adopt a similar drum magazine for their PPD-40 and PPSH-41 after encountering it during their invasion of Finland in 1939?

   a. Suomi KP-31
   b. Thompson M1
   c. Carl Gustaf
   d. MP-38

52. Which U.S. Army general was forced to leave the U.S. Military Academy at West Point in 1906 because he failed geometry?

    a. Major General Lucian Truscott

    b. Major General James M. Gavin

    c. Lieutenant General Courtney H. Hodges

    d. Major General John P. Lucas

53. What was the cause of most civilian deaths during the attack on Pearl Harbor?

    a. Japanese bombs

    b. Antiaircraft fire

    c. Exploding debris

    d. Panic in the streets

54. Which article of the Treaty of Versailles stated that nations were to disarm "to a level that is consistent with national safety"?

    a. Article 16

    b. President Wilson's 14 points

    c. "The Disarmament White Paper"

    d. Article 8

55. What was the U.S. Navy's first aircraft carrier?

    a. U.S.S. *Langley*

    b. U.S.S. *Hornet*

    c. U.S.S. *Enterprise*

    d. U.S.S. *Saratoga*

56. What was the Allied code name for the island of Guadalcanal?

    a. Wildflower

    b. Excelsior

    c. Bird Island

    d. Cactus

57. The German code name for their offensive against the Russian city of Sevastopol was:

   a. Barbarossa

   b. Black Power

   c. Citadel

   d. Sturgeon Catch

58. The Allied code name for the invasion of the Marshall Islands was Operation:

   a. Husky

   b. Strangle

   c. Flintlock

   d. Battleaxe

59. On which date did Germany and Italy declare war on the United States?

   a. January 6, 1942

   b. December 8, 1941

   c. December 11, 1941

   d. December 6, 1941

60. Name the British airborne divisions that parachuted into Normandy with the American 101st Airborne and Eighty-second Airborne:

   a. Twenty-second SAS Regiment

   b. Thirteenth Airborne

   c. Seventeenth Airborne

   d. Sixth Airborne

61. Admiral Yamamoto, the planner behind the sneak attack on Pearl Harbor, was shot down by P-38 fighters while inspecting:

   a. Guadalcanal

   b. Midway

   c. Tarawa

   d. Bougainville

62. Who was Morris "Two Gun" Cohen?

    a. A general in the Chinese Army

    b. A spy for the Soviet Union

    c. Both of the above

    d. None of the above

63. What is the German word for "final solution"?

    a. *Endergebnis*

    b. *Endlösung*

    c. *Finallösung*

    d. *Finalergebnis*

64. The night before the Russians attacked at Kursk, they opened up with a huge artillery barrage, but the Germans had already moved. Why had they relocated?

    a. An intercepted radio transmission

    b. A captured Russian soldier had warned them

    c. A lucky change in battle plans

    d. None of the above

65. How many pints of water did the Vickers HMG hold in its water jacket?

    a. 8

    b. 7.5

    c. 9

    d. 5

66. What was the nickname of the Boyes .55 antitank rifle?

    a. Big Kicker

    b. Armor Bouncing Gun

    c. Bloody Useless

    d. Charley the Bastard

67. During the Battle of Midway, which aircraft carrier was the first to strike against the Japanese fleet with its dive-bombers?

    a. U.S.S. *Wasp*

    b. U.S.S. *Yorktown*

    c. U.S.S. *Enterprise*

    d. U.S.S. *Hornet*

68. Who was the doctor aboard the U.S.S. *Indianapolis*?

    a. Edward Brown

    b. Giles McCoy

    c. Lewis Haynes

    d. Mike Kuryla

69. What was the original caliber of the main gun of the Panzer III (Panzerkampfwagen III)?

    a. 88 millimeter

    b. 37 millimeter

    c. 50 millimeter

    d. 75 millimeter

70. Which German warship was almost cut in two by another German ship?

    a. *Admiral Hipper*

    b. *Prinz Eugen*

    c. *Karlsruhe*

    d. *Leipzig*

71. Of the 1,100 men on board the U.S.S. *Indianapolis* when it was torpedoed, approximately how many made it into the water safely?

    a. About 500

    b. About 800

    c. About 700

    d. About 900

72. Why did it take so long for the U.S.S. *Indianapolis* to be reported as missing?

    a. Navy was waiting for its next supply order

    b. Navy thought it had arrived safely

    c. Navy foul-up

    d. It was on a secret mission

73. How many of the U.S. carriers in service at the beginning of the war made it to the end of the war?

   a. Two

   b. Three

   c. Four

   d. One

74. How many Essex-class carriers were commissioned?

   a. Twenty-four

   b. Thirty-two

   c. Twenty

   d. Sixteen

75. Where was the German U-boat U-372 sunk?

   a. Mediterranean Sea

   b. North Sea

   c. North Atlantic Ocean

   d. Baltic Sea

76. What was the only Japanese battleship to be sunk by submarines?

   a. *Kongo*

   b. *Ise*

   c. *Haruna*

   d. *Musashi*

77. The U.S. Army Air Force designed a bomber escort based on the B-17 airframe, with sixteen machine guns and a bomb bay that was converted to a magazine, which was called the:

   a. YB-36

   b. YB-20

   c. B-41

   d. YB-40

78. The French interceptor Caudron C.714 had a design flaw, which was its:

  a. Low firepower
  b. Wooden construction
  c. Unavailability of construction materials
  d. None; the pilots were flawed

79. The Royal Navy developed a turret fighter (a two-seat fighter in which all the armament was placed in a powered dorsal turret) called the:

  a. Blackburn Skua
  b. Hawker Demon
  c. Hawker Hotspur
  d. Blackburn Roc

80. The Me 163D was taken over by another aircraft manufacturer and redesignated the:

  a. Fi 103
  b. Hs 132
  c. He 280
  d. Ju 248

81. The German Technisches Amt of the RLM accepted a design study for a jet dive-bomber with a prone position for the pilot, designated the:

  a. He 280
  b. Me 263
  c. Hs 132
  d. Ba 349

82. In the Messerschmitt Bf 109F-4/R1, the R was an abbreviation of *Rustsatz*, which stands for:

  a. Rebuilt
  b. Field conversion kit
  c. Two-seat trainer conversion
  d. Factory-installed conversion kit

83. The German night fighter He 219 was first operationally flown from the Dutch airfield at:

   a. Leeuwarden
   b. Venlo
   c. Soesterberg
   d. Twenthe

84. What aircraft succeeded the Fairey Swordfish in the Fleet Air Arm?

   a. Fulmar
   b. Albacore
   c. Barracuda
   d. Skua

85. When the Royal Air Force returned P-39s to the U.S. Army Air Force, what designation did they receive?

   a. P-400
   b. P-45
   c. P-390
   d. P-39(Br)

86. The "Ann" was officially known as the:

   a. Mitsubishi Ki-21
   b. Mitsubishi Ki-67 Hiryu
   c. Mitsubishi Ki-30
   d. Nakajima Ki-49 Donryu

87. After the fall of France, the French transferred their Hawk 75As to the Royal Air Force. What was their new designation?

   a. Mohawk
   b. Kittyhawk
   c. Tomahawk
   d. Warhawk

88. The Handley Page Halifax used an engine manufactured by:

   a. Merlin-Hercules
   b. Mercury-Sabre
   c. Griffon-Hercules
   d. Pegasus-Merlin

89. Which company manufactured the P-35?

   a. Republic
   b. Seversky
   c. Lockheed
   d. Martin

90. Who was the commander of the German II SS Panzerkorps at the Battle of Arnhem?

   a. Oberstgruppenführer Dietrich
   b. Field Marshal Model
   c. SS Major General Meyer
   d. Obergruppenführer Bittrich

91. In 1943, the Pacific Fleet launched an offensive against a ring of coral atolls in the Pacific in their drive toward the Japanese mainland, which became known as the battle of:

   a. Tarawa/Betio
   b. Guadacanal/Leyte
   c. Wokomano/Niaagri
   d. Yitiian/Naman

92. What was the weekly tea ration for each person in England?

   a. 6 oz
   b. 4 oz
   c. 10 oz
   d. Unlimited

93. In what year did they begin rationing butter in the United States?

   a. 1940
   b. 1941
   c. 1943
   d. 1942

94. Which tank was created by the Germans to counter the Russian T-34 and the KV series tanks?

   a. Tiger
   b. Jagdtiger
   c. Stug III
   d. Panther

95. What was the Kellogg-Briand Pact?

   a. Agreement between U.S. Secretary of State Kellogg and French Foreign Minister Briand
   b. Document that renounced war as a means of national policy
   c. Pact among fascist powers to invade the U.S.S.R.
   d. Economic plan to get Italy out of the Great Depression

96. Which Hilfskreuzer sank the Australian cruiser HMAS Sydney?

   a. *Orion*
   b. *Komet*
   c. *Kormoran*
   d. *Pinguin*

97. Name the German U-boat commander who succeeded in penetrating the British anchorage at Scapa Flow:

   a. Otto Kretschmer
   b. Hans-Gunther Lange
   c. Wolfgang Luth
   d. Günther Prien

98. What ocean liner was sunk by a German U-boat, which helped bring the United States into the war?

   a. SS *Mauetania*
   b. SS *Athenia*
   c. SS *Erethusa*
   d. SS *New York*

99. Which Allied leader strongly disagreed with trying the Nazi leaders and advocated summary executions of those accused?

    a. Roosevelt
    b. Truman
    c. Stalin
    d. Churchill

100. Albert Speer, Hitler's architect and minister of armaments, was sentenced to twenty years at Nuremberg. Who was his assistant in the slave labor program who was sentenced to death?

    a. Sauckel
    b. Rosenberg
    c. Frick
    d. Funk

101. The Battle of Manchuria, which began on August 8, 1945, was known as Operation:

    a. August Rain
    b. August Flash
    c. August Storm
    d. August Typhoon

102. Who commanded the Big Red One during the Normandy landing?

    a. Clarence R. Huebner
    b. Leonard T. Gerow
    c. Theodore Roosevelt Jr.
    d. Russell P. Hartle

103. Which U.S. general commanded all Allied air forces in the southwest Pacific theater, carrier-based aircraft of the U.S. Third and Seventh Fleets, land-based aircraft of the Seventh Fleet, B-29s of the Twentieth Air Force, and operations of the Royal Air Force?

    a. Lewis H. Brereton
    b. George C. Kenney
    c. George H. Brett
    d. Ennis C. Whitehead

104. What two bases were bombed by the Japanese in addition to Pearl Harbor on December 7, 1941?

  a. Philippines and Guam
  b. Philippines and Midway
  c. Midway and Guam
  d. Wake Island and Guam

105. What was the name of British Field Marshal Bernard Montgomery's dog?

  a. Willie
  b. Rommel
  c. Blackie
  d. Telek

106. What was the first submarine captured by the U.S. Navy?

  a. I-178
  b. U-571
  c. U-505
  d. I-86

107. When did the Pz VI Tiger Tank first go into production?

  a. August 1941
  b. August 1942
  c. August 1943
  d. August 1940

108. What was the full name of Field Marshal Erwin Rommel, the Desert Fox?

  a. Erwin Johannes Rommel
  b. Erwin Eugen Rommel
  c. Erwin Johannes Eugen Rommel
  d. Erwin Eugene Hans Rommel

109. Which village was at Omaha Beach?

  a. Courseulles
  b. Colleville
  c. La Madeleine
  d. Arromanches

110. How close did the Nazis get to Moscow?

    a. Five miles
    b. Sniper range
    c. Seven miles
    d. Artillery range

111. On what date did France and Germany sign the armistice?

    a. June 21, 1940
    b. June 22, 1940
    c. June 11, 1940
    d. June 12, 1940

112. The first investigation into the Japanese attack on Pearl Harbor was called the:

    a. Army Pearl Harbor Board
    b. Hart Inquiry
    c. Roberts Commission
    d. Hewitt Investigation

113. What ship was supposed to deliver the atomic bomb to the Pacific, but was disqualified after failing to perform adequately during maneuvers?

    a. U.S.S. *Birmingham*
    b. U.S.S. *Idaho*
    c. U.S.S. *Pensacola*
    d. U.S.S. *Missouri*

114. Which carrier of the Essex class saw the longest service in the U.S. Navy?

    a. CV-19 *Hancock*
    b. CV-34 *Oriskany*
    c. CV-16 *Lexington*
    d. CV-11 *Intrepid*

115. The German company Fiesler developed a torpedo carrier aircraft designated the:

  a. Fi 156
  b. Fi 109
  c. Fi 103
  d. Fi 167

116. The British troop ship *Lancastria* was sunk by German aircraft approximately ten miles off the French port of:

  a. Calais
  b. Dunkirk
  c. St. Nazaire
  d. Brest

117. What was the original nickname for the B-17 bomber coined by reporter Richard L. Williams?

  a. 10 gun flying fortress
  b. 4,000 horsepower flying fortress
  c. 3 turret flying fortress
  d. 15 ton flying fortress

118. The Focke-Wulf Fw 300 was based on the:

  a. Fw 200
  b. He 177
  c. Captured B-17s
  d. Fw 210

119. What made the Republic P-43 Lancer aircraft unsuitable for combat?

  a. No self-sealing fuel tanks
  b. Bad high-altitude performance
  c. Bad roll rate
  d. Flammability

120. Which air force employed both the Spitfire and the Focke-Wulf Fw 190 at the same time?

- **a.** Turkey
- **b.** Switzerland
- **c.** Spain
- **d.** Sweden

121. The air force of which nation was known as Zrakoplovsto Nezavisna Drzava Hrvatska?

- **a.** Slovakia
- **b.** Croatia
- **c.** Poland
- **d.** Bulgaria

122. Which manufacturer built the Bristol Bolingbroke, a version of the Bristol Blenheim light bomber?

- **a.** Commonwealth
- **b.** CCF
- **c.** Fairchild
- **d.** DAP

123. What percentage of Lancaster bombers were lost in action?

- **a.** 17
- **b.** 37
- **c.** 66
- **d.** 53

124. What was the most modern bomber the Armee de l'Air (French Air Force) fielded in the war?

- **a.** LeO451
- **b.** Caudron 203
- **c.** MB323
- **d.** G.21

125. How many members of the South African Air Force died in action during the six years of the Second World War?

    a. 2,300
    b. 7,400
    c. 5,250
    d. 1,350

126. What type of aircraft was the Fokker T.8W?

    a. Transport
    b. Communication
    c. Trainer
    d. Seaplane

127. Who was the vice president when the United States entered the war in December 1941?

    a. Harry S Truman
    b. Henry A. Wallace
    c. John N. Garner
    d. Alben W. Barkley

128. Who was commander in chief of the German Army from 1938 to 1941?

    a. Walther von Brauchitsch
    b. Franz Halder
    c. Wilhelm Keitel
    d. Werner von Fritsch

129. What was the original unit designation of Merrill's Marauders, before they were placed under the command of Major General Frank Merrill?

    a. 5307th Composite
    b. Eighth Mountain Division
    c. 670th Composite Unit
    d. First U.S. Special Forces Division

130. How many officials were sentenced to death in the initial Nuremburg war crime trials?

    a. Eleven
    b. Twelve
    c. Twenty
    d. Twenty-two

131. Who or what killed well-known war journalist Ernie Pyle?

    a. Japanese sniper
    b. Explosion at a fuel dump
    c. German artillery round
    d. Friendly fire

132. What was the nickname of the Japanese torpedo bomber?

    a. Kate
    b. Betty
    c. Zeke
    d. Val

133. By 1945, which country had the third largest Allied navy?

    a. Soviet Union
    b. Canada
    c. Australia
    d. New Zealand

134. Who commanded the Russian Sixty-second Army?

    a. Vasilyev
    b. Rokossovsky
    c. Chuikov
    d. Yeremenko

135. During the movie *The Longest Day*, you see two German fighters machine-gun the invading troops on the beach on D-day. In real life, who were the pilots?

    a. Josef Priller and Kurt Buhligen
    b. Adolf Galland and Franz Kunz
    c. Werner Molders and Hans Schafer
    d. Josef Priller and Heinz Wodarczyk

136. What was Operation Frankton?

    a. St. Nazaire raid

    b. Allied invasion of Madagascar

    c. "Cockleshell Heroes" raid on Bordeaux harbor

    d. Dieppe raid

137. Who commanded the German Twelfth Army, which was ordered by Hitler to break the Russian encirclement of Berlin in April 1945?

    a. Walther Wenck

    b. Georg Von Kuchler

    c. Werner Kempf

    d. Walter Model

138. Which one of the following actors served in the Navy?

    a. Al Hirt

    b. Robert Mitchum

    c. Steve Allen

    d. Tony Curtis

139. How did Corregidor control the minefield guarding the entrance to Manila Bay?

    a. Switched on and off electrically

    b. Cables to the mines could be remotely cut

    c. Mines could be remotely detonated

    d. Mines could be moved around by radio control

140. Which of the following was a Japanese sidearm?

    a. Type 99

    b. Type 100

    c. Type 2

    d. Type 14

141. Who was the highest ranking U.S. admiral killed in the war?

    a. John W. Wilcox

    b. Isaac C. Kidd

    c. Arthur Radford

    d. Thomas C. Kinkaid

142. What was the worst time of day for shark attacks for the men in the water after the sinking of the U.S.S. *Indianapolis*?

    a. Night
    b. Midday
    c. Morning
    d. Evening

143. When did the U.S. Marines attack the Marshall Islands?

    a. January 31, 1944
    b. August 21, 1945
    c. May 12, 1943
    d. December 30, 1942

144. When did the Marines attack the Palau Islands?

    a. October 11, 1941
    b. March 6, 1943
    c. January 30, 1944
    d. September 15, 1944

145. Which tank was often wrongly identified by Allied troops as a Tiger?

    a. PzKpfw III
    b. PzKpfw VII
    c. PzKpfw V
    d. PzKpfw IV

146. How many rotating turrets were on the T-28 medium tank?

    a. None
    b. Two
    c. One
    d. Three

147. During the Battle of Leyte Gulf, Admiral Kurita led his depleted Centre Force up the Palawan passage and then turned eastward to proceed through the central Philippines across the:

a. Sulu Sea
b. Philippine Sea
b. South China Sea
d. Sibuyan Sea

148. During the Battle of Leyte Gulf, as the Third Fleet prepared to launch the first strikes on Kurita's Centre Force, incoming land-based Japanese aircraft bombed this carrier:

a. *Franklin*
b. *Bunker Hill*
b. *Essex*
d. *Princeton*

149. Name the Dutch submarine that torpedoed the Vichy French ship *Oued Yquem* on October 3, 1941, in the sea area of Terra Nova.

a. O 21
b. O 23
c. O 22
d. O 24

150. What Dutch gunboat captured the Danish tankers *Christian Holm* and *Scandia*?

a. *Van Kinsbergen*
b. *De Ruyter*
c. *Van Speyck*
d. *Java*

151. At Guadalcanal, this battleship fired seventy-five shells in seven minutes at close range into the Japanese battleship *Kirishima*:

   a. *Alabama*
   b. *Washington*
   c. *South Dakota*
   d. *North Carolina*

152. What was the last battleship ever sunk by gunfire in a battle-ship-to-battleship engagement?

   a. IJN *Nagato*
   b. IJN *Yamashiro*
   c. KMS *Scharnhorst*
   d. KMS *Tirpitz*

153. What was the code name given to the sortie by the battle-ship *Tirpitz* and the heavy cruisers *Admiral Hipper* and *Admiral Scheer* against convoy PQ17?

   a. Rösselsprung
   b. Nordmark
   c. Sportpalast
   d. Sizilien

154. Which two German destroyers were sunk by friendly fire during Operation Viking?

   a. *Theodor Riedel* and *Friedrich Eckoldt*
   b. *Richard Beitzen* and *Max Schultz*
   c. *Leberecht Maass* and *Erich Koelner*
   d. *Max Schultz* and *Leberecht Maass*

155. How many ships were in the light carrier Independence class?

   a. Seven
   b. Six
   c. Nine
   d. Ten

156. The battleship *Roma* was the first:

    a. Italian battleship to mount 15 inch guns
    b. Ship hit by a guided missile
    c. Battleship with twin turrets firing over triples
    d. Axis capital ship sunk in the war

157. What was the first U.S. submarine to be sunk?

    a. U.S.S. *Seadragon*
    b. U.S.S. *Sea Lion*
    c. U.S.S. *Snapper*
    d. U.S.S. *Skate*

158. The submarine sent by the Germans to Japan with uranium and other German advanced weapons technology was called:

    a. U-1708
    b. U-496
    c. U-2534
    d. U-234

159. What American aircraft benefited from the German research for the Amerika Bomber project?

    a. B-2
    b. B-1
    c. B-52
    d. Tu-160

160. What Japanese single-engine dive-bomber, designed by Aichi, with fixed landing gear, became well known for its role in the attack on Pearl Harbor?

    a. A6M
    b. B5A1
    c. D4Y
    d. D3A

161. What model B-17 was the Memphis Belle?

    a. B-17G
    b. B-17F
    c. B-17E
    d. B-17B

162. The U.S. Navy used an improved B-24 model called the:

    a. Neptune
    b. Vindicator
    c. Privateer
    d. Marlin

163. How many regiments did the Belgian Air Force have at the start of May 1940?

    a. Five
    b. Four
    c. Three
    d. Nine

164. Which Army fighter was never used in combat by the United States?

    a. P-36 Hawk
    b. P-70 Nighthawk
    c. P-63 King Cobra
    d. None of the above

165. When were the last bombs dropped by the South African Air Force in the African area of operations?

    a. June 10, 1944
    b. May 12, 1943
    c. August 11, 1942
    d. July 10, 1943

166. During the invasion of Italy, when the Germans were pushed back by reinforcments from airborne divisions, the Germans fell back to a series of fortified positions known as the:

   a. Chiunzi Pass
   b. Winter Line
   c. Difensa Line
   d. Volturno River Line

167. When was the final evacuation of the First Airborne Division completed after the Battle of Arnhem?

   a. Sunday, September 24, 1944
   b. Friday, September 22, 1944
   c. Wednesday, September 27, 1944
   d. Monday, September 25, 1944

168. What was Hitler's private railroad car called?

   a. Eva
   b. Amerika
   c. Napoleon
   d. Freedom

169. Ironically, at the beginning of the war, the Forty-fifth Infantry, New Mexico National Guard, wore this as their shoulder insignia:

   a. Gold swastika
   b. German Maltese cross
   c. Rising sun
   d. Jewish star

170. British rationing continued until:

   a. 1945
   b. 1948
   c. 1959
   d. 1954

171. What year was the Treaty of Locarno signed?

    a. 1925

    b. 1922

    c. 1919

    d. 1929

172. How many awards and decorations did Audie Murphy wear when he returned home to Texas in June 1945?

    a. Thirty

    b. Thirty-one

    c. Twenty-six

    d. Thirty-three

173. Audie Murphy finished the war as a first lieutenant and was commissioned in the Thirty-sixth Infantry Division, Texas Army National Guard, ultimately rising to the rank of:

    a. Lieutenant colonel

    b. Captain

    c. Major

    d. Colonel

174. In which Allied invasion were the beaches code named Cent, Dime, and Joss?

    a. North Africa (Operation Torch)

    b. Sicily (Operation Husky)

    c. Normandy (Operation Overlord)

    d. Southern France (Operation Dragoon)

175. Of the twenty-two Nazis that were tried for war crimes at Nuremberg, how many were found not guilty?

    a. Three

    b. One

    c. Two

    d. None

176. What is famous about the military designation F-7?

    a. First U.S. jet aircraft built by Boeing

    b. Berth of the U.S.S. *Arizona* on battleship row

    c. Designator for the chief of the O.S.S.

    d. First helicopter built by Igor Sikorsky

177. Hitler's code name for his second campaign in Russia was Operation:

    a. Citadel

    b. Haystack

    c. Barbarossa

    d. Triumvirate

178. On what date was the *Yamato*'s sister ship the *Musashi* sunk?

    a. October 20, 1944

    b. November 1, 1944

    c. September 21, 1944

    d. October 24, 1944

179. Japan began training paratroopers in what year?

    a. 1934

    b. 1936

    c. 1940

    d. 1938

180. Which Japanese army fought in Bataan?

    a. Thirteenth Imperial Army

    b. Fourteenth Imperial Army

    c. Fifteenth Imperial Army

    d. Third Imperial Army

181. What was the Bataan Death March called by the prisoners who survived?

    a. Trek

    b. Journey

    c. Hike

    d. Crawl

182. The Panzerjäger I was based on the tank chassis of the:

   a. Panzer II

   b. Panzer I

   c. Panzer 38(t)

   d. Panzer 35(t)

183. After the fall of Dunkirk, the Germans captured British wheeled vehicles that they liked so much that Rommel and members of his staff used them as their personal vehicles. What was the name of this vehicle?

   a. Land Rover Freelander

   b. A.E.C. Mark I Armored Command Vehicle

   c. Morris Mark II Light Reconnaissance Car

   d. Daimler Mark I Armored Car

184. How many combat-capable U-boats did the Kriegsmarine have in service at the beginning of the war?

   a. 145

   b. 89

   c. 36

   d. 57

185. Which warship had rendezvous at sea with Hilfskreuzers *Atlantis, Thor, Pinguin,* and *Kormoran*?

   a. *Deutschland*

   b. *Admiral Hipper*

   c. *Admiral Scheer*

   d. *Admiral Graf Spee*

186. Which cruiser was sunk by Royal Air Force dive-bombers at Bergen?

   a. *Leipzig*

   b. *Blücher*

   c. *Karlsruhe*

   d. *Königsberg*

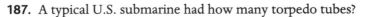

187. A typical U.S. submarine had how many torpedo tubes?

    a. Ten

    b. Six

    c. Four

    d. Eight

188. What happened to the *Hotspur* and the *Hunter*?

    a. Fired at each other

    b. Were beached

    c. Were damaged by their own depth charges

    d. Collided

189. Where did the designer of the Spitfire get his idea to use an elliptical wing?

    a. Typhoon

    b. He 70

    c. A5M

    d. Ar 68

190. The difference between the North American P-51D and the P-51K Mustangs was that:

    a. One was more heavily armed

    b. They were built at different factories

    c. One was faster

    d. One had a bubble-top canopy

191. What company designed the V-1 Flying Bomb?

    a. Blohm und Voss

    b. Arado

    c. Fiessler

    d. Horten

192. Approximately how many Me 262s were ultimately built for the Luftwaffe?

   a. 1,400

   b. 1,800

   c. 1,200

   d. 2,200

193. The Kawasaki Ki-61 Hien (Tony) fighter had engine production problems, so they created another version with an Ha-112 radial engine designated the:

   a. Ki-71

   b. Ki-100

   c. Ki-61

   d. Ki-96

194. Which British night fighter first went into combat as an intruder over Malta in the spring of 1942?

   a. Beaufighter MKIF

   b. Mosquito NF MKII

   c. Blenheim MKIVF

   d. Mosquito NF MK30

195. Who were the two scientists who sent a letter to President Roosevelt in 1939, warning him that Germany could be developing a nuclear weapon?

   a. Einstein and Bohr

   b. Einstein and Szilard

   c. Rutherford and Bohr

   d. Oppenheimer and Feynmann

196. Name a delaying battle fought by the Germans after Stalingrad that greatly slowed down the Soviets in their northern drive to Berlin:

   a. Battle of Lutzow

   b. Siege of Prenzlauer Berg

   c. Battle for the Seelow Heights

   d. Battle of Koenigsberg

197. What was the fate of the German heavy cruiser the *Prinz Eugen*?

    a. Scuttled by its own crew

    b. Sunk by an aircraft carrier

    c. Destroyed by the HMS *Hood*

    d. Target at the Bikini atomic tests

198. The day on which the Sullivan brothers were killed was ironic because it was:

    a. December 7 (Pearl Harbor)

    b. 4 of July

    c. George's birthday

    d. Friday the thirteenth

199. Who was the first British general to land in Normandy on D-day?

    a. Lieutenant General Fredrick Morgan

    b. Major General Richard Gale

    c. Field Marshal Bernard L. Montgomery

    d. Lieutenant General Frederick Browning

200. The Hilfskreuzer *Thor* sank this heavily armed British merchant cruiser:

    a. HMS *Alcantara*

    b. HMS *Voltaire*

    c. HMS *Rawalpindi*

    d. HMS *Carnarvon Castle*

201. Which U.S. Army division made the greatest advances inland on D-day?

    a. Twenty-ninth Infantry Division

    b. First Infantry Division

    c. Fourth Infantry Division

    d. Second Infantry Division

202. What was the nickname given to newscaster H. V. Kaltenborn?

   a. Voice of Hope
   b. Kalty's Voice
   c. Voice of Doom
   d. Baritone

203. Adolf Hitler had two personal railroad trains, the Brandenburg and the:

   a. Hindenburg
   b. Ludendorff
   c. Bismarck
   d. Amerika

204. The U.S. Marines at Henderson Field on Guadalcanal suffered the worst bombardment of the campaign on the night of October 13–14 when they were shelled by these battleships:

   a. *Hiei* and *Kirishima*
   b. *Shokaku* and *Zuikaku*
   c. *Yamato* and *Musashi*
   d. *Haruna* and *Kongo*

205. How many days was the Battle of Iwo Jima?

   a. Thirty
   b. Thirty-five
   c. Forty-two
   d. Forty-seven

206. The Combat Intelligence Unit in Hawaii was called Station:

   a. Cast
   b. Hula
   c. Sugar
   d. Hypo

207. How many troops were sent to the north end of Makin Island, in the Gilberts, on November 20, 1943?

    a. 7,000

    b. 5,000

    c. 9,400

    d. 11,000

208. Which Dutch destroyer fought in the Battle of Cape Bon?

    a. *Isaac Sweers*

    b. *Doymaer van Twist*

    c. *Brabant*

    d. *Jacob van Heemskerck*

209. What was the only Italian heavy cruiser to survive the disaster at Cape Matapan?

    a. *Pola*

    b. *Gorzia*

    c. *Zara*

    d. *Fiume*

210. What was the Scourge of the Atlantic?

    a. Area with no air coverage in the mid-Atlantic

    b. Fw 200

    c. Otto Kretschmer

    d. German sailors' "Happy Time"

211. Which U.S. submarine commander did not receive the Congressional Medal of Honor?

    a. Howard Gilmore

    b. Richard O'Kane

    c. Walter T. Griffith

    d. Red Ramage

212. What type of engines were used in the B-17 Flying Fortress?

   a. Allison V-1710
   b. Pratt and Whitney R-2800
   c. Wright R-1820 Cyclone
   d. Pratt and Whitney R-1830

213. The Amiot 351 and 354 versions of the French Amiot 350 bomber differed in that one:

   a. Had a twin tailplane; the other was single tailed
   b. Had twin engines; the other had four engines
   c. Had radial engines; the other had inline engines
   d. Was a biplane

214. A twin-engine British medium bomber with very cramped accommodation was the:

   a. Hampden
   b. Heyford
   c. Manchester
   d. Beaufort

215. Name the British torpedo bomber designed at the same time and to the same specifications as the Bristol Beaufort, but which turned out to be possibly the worst design to enter service with the Royal Air Force:

   a. Blackburn Shark
   b. Blackburn Botha
   c. Vickers Vildebeest
   d. Blackburn Ripon

216. Only two fighter aces brought down more than 300 enemy planes—Erich Hartmann and:

   a. Gerhard Barkhorn
   b. Gunther Rall
   c. Hermann Graf
   d. Helmut Lipfert

217. What German bomber was designed with forward-swept wings?

    a. Ju 248
    b. Ju 287
    c. Me 263
    d. Ba 349

218. How many Ar 234Bs were delivered to the Luftwaffe?

    a. 168
    b. 312
    c. 287
    d. 210

219. The Buckmaster was a two-seat training version of the:

    a. Blenheim
    b. Beaufort
    c. Buckingham
    d. Boston

220. What was the British Blackburn Dart?

    a. Single-seat carrier torpedo bomber
    b. Carrier spotter aircraft
    c. Single-wing twin-engine trainer aircraft
    d. All-wood aircraft designed for catapult launch

221. To achieve nuclear detonation of an atomic bomb, it is necessary to compress the required critical mass in microseconds before the developing chain reaction blows the components apart. This is done with:

    a. Compression and explosion
    b. Gun and explosion
    c. Compression and detonation
    d. Gun and implosion

222. Winston Churchill called it "not the beginning of the end, but, perhaps, the end of the beginning." What was he referring to?

   a. Battle of Stalingrad
   b. Battle of Kursk
   c. Battle of Britain
   d. Battle of El Alamein

223. How many miles did the First Airborne have to hike from their landing zone to Arnhem Bridge?

   a. Eight miles
   b. Ten miles
   c. Four miles
   d. Seven miles

224. Which handgun was used in large numbers by both the Axis and Allied military forces?

   a. Walther PPK
   b. Lahti L-35
   c. Colt M1911A1
   d. FN Browning High Power

225. Which British warship was the first to be sunk?

   a. HMS *Nelson*
   b. HMS *Courageous*
   c. HMS *Bulldog*
   d. HMS *Hood*

226. Which country captured the greatest number of enemy troops in one engagement?

   a. Germany
   b. Japan
   c. Britain
   d. Russia

227. The code name for the German offensive in the Ardennes, the Battle of the Bulge, was Operation:

  a. Merkur, "Mercury"
  b. Taifun, "Typhoon"
  c. Nordlight, "Northern Lights"
  d. Herbstnebi, "Autumn Mist"

228. Who was the leader of the Cetniks, the Yugoslavian resistance?

  a. Ion Antonescu
  b. Josep Broz Tito
  c. Draza Mihailovic
  d. Laszlo Bardossy

229. The first prime minister of the Polish government in exile in London died under mysterious circumstances. Who was he?

  a. Wladyslaw Anders
  b. Jozef Beck
  c. Stanislaw Mikolajczyk
  d. Wladyslaw Sikorski

230. British paratrooper Sergeant-Major Charles Coward was captured in May 1940 near Calais, while serving with the Eighth Reserve Regimental Royal Artillery as quartermaster battery sergeant major. He managed to make two escape attempts before even reaching a prisoner of war camp, and then made seven further escapes. When in captivity he was equally troublesome, organizing numerous acts of sabotage while out on work details. What else happened to him?

  a. He was the first soldier taken prisoner at Arnhem
  b. He was awarded the German Iron Cross by accident, while posing as a wounded soldier in a German field hospital
  c. He received a battlefield commission directly to major
  d. He landed in his sister's yard in France on D-day

231. The Zoot Suit Riots were a series of street fights that erupted during World War II between sailors and Marines and Latino youths, who were recognizable by the zoot suits they favored. While Mexican Americans were the primary targets of military servicemen, African American and Filipino or Filipino American youths were also targeted. In what city did the Zoot Suit Riots occur?

   a. San Antonio
   b. Houston
   c. New Orleans
   d. Los Angeles

232. Who was Germany's greatest tank ace?

   a. Sepp Dietrich
   b. Otto Graham
   c. Kurt Meyer
   d. Michael Wittman

233. Who was the commander that Admiral Yamamoto entrusted with his attack on Pearl Harbor?

   a. Commander Fuchida
   b. Commander Minami
   c. Commander Fujita
   d. Commander Genda

234. According to Japanese military doctrine, what had to precede the drop of airborne troops?

   a. Nothing
   b. Naval bombardment
   c. Aerial bombardment
   d. Complete surrender of the enemy

235. How many of the 32,000 Japanese soldiers of the Saipan garrison survived the battle?

   a. 100 soldiers
   b. 15,000 soldiers
   c. 500 soldiers
   d. 1,000 soldiers

236. What was the fastest tank in service during the war, with a top speed of 40 miles per hour?

    a. Cromwell tank

    b. M4 Sherman

    c. T-34

    d. Panther

237. Which Dutch submarine sank the Japanese destroyer *Sagiri* on December 24, 1941?

    a. K XVII

    b. K XVI

    c. O 16

    d. K X

238. What warship, whose superstructure was still above water although it had sunk, was used as a gun platform against the advancing Soviet Army?

    a. *Lützow*

    b. *Leipzig*

    c. *Admiral Scheer*

    d. *Köln*

239. How did the light cruiser *Köln* end the war?

    a. Surrendered at Copenhagen

    b. Bombed and capsized in its dock at Kiel

    c. Torpedoed and sunk in the Baltic Sea

    d. Sunk in its dock at Wilhelmshaven

240. On March 31, 1940, this warship was the first of the Kriegs-marine's Hilfskreuzer (auxiliary cruisers) to set out on a combat cruise:

    a. HK *Pinguin*

    b. HK *Atlantis*

    c. HK *Thor*

    d. HK *Orion*

241. How many ships were sunk by submarines in the Atlantic during 1942?

    a. 952
    b. 452
    c. 1,404
    d. 1,160

242. Which submarine sank the battleship the HMS *Barham* on November 25, 1941, in the eastern Mediterranean?

    a. U-331
    b. U-232
    c. U-121
    d. U-313

243. Which submarine sank the British carrier the HMS *Eagle*, on August 11, 1942, in the western Mediterranean, north of Algiers?

    a. U-73
    b. U-56
    c. U-47
    d. U-81

244. How was the battleship *Gneisenau* ultimately destroyed?

    a. Bombed in dry dock in Kiel
    b. Scuttled in Swinemünde
    c. Sunk in a battle off North Cape
    d. Scuttled as a block-ship in Gotenhafen

245. What was the new and improved U-boat that came into service near the end of the war?

    a. Scamperboot
    b. Schnorchelboot
    c. Electroboot
    d. Enduroboot

246. What class of Russian submarines has a hull made of titanium?

    a. Akula

    b. Golf

    c. Typhoon

    d. Alfa

247. Who was the captain of the *Lancastria*?

    a. Captain Rudolph Sharp

    b. Captain John Hawkins

    c. Captain Randal Hopkirk

    d. Captain James Whale

248. What two major changes were salient features of the D model Mustang?

    a. Bubble canopy, reduced weight

    b. Bubble canopy, new engine

    c. Armament, bubble canopy

    d. Increased armor, bubble canopy

249. Name the four-engine German heavy bomber built to the requirements of both a heavy bomber and a dive-bomber:

    a. He 177

    b. Do 17

    c. Ju 88

    d. He 111

250. What company, besides Vought, produced the Corsair for the U.S. Navy?

    a. General Motors

    b. Goodyear

    c. Grumman

    d. Curtiss

251. How many Belgian pilots were killed in the Battle of Britain?

    a. Three

    b. Twelve

    c. Seven

    d. Eight

252. What was the first aircraft designed to have a compressed air ejection seat?

    a. Go 229

    b. He 280

    c. Hs 132

    d. Me 262

253. Which town was bombed on September 19, 1944, by the Germans to interrupt the Allied advance during Operation Market Garden?

    a. Arnhem

    b. Eindhoven

    c. Nijmegen

    d. Grave

254. What type of aircraft was the VIP transport Ascalon, used by both Churchill and King George VI?

    a. York

    b. Rapide

    c. Dakota

    d. Liberator

255. Which twin-engine Saro seaplane saw service with the Royal Air Force?

    a. Catalina

    b. London

    c. Lerwick

    d. Cloud

256. What was Japan's most effective mass-produced fighter?

    a. KI-44 Shoki
    b. J2M Raiden
    c. KI-84 Hayate
    d. KI-29 Hayabusa

257. What radar-equipped Royal Air Force fighter was instrumental in the defense of Britain against German "blitz" bombing?

    a. Defiant MKIIF
    b. Beaufighter MKIIF
    c. Beaufighter MKIF
    d. Blenheim MKIF

258. Name the Royal Air Force day fighter experimentally fitted with AI radar in the spring of 1943:

    a. Hawker Hurricane
    b. Hawker Typhoon
    c. Spitfire V
    d. Spitfire IX

259. Who was Constance Babington-Smith?

    a. Royal Air Force pilot who never saw combat
    b. Mistress of General George Patton
    c. British Women's Air Force photo-reconnaissance expert
    d. Englishwoman who made German propaganda broadcasts

260. Who was Norman Baillie-Stewart?

    a. Greatest Royal Air Force ace
    b. British Army officer who made German propaganda broadcasts
    c. Member of parliament who gave Churchill his bulldog
    d. Only British general killed during Normandy

261. Which of the following was true of modernist poet Ezra Pound?

   a. He was an Axis propagandist while living in Italy
   b. He wrote many poems criticizing man's inhumanity to man
   c. He was President Roosevelt's special "Ambassador to the Arts"
   d. He had no connection with the war

262. How did U.S. and British brides buy a wedding cake when sugar was rationed to just 4 ounces per person?

   a. They didn't have wedding cakes
   b. Brides received a special exemption
   c. They bribed the bakers with sex
   d. They saved their ration for months, and then provided their own sugar

263. Which of the following was not a Japanese weapon?

   a. Type 11
   b. Type 53
   c. Type 99
   d. Samurai swords

264. The code name in 1942 for the plan to surround the German Sixth Army was Operation:

   a. Ring
   b. Uranus
   c. Saturn
   d. Little Saturn

265. The Battle of Stalingrad began on what date?

   a. November 12, 1942
   b. September 13, 1942
   c. August 14, 1942
   d. December 15, 1942

266. How many different badges (denoting Jews, homosexuals, etc.) were there for persons in Nazi concentration camps?

   a. Ten
   b. Eleven
   c. Eight
   d. Nine

267. Who was the only civilian casualty of the Japanese invasion of Attu and Kiska, islands in the Aleutians?

   a. Etta Ramirez, a Mexican tourist
   b. Charles Foster Jones, a radio operator
   c. Isqalit, an Aleut Native
   d. Dave Johnson, a Mormon missionary

268. Who commanded the Third Marines on Iwo Jima?

   a. Major Samuel Nichols
   b. Major General Merrit Edson
   c. General Graves Erskine
   d. Brigadier General Archibald Henderson

269. In a daring harbor raid, Italian frogmen using piloted torpedoes sank this ship in shallow waters at Alexandria on December 19, 1941:

   a. *Valiant*
   b. *Queen Elizabeth*
   c. *Malaya*
   d. *Barham*

270. How much tonnage did the U-boats sink in the period from June to October 1940?

   a. 1,230,000 tons
   b. 1,100,000 tons
   c. 1,400,000 tons
   d. 900,000 tons

271. How many U-boats were sent to the eastern seaboard of the United States for Operation Paukenschlag?

    a. Five

    b. Twenty-three

    c. Thirty-one

    d. One

272. How many aircraft were deployed aboard the *Enterprise*?

    a. 70–80

    b. 50–60

    c. 60–70

    d. 80–90

273. Name the cruiser that fought the *Bismarck* in its final battle:

    a. HMS *Suffolk*

    b. HMS *Belfast*

    c. HMS *Exeter*

    d. HMS *Norfolk*

274. On which date was the British battleship HMS *Prince of Wales* sunk?

    a. December 9, 1941

    b. December 12, 1941

    c. December 11, 1941

    d. December 10, 1941

275. What U.S. submarine was commanded by "Sam" Dealy and was lost in combat in 1944?

    a. U.S.S. *Harder*

    b. U.S.S. *Gato*

    c. U.S.S. *Tang*

    d. U.S.S. *Seawolf*

276. Which British warship was not a member of the King George V–class battleships?

    a. *Nelson*

    b. *Duke of York*

    c. *Anson*

    d. *Prince of Wales*

277. Which fighter was designed to counteract daylight bombing?

    a. Focke Wulf Fw 191

    b. Arado Ar 231

    c. DFS 228

    d. Blohm und Voss Bv 40

278. The Arado 232 transport aircraft had so many inboard wheels (to make loading the aircraft easier) that it earned this nickname:

    a. Centipede

    b. Millipede

    c. Caterpillar

    d. 4×4

279. The He 177 started out as a great aircraft, but the RLM (Reichsluftministerie) made what change that ruined the design?

    a. Changed to underpowered BMW 132 Bramo engines

    b. Switched from aluminum to wood

    c. Eliminated the evaporative cooling system

    d. Changed to underpowered French engines

280. The Arado Ar 234 flew operationally with which Kampfgeschwader?

    a. KG6

    b. KG51

    c. KG76

    d. KG54

281. What was the project name of the Luftwaffe's Mistel composite weapons system?

    a. Beethoven

    b. Roetkap

    c. Sondergerat S-1

    d. Freya

282. Which twin-engine Blackburn aircraft entered service as a torpedo bomber?

   a. Blenheim

   b. Botha

   c. Brigand

   d. Blandford

283. The designation of the photo-recon version of the Lockheed P-38 fighter was:

   a. F-6

   b. FP-38

   c. RP-38

   d. F-5

COLONEL ANSWERS

1. a.	**21.** a.	**41.** d.	**61.** d.	**81.** d.
2. a.	**22.** b.	**42.** c.	**62.** c.	**82.** b.
3. d.	**23.** c.	**43.** c.	**63.** b.	**83.** b.
4. d.	**24.** d.	**44.** a.	**64.** b.	**84.** b.
5. c.	**25.** d.	**45.** c.	**65.** b.	**85.** a.
6. b.	**26.** b.	**46.** c.	**66.** d.	**86.** c.
7. d.	**27.** b.	**47.** b.	**67.** c.	**87.** a.
8. b.	**28.** a.	**48.** d.	**68.** c.	**88.** a.
9. c.	**29.** d.	**49.** a.	**69.** b.	**89.** b.
10. b.	**30.** b.	**50.** a.	**70.** d.	**90.** d.
11. d.	**31.** c.	**51.** a.	**71.** d.	**91.** a.
12. d.	**32.** d.	**52.** c.	**72.** c.	**92.** b.
13. a.	**33.** a.	**53.** b.	**73.** b.	**93.** c.
14. b.	**34.** b.	**54.** d.	**74.** a.	**94.** d.
15. b.	**35.** b.	**55.** a.	**75.** a.	**95.** b.
16. b.	**36.** b.	**56.** d.	**76.** a.	**96.** c.
17. a.	**37.** a.	**57.** d.	**77.** d.	**97.** d.
18. a.	**38.** d.	**58.** c.	**78.** b.	**98.** b.
19. d.	**39.** a.	**59.** c.	**79.** d.	**99.** d.
20. d.	**40.** b.	**60.** d.	**80.** b.	**100.** a.

101. b.	138. d.	175. a.	212. c.	249. a.
102. a.	139. a.	176. b.	213. a.	250. b.
103. b.	140. d.	177. a.	214. a.	251. c.
104. d.	141. b.	178. a.	215. b.	252. b.
105. b.	142. a.	179. c.	216. a.	253. b.
106. c.	143. a.	180. b.	217. a.	254. a.
107. b.	144. d.	181. c.	218. d.	255. c.
108. c.	145. d.	182. b.	219. c.	256. c.
109. b.	146. d.	183. b.	220. a.	257. c.
110. d.	147. d.	184. d.	221. d.	258. b.
111. b.	148. d.	185. c.	222. d.	259. c
112. c.	149. a.	186. d.	223. a.	260. b.
113. c.	150. a.	187. a.	224. d.	261. a.
114. c.	151. b.	188. d.	225. b.	262. d.
115. d.	152. b.	189. b.	226. a.	263. b.
116. c.	153. a.	190. b.	227. d.	264. b.
117. d.	154. d.	191. c.	228. c.	265. b.
118. a.	155. c.	192. a.	229. d.	266. d.
119. a.	156. b.	193. b.	230. b.	267. b.
120. a.	157. b.	194. b.	231. d.	268. c.
121. b.	158. d.	195. b.	232. d.	269. b.
122. c.	159. c.	196. c.	233. d.	270. c.
123. d.	160. d.	197. d.	234. c.	271. a.
124. a.	161. b.	198. d.	235. d.	272. d.
125. a.	162. c.	199. b.	236. a.	273. d.
126. d.	163. c.	200. b.	237. b.	274. d.
127. b.	164. c.	201. c.	238. a	275. a.
128. a.	165. b.	202. c.	239. d.	276. b.
129. a.	166. b.	203. d.	240. b.	277. d.
130. b.	167. d.	204. d.	241. d.	278. b.
131. a.	168. b.	205. b.	242. a.	279. c.
132. a.	169. a.	206. d.	243. a.	280. c.
133. b.	170. a.	207. a.	244. d.	281. a.
134. c.	171. a.	208. a.	245. c.	282. b.
135. d.	172. d.	209. b.	246. d.	283. d.
136. c.	173. c.	210. b.	247. a.	
137. a.	174. b.	211. c.	248. c.	

GENERAL

1. Who designed the fastest fighter of the war, the rocket-powered Me 163, whose unique design included a tailless body?

   a. Hugo Junkers
   b. Kurt Tank
   c. Alexander Lippisch
   d. Willy Messerschmitt

2. Who was Barnes Wallis?

   a. An ex–fighter pilot and the uncle of Douglas Bader
   b. An adviser in the skip bombing of the Eder dam
   c. The designer of the first swing wing aircraft
   d. The designer of a flying torpedo called the victory seeker

3. Who succeeded Reinhard Heydrich as chief of the SD and RSHA in January 1943?

   a. Hans Frank
   b. Adolf Eichmann
   c. Ernst Kaltenbrunner
   d. Odilo Globocnik

4. What advantage did the British PIAT have over the U.S. Bazooka M1A1 and the German Panzerschreck RPzB.54?

   a. Greater armor penetration
   b. Smaller backblast
   c. Lighter weight
   d. Longer effective range

5. Which was the first U.S. island to fall to the Japanese?

   a. Midway
   b. Guam
   c. Wake Island
   d. Kiska in the Aleutians

6. Which Hilfskreuzer commander was charged with war crimes in 1946?

   a. Robert Eyssen
   b. Kurt Weyher
   c. Theodor Detmers
   d. Hellmuth von Ruckteschell

7. How many submarines did the U.S. Navy lose during the war?

   a. Forty-four
   b. Fifty-two
   c. Sixty-one
   d. Thirty-eight

8. What was the only U.S. Navy submarine to be sunk by a Japanese submarine?

   a. U.S.S. *Corvina* SS-226
   b. U.S.S. *Golet* SS-361
   c. U.S.S. *Cisco* SS-290
   d. U.S.S. *Kete* SS-369

9. Who was the first to use the term *axis*, in reference to the Axis Powers?

    a. Adolf Hitler
    b. Benito Mussolini
    c. Hirohito
    d. Franklin D. Roosevelt

10. Name the U.S. general that commanded the initial Allied landing at Anzio:

    a. Ernest J. Dawley
    b. John P. Lucas
    c. Lucian K. Truscott
    d. Lyman L. Lemnitzer

11. Who was the president of the Reichsbank and the German economics minister?

    a. Walther Funk
    b. Adolf Eichmann
    c. Hans Frank
    d. Wilhelm Frick

12. The British and French evacuation from Dunkirk began on what date?

    a. May 25, 1940
    b. May 26, 1940
    c. May 16, 1940
    d. May 15, 1940

13. What was the only British machine carbine at the beginning of the war?

    a. Lanchester
    b. Thompson
    c. Sten
    d. Lancaster

14. The U.S. ration designed to sustain a soldier in the field for one day was called:

   a. C-rations
   b. Field rations
   c. Alpha rations
   d. K-rations

15. Who was the chief of naval operations on December 7, 1941?

   a. Ernest J. King
   b. Harold R. Starke
   c. William S. Pye
   d. H. Kent Hewitt

16. In the Mediterranean, the Australian cruiser HMAS *Sydney* pursued two Italian light cruisers and destroyed one before they could make use of their high speed to get away. Which one was destroyed?

   a. *Bolzano*
   b. *Guiseppe Garibaldi*
   c. *Bartolomeo Colleoni*
   d. *Scipione Africano*

17. In an action during which the *Scharnhorst* and the *Gneisenau* sank the British aircraft carrier HMS *Glorious*, the *Scharnhorst* was damaged by a torpedo from which British destroyer?

   a. HMS *Acasta*
   b. HMS *Acheron*
   c. HMS *Ardent*
   d. HMS *Achates*

18. On December 26, 1943, which two ships finally sank the *Scharnhorst*?

   a. Destroyers HMS *Saumarez* and HMS *Savage*
   b. Cruisers HMS *Sheffield* and HMS *Belfast*
   c. Cruisers HMS *Belfast* and HMS *Jamaica*
   d. Cruisers HMS *Jamaica* and HMS *Norfolk*

19. How many aircraft carriers had been commissioned in the U.S. Navy before the Japanese attack in Pearl Harbor?

   a. Nine
   b. Seven
   c. Eight
   d. Ten

20. This ship captured a total of 1,776 Japanese:

   a. U.S.S. *Cassin Young*
   b. U.S.S. *Charrette*
   c. U.S.S. *Indianapolis*
   d. U.S.S. *Enterprise*

21. Which U.S. submarine sank the Japanese aircraft carrier *Soryu* during the Battle of Midway?

   a. U.S.S. *Tang*
   b. U.S.S. *Archerfish*
   c. U.S.S. *Harder*
   d. U.S.S. *Nautilus*

22. What is the main difference between the Ho XVIII A and B variants?

   a. Landing gear and defensive weaponry
   b. Offensive payload and internal structure
   c. Number of engines and crew accommodation
   d. Number of engines and landing gear

23. How many Schneider racing trophies did the Spitfire win?

   a. Three
   b. Four
   c. Five
   d. Two

24. Which of the following countries never used the P-51 aircraft?

   a. Saudi Arabia
   b. Cuba
   c. Israel
   d. China

25. Who was the top female ace of the war?

    a. Yekaterina Budanova

    b. Lidiya Litvak

    c. Olga Yamschikova

    d. Valeria Khomiakova

26. Italian aircraft had a prefix before their production number, which was:

    a. Code for the type of aircraft

    b. Initials of the designer

    c. City in which it was built

    d. Roman numeral to indicate the main series

27. What was special about the De Havilland Mosquitoes made in Australia?

    a. Frame was made from metal

    b. Serial number began with A52

    c. Two extra machine guns

    d. Night vision scope

28. Which weapon was used in the armed forces of the United States, Belgium, and Poland?

    a. M1903 Springfield

    b. M1 Garand

    c. Browning Automatic Rifle

    d. M1A1 Thompson

29. The first controlled nuclear chain reaction was conducted at the University of Chicago in 1942 by Enrico Fermi, using uranium 238. In what kind of room was this first atomic pile located?

    a. Tennis court

    b. Swimming pool

    c. Handball court

    d. Squash court

30. Of the 10,600 men of the First Airborne who fought at Arnhem, how many survived the battle?

   a. 6,935

   b. 2,429

   c. 2,398

   d. 4,336

31. The Polish Ckm wz.30 machine gun was a copy of which gun?

   a. Schwarzlose M.7/12

   b. Browning M1917

   c. .303 Vickers

   d. Bren

32. Which aircraft was produced in the largest quanities?

   a. Messerschmitt BF 109

   b. B-24 Liberator

   c. Japanese Zero

   d. DC-3 (C-53 and C47 versions included)

33. Which general was the commanding officer of the first Allied troops to cross the Strait of Messina in the invasion of Italy?

   a. Major General Lucian Truscott

   b. Lieutenant General Frederick Browning

   c. Field Marshal Bernard L. Montgomery

   d. Lieutenant General George S. Patton Jr.

34. Name the SAS/Commandos rifle/carbine that was silenced for covert operations:

   a. Enfield Carbine

   b. No. 7 Carbine SD

   c. Vickers Light Rifle (S) .303

   d. De Lisle C

35. What was the only U.S. submarine to sink a battleship?

   a. U.S.S. *Sealion* II SS-315

   b. U.S.S. *Perch* SS-313

   c. U.S.S. *Batfish* SS-310

   d. U.S.S. *Tang* SS-306

36. Who was Japanese chief of the Naval General Staff between 1941 and 1944?

   a. Takijiro Onishi

   b. Shigetaro Shimada

   c. Osami Nagano

   d. Tamon Yamaguchi

37. What was the Gooney Bird?

   a. B-29 Superfortress

   b. PBY Catalina

   c. B-17 Flying Fortress

   d. C-47 Dakota Transport

38. What was the code name for the German offensive to destroy the Russian oil fields in the Caucasus Mountains?

   a. Blue

   b. Yellow

   c. Red

   d. Black

39. Avant-garde composer George Antheil, a son of German immigrants, and his neighbor, a famous Hollywood actress, experimented with the automated control of instruments. Together, on August 11, 1942, they were granted U.S. Patent 2,292,387. This early version of frequency hopping used a piano roll to change between eighty-eight frequencies and was intended to make radio-guided torpedoes harder for enemies to detect or jam. The idea was ahead of its time, and not feasible due to the state of mechanical technology in 1942. Today their frequency-hopping idea serves as the basis for modern spread-spectrum communication technology, such as that used in WiFi network connections and cordless and wireless telephones. The actress wanted to join the National Inventors Council, but she was told that she could better help the war effort by using her celebrity status to sell war bonds. She once raised $7,000,000 at just one event. Who was this actress?

a. Hedy Lamarr
b. Joan Crawford
c. Veronica Lake
d. Olivia de Havilland

40. Vice Admiral Mikawa of the Imperial Japanese Navy inflicted one of the worst defeats of the war on the U.S. Navy at the Battle of:

a. Tokyo Bay
b. Coral Sea
c. Savo Island
d. Leyte Gulf

41. What did Ernest Childers, an American Indian, George H. Cannon, a Marine, Desmond T. Doss, a conscientious objector, and Joseph T. O'Callaghan, a chaplain, have in common?

a. All killed by the same bullet
b. Received the Medal of Honor
c. Tried for treason
d. Received battlefield commissions

42. When did the First Battle of El Alamein take place?

    a. September 1942
    b. December 1942
    c. July 1942
    d. March 1942

43. Which of the following was not an aircraft carrier?

    a. U.S.S. *Forestall*
    b. U.S.S. *Lexington*
    c. U.S.S. *Lake Champlain*
    d. U.S.S. *Ranger*

44. What was the official designation of the Vickers .303 HMG?

    a. Machine Gun, Type: Vickers .303 British
    b. Gun, Machine. Vickers, calibre .303 Mark1 (Class C)
    c. Vickers Heavy Machine Gun, .303
    d. Vickers Watercooled .303 Heavy Machine Gun Mark 1

45. *Yamato*, the world's largest battleship, was sunk on what date?

    a. April 10, 1945
    b. May 10, 1945
    c. May 7, 1945
    d. April 7, 1945

46. During the war, how many U.S. Navy aircraft carriers and escort carriers were sunk?

    a. Eight
    b. Nineteen
    c. Fifteen
    d. Twelve

47. Who was chief of the Japanese Naval General Staff at the outbreak of the war?

    a. Shigeru Fukudome
    b. Mitsumi Shimizu
    c. Chuichi Nagumo
    d. Osami Nagano

48. How many minutes did it take for the U.S.S. *Indianpolis* to sink?

    a. Nine

    b. Fourteen

    c. Eleven

    d. Twelve

49. How many of the thirty-nine Marines aboard the U.S.S. *Indianapolis* survived?

    a. Seventeen

    b. Twenty-two

    c. Four

    d. Nine

50. The most successful Dutch submarine in the war, which torpedoed the *Itala Balbo* on September 9, 1941, off Elba, was:

    a. O 23

    b. O 21

    c. O 24

    d. O 22

51. What was the caliber of the main armament of the *Wilhelm Heidhamp*?

    a. 5

    b. 4

    c. 5.25

    d. 3.3

52. The commander of the U-boat that sank the liner *Laconia* in September 1942 was engaged in rescuing the survivors when he was attacked by an Allied fighter aircraft and had to abandon the survivors to their fate. Who was he?

    a. Kapitänleutnant Erich Würdemann

    b. Korvettenkapitän Harro Schacht

    c. Fregattenkapitän Werner Hartmann

    d. Korvettenkapitän Werner Hartenstein

53. Which of the following statements about the Type XXI U-boat is false?

   a. Employed a revolutionary propulsion system
   b. Employed a hydraulic reloading system for its torpedo tubes
   c. Design was derived from the "Walter-Boot"
   d. Carried the first "Stealth" materiel ever used operationally

54. Name the only one of the nine Hilfskreuzer commanders who completed raider cruises not to receive the Knight's Cross:

   a. Theodor Detmers
   b. Kurt Weyher
   c. Günther Gumprich
   d. Horst Gerlach

55. Which of the following destroyer escorts was a member of the Cannon class?

   a. U.S.S. *Abercrombie* (DE-343)
   b. U.S.S. *Lovelace* (DE-198)
   c. U.S.S. *Weiss* (DE-719)
   d. U.S.S. *O'Neill* (DE-188)

56. Which of the following officers received the Congressional Medal of Honor?

   a. Mush Morton
   b. C. W. Coe
   c. Howard Gilmore
   d. Charles Lockwood

57. Of the approximately 9,000 men aboard the *Lancastria*, how many are estimated to have survived?

   a. Fewer than 100
   b. Between 100 and 1,000
   c. Almost 5,000
   d. Fewer than 3,000

58. Of the 291 B-17s sent to attack the Schweinfurt ball bearing factories, how many were shot down on Black Thursday?

   a. 82

   b. 59

   c. 100

   d. 291

59. Which was the first Mustang variant to see action with the U.S. Army Air Corps?

   a. Mustang I

   b. P-51B/Mustang II

   c. P-51A

   d. A-36 Apache

60. ED 888 flew more operational sorties than any other Lancaster. How many missions was it credited with?

   a. 109

   b. 99

   c. 129

   d. 139

61. The Soviet Ilyushin Il-2 (Sturmovik) was succeeded by the:

   a. Il-6

   b. Il-10

   c. Il-8

   d. Il-12

62. Which aircraft should have been Italy's most effective fighter-bomber but spent most of its career on the ground as a decoy aircraft in North Africa?

   a. Breda Ba.88

   b. Reggiane Re.2000

   c. Savoia-Marchetti SM.79

   d. Fiat G.50

63. The largest number of Me 262 fighter sorties flown on a single day was:

   a. 104

   b. 68

   c. 26

   d. 57

64. Which digit of the Japanese A6M2 Zero aircraft designation indicated that it was a carrier-based fighter aircraft?

   a. 2

   b. 6

   c. A

   d. M

65. What submachine gun had the highest rate of fire?

   a. Beretta Modello 1938A

   b. MP 40

   c. PPSH-41

   d. Thompson M1

66. The German MP 3008 was a copy of the:

   a. Sten

   b. Bren

   c. Thompson

   d. BAR

67. What was the first Japanese carrier to be sunk by the United States?

   a. *Shoho*

   b. *Zuikaku*

   c. *Nagato*

   d. *Shokaku*

68. How many World War II movies starred John Wayne?

   a. Fourteen

   b. Seventeen

   c. Twenty-five

   d. Thirty

69. What mistake did three German pilots make at Comiso Airfield in Sicily?

   a. They landed there by mistake, after the United States had already taken the field
   b. They collided on approach
   c. They bombed too low and blew themselves up
   d. They strafed their own field

70. On what date was the last internment camp closed?

   a. December 5, 1945
   b. November 27, 1947
   c. January 12, 1948
   d. March 20, 1946

71. Who was the commander of the U.S. Navy during World War II?

   a. Admiral King
   b. Admiral Halsey
   c. Admiral Nimitz
   d. Admiral Spruance

72. Who said, "Blood alone moves the wheels of history"?

   a. Adolf Hitler
   b. Josef Stalin
   c. Winston Churchill
   d. Benito Mussolini

73. The massive Soviet summer offensive of 1944 was called Operation:

   a. Whirlwind
   b. Spark
   c. Bagration
   d. Typhoon

74. When did the P51 Mustang begin combat operations?

   a. April 1940
   b. April 1942
   c. April 1943
   d. April 1941

75. When and where was Hermann Goering born?

    a. May 14, 1896, in Hamburg, Germany
    b. January 12, 1893, in Rosenheim, Germany
    c. Janary 17, 1893, in Essen, Germany
    d. February 17, 1891, in Bonn, Germany

76. Who was commander of the U.S.S. *Hornet* for both the Doolittle raid and the Battle of Midway?

    a. Marc Mitscher
    b. Frank Fletcher
    c. Raymond Spruance
    d. William Halsey

77. Who was commander of the German Sixth Paratroop (Fallshirmjäger) regiment in Normandy on D-day?

    a. Baron von der Heydt
    b. Siegfried Knappe
    c. Walther Wenck
    d. Werner Henke

78. Japan unconditionally surrendered on what day?

    a. August 16, 1945
    b. August 10, 1945
    c. August 14, 1945
    d. August 12, 1945

79. Axis Sally's real name was:

    a. Mildred Gillars
    b. Hildegarde Von Eichman
    c. Anna Berg
    d. Jane Bartlett

80. What was the size of the secondary gun on the Japanese heavy tank type 5 Chi Ri?

    a. 20 millimeter
    b. 50 millimeter
    c. 40 millimeter
    d. 37 millimeter

81. Which Japanese carriers were sunk at the Battle of Leyte Gulf?

   a. *Shokaku, Hosho, Shoho, Ryujo*
   b. *Soryu, Hiryu, Kaga, Akagi*
   c. *Zuikaku, Zuiho, Chiyoda, Chitose*
   d. *Hiyo, Taiho, Shokaku, Shinano*

82. Which two British destroyers were sunk while trying to defend HMS *Glorious* against the German battleships *Scharnhorst* and *Gneisenau*?

   a. *Gurkha* and *Maori*
   b. *Acasta* and *Ardent*
   c. *Glowworm* and *Gipsy*
   d. *Ardent* and *Acheron*

83. When Kapitänleutnant Günther Prien penetrated the British fleet anchorage at Scapa Flow in his U-boat in October 1939, he found it deserted. Where were the major ships of the Home Fleet?

   a. Taking part in Fleet exercises
   b. At anchor at Lough Ewe
   c. Responding to a rumored German attack on the Northern Patrol
   d. Searching for the *Gneisenau*, *Köln*, and destroyer escorts in the North Sea

84. Which German ship was sunk by a U-boat in March 1943?

   a. *Alsterufer*
   b. *Uckermark*
   c. *Coburg*
   d. *Doggerbank*

85. Early in the war, the majority of the aircraft in the Royal Air Force Coastal Command were:

   a. Handley Page Hampden
   b. Avro Anson
   c. Armstrong Whitworth Whitley
   d. Bristol Blenheim

86. How many German U-boats were in commission by 1943?

   a. 300–325

   b. 250–300

   c. 400–425

   d. Over 550

87. The submarine U.S.S. *Jack* was famous for:

   a. Sinking Japanese warships

   b. Destroying Japanese oil tankers

   c. Sinking a U.S. submarine

   d. Surrendering on the high seas

88. How many battleships were deployed in Operation Neptune on D-day?

   a. Five

   b. Six

   c. Seven

   d. Eight

89. The *Lancastria* was previously known as the:

   a. *Princess Eugene*

   b. *Windsor Castle*

   c. *Tyrrhenia*

   d. *Britannic*

90. Which battleship never fired its guns at another battleship?

   a. *West Virginia*

   b. *California*

   c. *Pennsylvania*

   d. *Maryland*

91. The Spitfire Mk.V was a major variant of the Spitfire, which included a change of power plant, armament, and:

   a. Malcolm hood

   b. Merlin 45 engine

   c. New "Trop" filter

   d. Universal wing

92. Apart from the Nazis, which two other European air forces employed a swastika-style design?

   a. Lithuania and Finland
   b. Finland and Estonia
   c. Latvia and Finland
   d. Estonia and Latvia

93. The PZL P.23B, the mainstay of the Polish light bomber force in 1939, was nicknamed the:

   a. Los
   b. Karas
   c. Zubr
   d. Wyzel

94. Name the Soviet twin-engine bomber which after the war earned the NATO reporting name of "Buck":

   a. SB
   b. Il-4
   c. Pe-2
   d. Tu-2

95. Which Italian single-engine fighter attacked the HMS *Victorious*?

   a. G.55
   b. Re.2005
   c. Re.2001
   d. MC.202

96. The German Focke-Wulf Fw 190 had a problem with:

   a. High-altitude performance
   b. Engine overheating
   c. Complex undercarriage system
   d. Bad gliding properties

97. The British squadron with the first Belgian flight was:

   a. 408th Squadron
   b. 609th Squadron
   c. 198th Squadron
   d. 131th Squadron

98. What was the designation of the night fighter version of the P-38 Lightning?

   a. P-38L

   b. P-38N

   c. P-38M

   d. P-38NF

99. Who were the German generals who arrested Rommel for treason for his complicity in the plot to kill Hitler?

   a. Heinz Guderian and Erich Hoepner

   b. Hermann Hoth and Hans Krebs

   c. Kurt Zeitzler and Wilhelm Burgdorf

   d. Wilhelm Burgdorf and Ernst Maisel

100. What was the last Hilfskreuzer to attempt to break out into the Atlantic?

   a. *Coronel*

   b. *Komet*

   c. *Hansa*

   d. *Coburg*

101. In the invasion of southern France, who was the commanding general of the Seventh U.S. Army?

   a. Lieutenant General William Simpson

   b. Lieutenant General George S. Patton

   c. Lieutenant General Alexander M. Patch

   d. Lieutenant General Courtney H. Hodges

102. Who coined the term *totalitarian*?

   a. Theodor Adorno

   b. Josef Stalin

   c. Benito Mussolini

   d. Max Horkheimer

103. The Audie Murphy of Germany, that is, the German soldier who received more combat military decorations than any other soldier, was:

   a. Werner Molders
   b. Joachim Peiper
   c. Gotthard Heinrici
   d. Erwin Rommel

104. What did the British soldiers call their Sherman medium tanks?

   a. Churchill
   b. Tiger
   c. Crusader
   d. Firefly

105. British actor David Niven rose to the rank of lieutenant colonel. What actor was his orderly?

   a. Trevor Howard
   b. Michael Caine
   c. Peter Ustinov
   d. Alec Guiness

106. Operation Galvanic was the U.S. invasion of the:

   a. Marshall Islands
   b. Iwo Jima
   c. Palau Islands
   d. Gilbert Islands

107. General Percival was blamed for what poor strategy in the defense of Singapore?

   a. Falling back too early to a secondary position
   b. Not spreading out his troops
   c. Spreading out his troops too far
   d. Not laying mines in the Straits of Jahor

108. Who was the German tank ace who destroyed nine Shermans with a damaged PzKpfw V Panther, and then made it back to his own lines?

   a. SS-Untersturmführer Karl Brommann
   b. SS-Haupsturmführer Michael Wittmann
   c. SS-Unterscharführer Ernst Barkmann
   d. Oberst Dr. Franz Bake

109. Which shipyard built the aircraft carrier HMS *Ark Royal*?

   a. Birkenhead
   b. Tyne
   c. Belfast
   d. Southampton

110. What was a direct result of the Battle of the Barents Sea, fought between elements of the German and Royal navies?

   a. Hitler abandoned his plans to invade England
   b. *Scharnhorst* was sunk
   c. Raeder resigned
   d. *Bismarck* was recalled

111. Name the Japanese prisoner of war ship sunk by mistake by the U.S. submarine *Sturgeon* off Cape Bojidoru, Luzon, in the Philippines as it headed to Japan from Rabaul, New Britain, carrying over a thousand Australian nationals:

   a. *Kobiashi Maru*
   b. *Montevideo Maru*
   c. *Hiryu*
   d. *Kuru Ashi*

112. The advanced Silbervogel "space-plane" bomber was designed by:

   a. Eugen Sanger
   b. Mistislav Keldysh
   c. Werner von Braun
   d. Fritz Sauter

113. How many fighter groups were equipped with the new P-51 B and C models in Europe?

   a. Fourteen
   b. Sixteen
   c. Fifteen
   d. Twenty

114. What type of aircraft was the Pathfinder?

   a. P-51
   b. No such craft
   c. F-4U
   d. P-38

115. Approximately how many Me 163 aircraft were delivered to the Luftwaffe?

   a. 220
   b. 364
   c. 412
   d. 463

116. What successful German night fighter wing was based mainly in the Netherlands from 1941 through 1944?

   a. Nachtjagdgeschwader 2
   b. Nachtjagdgeschwader 6
   c. Nachtjagdgeschwader 5
   d. Nachtjagdgeschwader 1

117. Who was Hitler's last chief of the Army General Staff?

   a. General Alfred Jodl
   b. General Kurt Zeitzler
   c. General Wilhelm Burgdorf
   d. General Hans Krebs

118. The first ship to be sunk on D-day was the:

   a. U.S.S. *John Paul Jones*
   b. U.S.S. *Tanny*
   c. U.S.S. *Fitch*
   d. U.S.S. *Corry*

119. What day was the Nazi-Soviet Pact signed?

 a. August 25, 1939
 b. September 1, 1939
 c. August 20, 1939
 d. August 23, 1939

120. Which U.S. Army unit had the first ground troops to see combat in Asia during the war?

 a. Seventy-seventh Infantry Division
 b. Eleventh Airborne Division
 c. 5307 Composite Group
 d. Twenty-fourth Infantry Division

121. Which general led the U.S. Alamo Force and the Sixth U.S. Army under MacArthur in the Pacific theater?

 a. Roger L. Eichelberger
 b. George C. Kenney
 c. Richard K. Sutherland
 d. Walter Krueger

122. Watching the U.S. flag being raised atop the mountain on Iwo Jima, Secretary of the Navy James Forrestal is said to have stated: "Holland, the raising of that flag on Suribachi means a Marine Corps for the next":

 a. 800 years
 b. 1,000 years
 c. 500 years
 d. 2,000 years

123. Which Russian general served under both the tsar and then the Communists, even though he was under a never-revoked death sentence?

 a. Konstantin Rokossovsky
 b. Ivan Koniev
 c. Georgiy Zhukov
 d. Erich von Manstein

124. The designer of the German Focke Wulf 190 fighter was:

    a. Kurt Tank

    b. Fritz Kurt

    c. Willy Messerschmitt

    d. Hugo Krass

125. During the Japanese attack on Pearl Harbor, what was the first target hit by a Japanese bomb?

    a. Hickham Field

    b. Battleship Row

    c. Ford Island

    d. Sub base

126. The Marines who raised the flag at Iwo Jima were from the:

    a. Twenty-eighth Regimental Command

    b. Fifty-seventh Regimental Command

    c. Fifty-sixth Regimental Command

    d. Fifth Regimental Command

127. Which U.S. submarine sank the Japanese aircraft carrier *Shokaku* during the Battle of the Philippine Sea?

    a. *Darter*

    b. *Wahoo*

    c. *Dace*

    d. *Cavalla*

128. What was the fate of the Japanese commander who ordered the Bataan Death March?

    a. Committed suicide

    b. Convicted of war crimes and shot

    c. Vanished into thin air

    d. Murdered by former prisoners

129. In what year was the T-34-85 tank Model 1943 introduced?

    a. 1941

    b. 1943

    c. 1942

    d. 1944

130. What was the size of the main gun on the NbFz-type tank?

    a. 57 millimeter

    b. 37 millimeter

    c. 88 millimeter

    d. 75 millimeter

131. Which German company designed and manufactured the Panther tank?

    a. Porsche

    b. Krupp

    c. Daimler-Benz

    d. MAN

132. Who was Hitler's naval adjutant?

    a. Admiral Hermann Boehme

    b. Admiral Hans-Georg Von Friedeburg

    c. Admiral Theodor Krancke

    d. Rear Admiral Karl Jesco von Puttkammer

133. The battleship with hull number BB-36 was:

    a. U.S.S. *Oklahoma*

    b. U.S.S. *California*

    c. U. S. S. *Arizona*

    d. U.S.S. *Nevada*

134. How many vessels were involved in Operation Neptune on D-day?

    a. 10,000

    b. 4,000

    c. 200

    d. 7,000

135. How many days did it take NAA to design and build the first P-51 Mustang?

   a. 120

   b. 117

   c. 116

   d. 124

136. What was the first U.S. fighter aircraft to fly from British bases in the European theater of operations?

   a. Lockheed P-38 Lightning

   b. North American P-51 Mustang

   c. Republic P-47 Thunderbolt

   d. Curtis P-40 Tomahawk

137. Which British company built the Lerwick, a twin-engine, smaller version of the Sunderland flying boat?

   a. Short

   b. Saro

   c. Avro

   d. Blackburn

138. The total number of Lightnings built was:

   a. 4,658

   b. 9,924

   c. 6,913

   d. 7,117

139. Tuba, a homemade whiskey popular on ships, was made from:

   a. Yams and coconuts

   b. Green eggs and ham

   c. Potatoes and plums

   d. Rice and raisins

140. In what year did Mussolini and the Fascist Party come to power in Italy?

   a. 1933

   b. 1923

   c. 1929

   d. 1922

141. One naval battle is incorrectly named, that is, it did not occur in the location for which it was named. This naval battle was fought in the Solomon Sea in May 1942, but is today known as the:

   a. Battle of the Coral Sea

   b. Battle of the Philippine Sea

   c. Battle of Midway

   d. Battle of Leyte Gulf

142. The commanding general of the U.S. Eighth Air Force in Britain was:

   a. General Henry H. Arnold

   b. General Hoyt Vandenberg

   c. General Curtis E. Lemay

   d. General Jimmy Doolittle

143. A U.S. general successfully commanded the Big Red One infantry division through North Africa and Sicily, but was relieved of his command by General Eisenhower for maintaining poor discipline. He was rescued from oblivion by General George C. Marshall and given the "Timberwolf" division. Who was he?

   a. Theodore Roosevelt Jr.

   b. George S. Patton

   c. Clarence Huebner

   d. Terry de la Mesa Allen

144. What German general brought tanks into the Ardennes Forest to capture France?

   a. Erich von Manstein

   b. Heinz Guderian

   c. Erwin Rommel

   d. Gerd von Rundstedt

145. Simon Christopher Joseph Fraser, the Fifteenth Lord Lovat, was known during the war as:

   a. An outspoken critic of the war

   b. A daring Commando officer

   c. Only member of Parliament to vote against war

   d. The infamous Lord Haw-Haw

146. The maximum weight for a soldier to start airborne training was:

   a. 145 pounds

   b. 170 pounds

   c. 155 pounds

   d. 165 pounds

147. Who was the commander of the U.S. Fifth Marines on Iwo Jima?

   a. General George Patton

   b. Brigadier General Archibald Henderson

   c. Major General Merrit Edson

   d. Lieutenant General Keller Rockey

148. The Tog II heavy tank was used primarily by:

   a. Greece

   b. Japan

   c. Great Britain

   d. Germany

149. What was the Type 1 Chi-He?

    a. Medium tank

    b. Heavy tank

    c. Light tank

    d. Amphibious tank

150. What was the Soviet Kyrliatyi tank?

    a. Multiturreted tank

    b. Flamethrower tank

    c. Airborne winged tank

    d. Light amphibious tank

151. Which was the first British aircraft carrier to attack the *Bismarck*?

    a. HMS *Illustrious*

    b. HMS *Victorious*

    c. HMS *Ark Royal*

    d. HMS *Formidable*

152. What Royal Navy submarine torpedoed two cruisers during a single attack?

    a. HMS *Trident*

    b. HMS *Clyde*

    c. HMS *Salmon*

    d. HMS *Truant*

153. In August 1942, the tactical advantage in the "Electron War" briefly swung back to the Germans with the introduction of a radio receiver installed on German U-boats that could detect ASV (air-to-surface vessel radar) transmissions from patrolling Allied aircraft. This receiver was called:

    a. Naxos

    b. Wanze

    c. Hohentwiel

    d. Metox

154. On April 8, 1940, in the Norwegian Sea, West Fjord, Norway, Lieutenant-Commander Roope commanding HMS *Glowworm* (1,345 tons) fought an unequal duel with the German cruiser *Admiral Hipper* (10,000 tons). In the encounter *Glowworm* was soon burning and as a last gesture of defiance, its commander decided to ram, which resulted in a good deal of damage to the cruiser. *Glowworm* then fired one more salvo, scoring a hit, before it capsized and sank. One officer and thirty men were picked up by *Admiral Hipper*'s captain, but Lieutenant-Commander Roope was lost. The commanding officer of the *Admiral Hipper* was so impressed by Roope's gallantry that he wrote via the Red Cross to the British authorities and gave a statement of the valiant courage he had shown while engaged in a close battle with a much superior ship, which ultimately resulted in the award of the Victoria Cross for outstanding bravery to Captain Roope. What was the name of the German captain?

a. Captain Theodor Krancke

b. Captain Kurt Hoffmann

c. Captain Harald Netzbandt

d. Captain Hellmuth Heye

155. Which warship was torpedoed, but refused to sink, and survived?

a. *Prinz Eugen*

b. *Leipzig*

c. *Karlsruhe*

d. *Lützow*

156. Name the German passenger liner that was transporting troops and horses to the invasion of Norway when it was torpedoed and sunk off Lillesund in southern Norway by the Polish submarine *Orzel*:

a. *Brasillia*

b. *Constance*

c. *Cameroon*

d. *Rio De Janeiro*

157. How many Essex-class carriers were named after aircraft carriers sunk earlier in the war?

    a. Five

    b. Three

    c. Four

    d. Two

158. Which U.S. aircraft carrier had the shortest period of service?

    a. CV-7 *Wasp*

    b. CV-13 *Franklin*

    c. CVL-23 *Princeton*

    d. CV-8 *Hornet*

159. What was the last all-gun cruiser to remain on the U.S. naval register?

    a. U.S.S. *Newport News*

    b. U.S.S. *Worcester*

    c. U.S.S. *Des Moines*

    d. U.S.S. *Salem*

160. Name one of only two World War II Canadian warships still in existence:

    a. HMCS *Toronto*

    b. HMCS *Sackville*

    c. HMCS *Magnificent*

    d. HMCS *Bonaventure*

161. A stripped-down Spitfire battled with this aircraft in the highest dogfight of the war:

    a. Bv 141

    b. Me 262

    c. Ju 86R

    d. He 111Z

162. What was the approximate air-to-air kill ratio for Mustangs in the European theater of operations?

   a. 6:1

   b. 8:1

   c. 5:1

   d. 10:1

163. The MiG series of fighters, which resembled a prototype German fighter developed by Kurt Tank, was designated the:

   a. Ta-183

   b. Ta-152

   c. Ta-154

   d. Ta-224

164. The Royal Air Force airbase at Habbaniyah defended itself with obsolete training aircraft against attacks by aircraft from:

   a. Persia

   b. Turkey

   c. Vichy France

   d. Iraq

165. About how many He 162 aircraft were ultimately delivered to the Luftwaffe?

   a. 200

   b. 120

   c. 84

   d. 282

166. What was the target of Operation Oyster on December 6, 1942?

   a. Amsterdam

   b. Eindhoven

   c. Rotterdam

   d. Den Helder

167. The fastest P-47 Thunderbolt variant to be put into service, it had an improved engine, reduced weight, and various aerodynamic improvements:

   a. P-47M
   b. P-47D-65
   c. P-47N
   d. P-47S

168. How many Belgian fighter squadrons supported the Royal Air Force on D-day?

   a. One
   b. Four
   c. Two
   d. Three

169. What Royal Air Force night fighter scored the first British intruder victory of the war?

   a. Blenheim MKIVF
   b. Defiant MKI
   c. Beaufighter MKIF
   d. Blenheim MKIF

170. What British general commanded the British Expeditionary Force in France and supervised the evacuation of his army from Dunkirk?

   a. General Lord Gort
   b. General Bernard Montgomery
   c. General Harold Alexander
   d. General Edmund Ironside

171. How many Reichstag seats did the Nazi Party gain in the 1933 German elections?

   a. 169
   b. 107
   c. 288
   d. 196

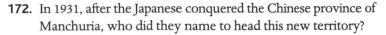
172. In 1931, after the Japanese conquered the Chinese province of Manchuria, who did they name to head this new territory?

    a. Henry Pu Yi

    b. Jisaburo Ozawa

    c. Takashi Hashiguchi

    d. Mitsuo Homma

173. The first generation of Japanese in the United States were called:

    a. Sansei

    b. Nisei

    c. Issei

    d. Kibei

174. What day did Italy surrender to the Allies?

    a. September 9, 1943

    b. September 10, 1943

    c. September 11, 1943

    d. September 8, 1943

175. Churchill addressed the U.S. Congress for the second time on:

    a. June 22, 1942

    b. February 17, 1943

    c. August 23, 1944

    d. May 19, 1943

176. The primary U.S. forces that invaded Okinawa were the:

    a. Tenth Army

    b. Second Marines

    c. Third Marines

    d. Fifth Marines

177. What part did the Japanese Ninth Division play in the defense of Okinawa?

   a. It opposed the United States on the invasion beaches
   b. It was annihilated near Naha
   c. It opposed the United States from underground bunkers
   d. It was moved from Okinawa to the Philippines before the battle

178. How many days did it take for the United States to conquer Attu during the Aleutian campaign?

   a. Thirty-four
   b. Five
   c. Eighteen
   d. Thirteen

179. On which island were Navy parachutists first deployed?

   a. Sumatra
   b. Izu Islands
   c. Iwo Jima
   d. Celebes

180. Who was the intelligence officer for the commander in chief of the Pacific Fleet at Pearl Harbor on December 7, 1941?

   a. Rufus C. Bratton
   b. Joseph J. Rochefort
   c. Edwin T. Layton
   d. James E. Stafford

181. When the U.S.S. *Indianapolis* was sunk, 900 men went into the water. How many survived?

   a. 317
   b. 323
   c. 316
   d. 321

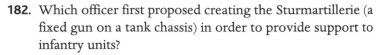

182. Which officer first proposed creating the Sturmartillerie (a fixed gun on a tank chassis) in order to provide support to infantry units?

   a. General Von Runstedt
   b. Lieutenant Colonel Heinz Guderian
   c. Colonel Erich von Manstein
   d. General Beck, chief of general staff

183. Which British cruiser was sunk in a collision with the passenger liner *Queen Mary* in October 1942?

   a. HMS *Carlisle*
   b. HMS *Curacoa*
   c. HMS *Calcutta*
   d. HMS *Coventry*

184. One of the many cruisers lost by the U.S. Navy in the Guadalcanal campaign was sunk in a night fight when the Japanese tried to reduce Henderson Field with battleship bombardment. Which ship was it?

   a. *Juneau*
   b. *San Francisco*
   c. *Helena*
   d. *Atlanta*

185. The Atlantic cruise of the *Scharnhorst* and *Gneisenau* in February 1941 was called Operation:

   a. Nordmark
   b. Juno
   c. Berlin
   d. Sizilien

186. Of the nine Hilfskreuzer, only two made more than one war cruise. Which two were they?

   a. *Komet* and *Orion*
   b. *Komet* and *Thor*
   c. *Orion* and *Michel*
   d. *Thor* and *Michel*

187. What was the last U.S. destroyer to be commissioned?

   a. U.S.S. *Hayler*

   b. U.S.S. *Fife*

   c. U.S.S. *Fletcher*

   d. U.S.S. *O'Brien*

188. As the *Lancastria* sank, hundreds of men clung to its sides, singing these songs:

   a. "God Save the King" and "Rule Britannia"

   b. "Rule Britannia" and "Abide with Me"

   c. "Jerusalem" and "Underneath the Arches"

   d. "Roll Out the Barrel" and "There'll Always Be an England"

189. How did the Handley Page Hereford differ from its sister aircraft, the Hampden?

   a. Different power plants

   b. Torpedo-carrying version

   c. Single tailplane instead of a twin

   d. Long-range version with extra fuel tanks

190. Which was the least successful of the four different design bureaus for Soviet single-engine fighters?

   a. Yakovlev

   b. Lavochkin

   c. Mikoyan Gurevich (MiG)

   d. Polikarpov

191. Which ace has the record number of kills for a single mission?

   a. Hans-Joachim Marseille, eight

   b. Emil "Bully" Lang, eighteen

   c. Erich Rudorffer, thirteen

   d. Hans-Joachim Marseille, seventeen

192. The fighter aces Egmont Zur Lippe-Weissenfeld (fifty-one victories), Constantin Cantacuzino (forty-three victories), and Heinrich Zu Sayn-Wittgenstein (eighty-three victories) were:

   a. Nachtjaegers (night fighters)
   b. Noblemen
   c. Killed in the defense against the Ploesti oil raids
   d. The only non-Germans to get the Eichenlaub decoration

193. The Me 262 unit with the highest score was:

   a. Kommando Nowotny
   b. JG7
   c. JV44
   d. NJG10/11

194. Which nation had the most expensive military decoration?

   a. Germany
   b. France
   c. Italy
   d. Soviet Union

195. What year was the Treaty of Rapallo signed between Germany and the Soviet Union?

   a. 1919
   b. 1926
   c. 1939
   d. 1922

196. The commander of which Hilfskreuzer subsequently became a rear admiral in the Bundesmarine?

   a. *Orion*
   b. *Komet*
   c. *Kormoran*
   d. *Atlantis*

197. The Hilfskreuzer Coronel was converted into a:

   a. Hospital ship

   b. Troop transport

   c. Gunnery training ship

   d. Night fighter direction ship

198. The first enemy ground troops faced by U.S. soldiers in the North African European theater of operations were nicknamed:

   a. Krauts

   b. Huns

   c. Spaghetti soldiers

   d. Frogs

199. How many ships were moored at Pearl Harbor Naval Base on Sunday, December 7, 1941?

   a. 24

   b. 61

   c. 189

   d. 96

200. How many Japanese aircraft were shot down at Pearl Harbor?

   a. Twenty-four

   b. Twenty-nine

   c. Twenty

   d. Thirteen

201. What day did Free French forces take Corsica?

   a. October 5, 1943

   b. October 7, 1942

   c. October 4, 1943

   d. October 11, 1943

202. The first U.S. Navy ship named in honor of an African American was the:

    a. U.S.S. *Carter* DE-112
    b. U.S.S. *Bates* DE-68
    c. U.S.S. *Harmon* DE-72
    d. U.S.S. *Thomas* DE-102

203. Oscar, the *Bismarck*'s cat, was mascot on the:

    a. *Bismarck, Dorsetshire,* and *Ark Royal*
    b. *Bismarck, Gurkha,* and *Illustrious*
    c. *Bismarck, King George V,* and *Furious*
    d. *Bismarck, Cossack,* and *Ark Royal*

204. Captain Lemp of U-30, who sank the passenger liner *Athenia* northwest of Ireland, is also known for:

    a. The "secret" capture of U-110
    b. Being the first to sink 50,000 GRT in one patrol
    c. The unsuccessful attack on HMS *Ark Royal*
    d. Being the only U-boat commander to survive the entire war

205. Which cruiser was handed over to the Soviet Union after the war?

    a. *Nürnberg*
    b. *Leipzig*
    c. *Lützow*
    d. *Köln*

206. Which U.S. submarine commander named his boat's four engines Matthew, Mark, Luke, and John?

    a. Sam Dealy
    b. Richard O'Kane
    c. Hiram Walker
    d. Roy Davenport

207. The Amerika Bomber project, designed to strike the United States, started with the Huckepack-Projekt, which entailed:

   a. Releasing a Do 217 over the Arctic for a one-way bombing run

   b. A suborbital rocket plane bomber

   c. Carrying small "parasite" fighters armed with bombs

   d. Large conventional bomber aircraft

208. Which two air forces adopted the Heinkel He 112 fighter, after it was rejected for service with the German Luftwaffe?

   a. Spain and Romania

   b. Bulgaria and Romania

   c. Romania and Hungary

   d. Spain and Hungary

209. The only Japanese aircraft to bomb the U.S. mainland was the:

   a. Mitsubishi G4M

   b. Yokosuka E14Y

   c. Kawasaki Ki.21

   d. Kawanishi H8K

210. When Italy invaded Greece in 1940, what was the main Greek Air Force fighter?

   a. Gloster Gladiator

   b. PZL P.24

   c. Avia B.534

   d. Bloch M.B.153

211. How many pilots served in the Belgian squadron of the Royal Air Force?

   a. Forty-three

   b. Forty-one

   c. Fifty-five

   d. Fifty-seven

212. Of the 521 Belgian officers who served as pilots or navigators in the Royal Air Force, how many were killed?

   a. 184

   b. 129

   c. 108

   d. 128

213. The U.S. Navy put out a length of anchor chain whose length was how many times the depth of the water?

   a. 3.5

   b. 4.5

   c. 4

   d. 5

214. Who developed the Modello 35, an Italian breech-loading mortar?

   a. Carcano

   b. Fiat

   c. Manlicher

   d. Brixia

215. Which Hilfskreuzer was sunk in the English Channel on its second raiding cruise while attempting to break out?

   a. *Michel*

   b. *Orion*

   c. *Thor*

   d. *Komet*

216. What was the last variant of the Panzer 3?

   a. Ausf P

   b. Ausf G

   c. Ausf K

   d. Ausf N

217. What was known as the Alliance of Animals?

    a. Nickname given to Hitler, Mussolini, and Tojo by Churchill

    b. Code name given to a pack of rabid dogs released by Soviet forces in Berlin

    c. Official intelligence bureau code name assigned to Hitler, Mussolini, and Tojo

    d. French organization that gathered information prior to the Normandy invasion

218. A Sonderkommando was:

    a. A German commando

    b. A squad of SS men

    c. A Romanian commando

    d. SS special forces

219. The commander of the Vichy forces in North Africa at the time of the Allied landings commanded French forces in Italy and ultimately became chief of staff following France's liberation. Who was he?

    a. Maxime Weygand

    b. Philippe LeClerc

    c. Thomas-Robert Bugeaud

    d. Alphonse Juin

220. On Okinawa, Japanese Colonel Yahara became a prisoner when he:

    a. Was wounded and found unconscious

    b. Was captured while posing as a civilian teacher

    c. Became confused and walked into a U.S. position

    d. Was driven mad by the shelling

221. How many types of national markings did the Slovaks use on their aircraft?

    a. Four

    b. One

    c. Three

    d. Two

222. The Beech Model 18 operated as a transport and training aircraft with both the U.S. Army Air Force and the Royal Air Force. The Kansan version was the:

a. AT-10
b. C-45
c. AT-11
d. AT-7

223. What was the first Royal Air Force aircraft to employ geodetic construction?

a. Wellington
b. Wellesley
c. Warwick
d. Whirlwind

224. The Boeing Fortress 3 was used by the Royal Air Force as a:

a. Bomber
b. Radio countermeasures aircraft
c. Transport
d. Air-sea rescue craft

225. Who did General Eisenhower, in September 1943, send on a secret mission to Italy?

a. General Mark Clark
b. General Maxwell Taylor
c. General Omar N. Bradley
d. General Lucius Clay

226. During the Battle of Midway in June 1942, the U.S. Navy sank four Japanese carriers but lost the *Yorktown*. What U.S. destroyer was sunk trying to rescue sailors from the *Yorktown*?

a. *Exetur*
b. *Johnson*
c. *Hammann*
d. *Hartman*

227. During the Battle of Britain, the largest number of German aircraft to attack Britain on a single day was:

a. 1,500

b. 1,000

c. 800

d. 500

228. The Auschwitz Concentration Camp was liberated on:

a. February 26, 1945

b. April 26, 1945

c. March 26, 1945

d. January 27, 1945

229. When the United States attacked Attu in the Aleutians on May 11, 1943, the southern invasion force landed at:

a. Beach Red

b. Massacre Bay

c. Blood Bay

d. Black Bay

230. The greatest aircraft carrier engagement of the war was the Battle of:

a. The Coral Sea

b. The Java Sea

c. Midway

d. The Philippine Sea

231. During the campaign on the island of Saipan, General Smith thought that the Army was moving too slowly, so he relieved their commander, General:

a. William Douglas

b. Ralph Smith

c. Simon Buckner

d. Douglas MacArthur

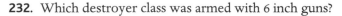
232. Which destroyer class was armed with 6 inch guns?

    a. Type 34

    b. Type 36

    c. Type 36a

    d. Type 36b

233. How many Essex-class carriers had their keel laid down, but were never completed because the war ended?

    a. Two

    b. Four

    c. Five

    d. One

234. What was the last U.S. warship to be sunk in combat?

    a. U.S.S. *Pirate*

    b. U.S.S. *Sarsi*

    c. U.S.S. *Magpie*

    d. U.S.S. *Pledge*

235. The Mk V Spitfire had the distinction of being the first to:

    a. Be used by a foreign country

    b. Serve in full squadron combat overseas

    c. Fly over Germany

    d. Use bombs and rockets

236. The successor to the He 112 was turned down by the Reichs Luftwaffe Ministerium in favor of improved variants of the Bf 109. What was it?

    a. Heinkel 100

    b. Heinkel 114

    c. Heinkel 162

    d. Heinkel 280

237. The Junkers 287 bomber was developed by the Germans late in the war to replace the Stuka. Ironically, one of the design features was "borrowed" from the United States. What was it?

    a. Guns from the P-51D
    b. Norden bombsight from the B-17
    c. Rockets from the P-47
    d. Landing gear from the B-24

238. The Me 262 first flew on:

    a. June 12, 1944
    b. March 25, 1942
    c. February 18, 1942
    d. April 18, 1941

239. Who was the highest scoring jet pilot ace?

    a. Johannes Steinhoff
    b. Adolf Galland
    c. Heinz Bar
    d. Kurt Welter

240. During the escape from POW Stalag Luft III, one of those escaping was this South African Air Force lieutenant:

    a. L. A. S. Waugh
    b. Mitch Mitchell
    c. Dan McGarr
    d. Staff Hope

241. Germany had a number of auxiliary cruisers, armed merchant ships that would generally fly the flag of a neutral nation while they were closing in on unsuspecting Allied ships. Once they were within range they would run up the German flag and deploy their hidden guns. What was the most successful auxiliary cruiser?

    a. *Atlantis*
    b. *Pinguin*
    c. *Orion*
    d. *Komet*

242. In 1942, a small town in North Africa was attacked by elements of the U.S. Eighteenth Infantry four times before it had to be bypassed. What was the event called?

   a. Battle for St. Cloud
   b. Battle for Zimbaque
   c. Operation Reservist
   d. St. Novueanu

243. Who was the commander of the Hilfskreuzer *Michel* on its second cruise?

   a. Hellmuth von Ruckteschell
   b. Ulrich Brocksien
   c. Ernst Thienemann
   d. Günther Gumprich

244. What was the size of the largest self-propelled gun of the war?

   a. 300 millimeter
   b. 88 millimeter
   c. 600 millimeter
   d. 152 millimeter

245. The United States exploded the first atomic bomb at the Trinity test site in Alamagordo, New Mexico, on July 16, 1945. This bomb was the same type used on:

   a. Nagasaki
   b. Hiroshima
   c. Neither
   d. Both

246. On Red Cross volunteer service ribbons, what color stripe designates 500 hours of volunteer work?

   a. Silver
   b. White
   c. Gold
   d. Blue

247. The most deadly air raids carried out by Allied strategic bombing forces were launched against which city?

   a. Tokyo
   b. Dresden
   c. Berlin
   d. Hiroshima

248. Who interrogated the most German prisoners at Stalingrad?

   a. Voronov
   b. Beria
   c. Suvorov
   d. Dyatlenko

249. On what date did Hitler order the evacuation of all forces from Greece?

   a. July 4, 1944
   b. September 23, 1944
   c. October 7, 1944
   d. March 5, 1944

250. The gross agricultural production of the U.S.S.R. dropped in 1941, and did not rise again until:

   a. 1945
   b. 1944
   c. 1946
   d. 1943

251. Who originally designed the Vickers Class K MG?

   a. Chauchat
   b. Berthier
   c. Hotchkiss
   d. St. Etienne

252. What German blockade runner was torpedoed by mistake by U-boat 43?

   a. *Spreewald*
   b. *Heddernheim*
   c. *Ajax*
   d. *Doggerbank*

253. What was the popular name of the Bristol 130?

    a. Blenheim

    b. Bombay

    c. Beaufort

    d. Beaufighter

254. What kind of weapon is a Type 94?

    a. Submachine gun

    b. Rifle

    c. Pistol

    d. Machine gun

255. On what date did the U.S. Eighth Air Force first bomb Berlin?

    a. January 25, 1945

    b. May 8, 1942

    c. March 4, 1944

    d. July 20, 1943

256. Who was the only U.S. Marine Corps general to command a field army?

    a. General Thomas Holcomb

    b. Major General Roy S. Geiger

    c. Lieutenant General Alexander A. Vandegrift

    d. Major General Harry Schmidt

257. The U.S. Army Air Force bombing of the Ploesti oil fields in Romania was called Operation:

    a. Plunder

    b. Boomerang

    c. Crossbow

    d. Tidalwave

258. Admiral King called him the smartest man in the Navy:

    a. Admiral William "Bull" Halsey

    b. Admiral Jack Fletcher

    c. Admiral Chester Nimitz

    d. Admiral Raymond A. Spruance

259. The western task force of the North African Campaign liberated which three cities in 1942?

　　a. Safi, Mazagan, and La Senia
　　b. Safi, Port-Lyautey, and La Senia
　　c. Port-Lyautey, Rabat, and Mazagan
　　d. Safi, Mazagan, and Port-Lyautey

260. The ZB vz26 (Bren) was adopted by Britain and what other country?

　　a. Italy
　　b. Austria
　　c. Germany
　　d. France

261. What was the standard weapon of the Japanese paratroopers?

　　a. Type 2
　　b. Type 100
　　c. Type 99
　　d. Type 14

262. Approximately how many Filipinos died on the Bataan Death March?

　　a. 2,500
　　b. 5,000
　　c. 11,000
　　d. 8,000

263. The Bataan Death March ended at a prison camp designed for 9,000 prisoners. How many POWs arrived?

　　a. 20,000
　　b. 65,000
　　c. 25,000
　　d. 50,000

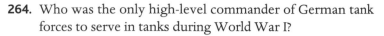

264. Who was the only high-level commander of German tank forces to serve in tanks during World War I?

   a. Erich von Manstein
   b. Heinz Guderian
   c. Walther Model
   d. Joseph Sepp Dietrich

265. What was the most successful U-boat of the war?

   a. U-99
   b. U-103
   c. U-47
   d. U-48

266. After PT boats evacuated General Douglas MacArthur from Corregidor in the spring of 1942, they brought him to the airfield at:

   a. Del Monte
   b. Clark
   c. Wheeler
   d. Buayan

267. The day the second atomic bomb was dropped, Nagasaki was the secondary target. The primary target was bypassed due to local weather conditions. What city was the primary target?

   a. Yahata
   b. Kyoto
   c. Niigata
   d. Kokura

268. What was the first post-Dreadnought battleship commissioned in the U.S. Navy?

   a. U.S.S. *Michigan*
   b. U.S.S. *Texas*
   c. U.S.S. *Maine*
   d. U.S.S. *Arkansas*

269. When was the first Series E Defense Bond sold?

    a. June 6, 1942
    b. January 1, 1942
    c. May 1, 1941
    d. December 26, 1941

270. The German *Fall Rot* (Operation Red) was the invasion of:

    a. Russia in 1941
    b. France in 1940
    c. Greece in 1941
    d. Denmark in 1940

271. What was the last U.S. airfield to be captured by the Japanese?

    a. Ormoc Bay, Philippines, 1942
    b. Henderson Field, Guadalcanal, 1942
    c. Kunmig, China, 1943
    d. Laohokow, China, 1945

272. What Navy aircraft used the laminar flow wing similar to the P-51?

    a. FJ Fury
    b. T-2 Buckeye
    c. F-2 Banshee
    d. F-86 Sabre

273. Who was Germany's great advocate for the development of long-range bombers?

    a. Ernst Udet
    b. Walter Wever
    c. Kurt Student
    d. Ernhard Milch

274. Which Jagdgeschwader was equipped with the He 162 at the end of the war?

    a. JG400

    b. JG7

    c. JG3

    d. JG1

275. What Russian general led a counterattack against German tanks armed only with a pistol?

    a. Kliment Voroshilov

    b. Ivan Konev

    c. Georgy Zhukov

    d. Vasily Chuikov

276. Georg Luger's Parabellum pistol, usually associated with Nazi officers, was most innovative in its:

    a. Ammunition

    b. Toggle breech locking system

    c. Use as a carbine with a shoulder stock

    d. Automatic grip safety

277. What was the greatest airborne operation of the war?

    a. German drop on Crete (Operation Mercury)

    b. U.S. drop on Sicily (Operation Husky)

    c. Allied drop on Holland (Operation Market Garden)

    d. Allied drop on Wesel, Germany (Operation Varsity)

278. On April 13, 1945, the Soviet army marched into:

    a. Budapest

    b. Vienna

    c. Berlin

    d. Prague

279. Who came up with the idea to reply "nuts" to a German request for the surrender of the 101st Airborne Division at Bastogne during the Battle of the Bulge?

   a. Brigadier General Anthony C. McAuliffe
   b. Colonel Harry W. O. Kinnard
   c. Colonel Julian J. Ewell
   d. Lieutenant Colonel John H. Michaelis

280. The first surface engagement fought by the U.S. Navy since the Spanish American War was the Battle of:

   a. Cape Esperance
   b. Savo Island
   c. Midway
   d. Balikpapan

281. What was the Allied nickname for the Japanese version of the DC-3?

   a. Tabby
   b. Rob
   c. Topsy
   d. Toby

282. What ship was known to German raider and U-boat crews as the Floating Delicatessen, because the U-boat crews lived off its refrigerated food after it was captured?

   a. *Nordmark*
   b. *Altmark*
   c. *Tannenfels*
   d. *Duquesa*

283. Name the campaign in which Marine Corsairs first used napalm canisters against entrenched Japanese troops:

   a. Saipan
   b. Peleliu
   c. Iwo Jima
   d. Tarawa

284. Which two nations used the obsolete Hawker Fury biplane fighter in combat?

   a. South Africa and Greece
   b. Hungary and Yugoslavia
   c. Yugoslavia and South Africa
   d. Greece and Romania

285. The Germans had originally decided to build one carrier, the *Graf Zeppelin*, and deploy on it two types of aircraft. What were they?

   a. Fi 167 and Ju 87C
   b. Ju 87T and Bf 109L
   c. He 115B and Bf 110E
   d. Fi 282 and Do 215

286. On what date was the Belgian section of the Royal Air Force transferred back to the Belgian Armed Forces?

   a. May 9, 1945
   b. July 21, 1946
   c. October 1, 1947
   d. October 15, 1946

287. The Allies used code names to aid recognition of Japanese aircraft. Men's names were given to fighters, women's names to bombers and reconnaissance aircraft, and this type of name to training aircraft:

   a. Birds
   b. Flowers
   c. Trees
   d. Animals

288. What was the last country to enter the war on the Allied side?

   a. Brazil
   b. Mongolia
   c. Bulgaria
   d. Vietnam

289. What was the first U.S. unit assigned to England during the war?

  a. Thirty-fourth Infantry Division
  b. First Infantry Division
  c. Twenty-ninth Infantry Division
  d. Third Infantry Division

290. Chester Nimitz, the son of Admiral Chester Nimitz, commanded which ship?

  a. U.S.S. *Bonefish*
  b. U.S.S. *Haddo*
  c. U.S.S. *Barbel*
  d. U.S.S. S-28

291. Who was the first U.S. general killed during the war?

  a. Gerald D. Bryant
  b. Lesley McNair
  c. Herbert Arthur Dargue
  d. Simon Bolivar Buckner Jr.

292. Allied "V-2" was a:

  a. Nickname given by the press to U.S.O. singer Dinah Shore
  b. Long-range rocket under development for use against Washington, DC
  c. Rocket jointly developed by Britain and the United States that was never used
  d. Code name for Princess Elizabeth of England

293. Whom did Berliners sarcastically refer to as "Groefaz"?

  a. Hermann Goering
  b. Adolf Hitler
  c. Josef Goebbels
  d. Erwin Rommel

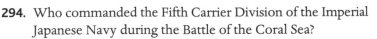

294. Who commanded the Fifth Carrier Division of the Imperial Japanese Navy during the Battle of the Coral Sea?

   a. Chuichi Nagumo

   b. Aritomo Goto

   c. Isoroku Yamamoto

   d. Hara Chuichi

295. The Sherman tank was the first tank:

   a. With a snorkel

   b. To be mass produced

   c. To introduce wet storage

   d. That could stand against the T-34

296. Which U.S. submarine held the record for the number of ships sunk during the war?

   a. U.S.S. *Flasher*

   b. U.S.S. *Tang*

   c. U.S.S. *Archerfish*

   d. U.S.S. *Bowfin*

297. What type of aircraft was downed by Spitfires on September 6, 1939, their first day of action?

   a. Curtis P-36 Hawk

   b. Hawker Hurricane

   c. Junker Ju 52

   d. Henshel Hs 123

298. In 1940, how often did a Briton get a fresh egg?

   a. Every week

   b. Every month

   c. Every two weeks

   d. Every two months

299. Hitler loved books about the Old West. Who was his favorite author?

    a. Zane Gray

    b. Karl May

    c. Jack London

    d. Ned Buntline

300. Who sank the Japanese battleship *Fuso* at the Battle of Leyte Gulf?

    a. R. E. Davison

    b. W. H. Rupertus

    c. J. G. Coward

    d. M. A. Mitscher

301. The sonar used by the HMS *Hunter* was Type:

    a. 123

    b. 124

    c. 121

    d. 44

302. What aircraft produced in Germany during the war had the longest range?

    a. Messerschmitt 323 "Gigant"

    b. Heinkel 177

    c. Blohm und Voss 222 "Wiking"

    d. Focke Wulf Condor

303. The largest attack in a single day by the Arado Ar 234, the very first purpose-built jet bomber, was flown by how many aircraft?

    a. Twelve

    b. Twenty-nine

    c. Fifty-four

    d. Thirty-seven

304. Which German Fighter Wing (Jagdgeschwader) was stationed in the Netherlands?

    a. Jagdgeschwader 26
    b. Jagdgeschwader 2
    c. Jagdgeschwader 1
    d. Jagdgeschwader 11

305. Before the war, British Field Marshal Earl Alexander of Tunis spent time doing something unusual. He was:

    a. A senior officer in the Baltic Landwehr
    b. Retrained and did a stint in the Navy before returning to the Army
    c. Commander of the Black and Tans
    d. A military adviser to the Chinese Nationalists

306. Academy award–winning actor Jimmy Stewart flew twenty-five combat missions in a bomber named:

    a. Windy City
    b. Four Yanks and a Jerk
    c. Sweet as She Can Be
    d. Sweet Baby Jane

307. The T-35b had how many turrets?

    a. Five
    b. Two
    c. Three
    d. Nine

308. The Red Army operation to encircle the German army at Stalingrad, code named Uranus, was spearheaded on three fronts, under the command of these generals:

    a. Zhukov, Eremenko, and Rokossovsky
    b. Vatutin, Eremenko, and Korobkov
    c. Korobkov, Zhukov, and Rokossovsky
    d. Rokossovsky, Vatutin, and Eremenko

309. What Red Army general was commander in charge of the Fourth Ukranian Front?

   a. Zhukov
   b. Vatutin
   c. Rokossovsky
   d. Tolbukhin

310. How many prisoners of war died from maltreatment at the Japanese POW camp on Bataan?

   a. 7,000
   b. 4,500
   c. 3,000
   d. 1,500

311. What was the lightest light tank used in the war?

   a. A4EII
   b. Fiat 3000
   c. M39
   d. T-13

312. Name the submarine that is not a member of the Ohio-class ballistic missile boats:

   a. U.S.S. *Oregon*
   b. U.S.S. *Henry M. Jackson*
   c. U.S.S. *Kentucky*
   d. U.S.S. *Pennsylvania*

313. What were the two major differences between the original Model 299 and the first B-17?

   a. Engines and payload
   b. Number of engines and top speed
   c. Payload and landing gear arrangement
   d. Crew and payload

314. Who designed the MP38/40?

   a. Hugo Schmeisser
   b. Follmer
   c. Herman Schmeisser
   d. Heydrich Schmeisers

315. What ship present during the attack on Pearl Harbor on December 7, 1941, was still in service on December 7, 1981, forty years later?

   a. *Phoenix* (CL-46)
   b. *Ward* (DD-139)
   c. *West Virginia* (BB-48)
   d. *Taney* (PG-37)

316. Who was the first German general to be killed in action after the Allied invasion of Normandy on June 6, 1944?

   a. Major General Wilhelm Falley
   b. Major General Heinz Furbach
   c. Lieutenant General Wilhelm Daser
   d. Lieutenant General Otto Elfeldt

317. Who was chief of staff of the British Royal Air Force from October 1940 until the end of the war?

   a. Arthur Harris
   b. Charles Portal
   c. Hugh Dowding
   d. Trafford Leigh-Mallory

318. What was the target of Russia's Operation Yaslo-Gorlice in 1943?

   a. German Sixth Army
   b. Italian Eighth Army
   c. Fourth Panzer Army
   d. Third Romanian Army

319. The atomic bomb dropped over Nagasaki detonated over the:

   a. Golf course
   b. Tennis court
   c. Gym
   d. School

320. Which plane did the Japanese use to drop paratroops over Palembang?

   a. Kawasaki Ki-56 ("Thalia")
   b. Yokosuka P1Y ("Frances")
   c. Lockheed Hudsons
   d. Mitsubishi Ki-57 ("Topsy")

321. The only Canadian aircraft carrier to be damaged during the war was torpedoed during an escort mission on August 22, 1944, but managed to limp into Halifax for repairs. What was it called?

   a. HMS *Nabob*
   b. HMCS *Majestic*
   c. HMS *Thunderer*
   d. HMCS *Tempest*

322. Which of the following Focke Wulf Fw 190 subtypes never existed?

   a. Fw 190D-4
   b. Fw 190A-0
   c. Fw 190S-8
   d. Fw 190G-8

323. What nation never instituted rationing during the war?

   a. France
   b. Italy
   c. Canada
   d. New Zealand

324. What was the dominant tank type used by the Sixth Panzer Division during the French campaign in 1940?

   a. PzKw III
   b. PzKw IV
   c. PzKw (35)ts
   d. PzKw (38)ts

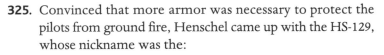
325. Convinced that more armor was necessary to protect the pilots from ground fire, Henschel came up with the HS-129, whose nickname was the:

    a. Flying armored car
    b. Flying assault gun
    c. Flying tank
    d. Armored Panzer destroyer

326. Which of the following tanks was the fastest?

    a. T-34
    b. Panzer MkIV
    c. Sherman
    d. Cromwell

327. Where and when was Field Marshal Bernard L. Montgomery born?

    a. Hampshire, England, on March 4, 1889
    b. Sandhurst, England, on May 29, 1890
    c. Glasgow, Scotland, on March 24, 1887
    d. London, England, on November 17, 1887

328. Of the twenty-two Nazi leaders accused of war crimes at the Nuremberg trials, how many were sentenced to death?

    a. Eighteen
    b. Twelve
    c. Fifteen
    d. Twenty-one

329. The Fiat BR.20 Cicogna medium bomber was used in substantial numbers by the air forces of Italy and what other country?

    a. Sweden
    b. Uruguay
    c. Japan
    d. Romania

330. An admiral said, "You will not only be unable to make up your losses but will grow weaker as time goes on. . . . We will not only make up our losses but will grow stronger as time goes on. It is inevitable that we shall crush you before we are through with you." Who said it?

    a. Raymond A. Spruance

    b. Husband E. Kimmel

    c. Harold Stark

    d. Chester W. Nimitz

331. Which U.S. Army general was the first choice to be commander of U.S. forces in Europe?

    a. Lieutenant General Omar N. Bradley

    b. Lieutenant General Frank M. Andrews

    c. Lieutenant General Mark Clark

    d. Lieutenant General George S. Patton Jr.

332. What was the code name used by General Eisenhower for his retreat outside of London?

    a. London Bridge

    b. Little Camp David

    c. Da De Da

    d. Tweedle De Dum

333. This flag officer graduated from a well-known U.S. military school in 1909 and held, among other awards, the Imperial Order of the Meiji, the Order of the Sacred Treasure, and the Order of the Rising Sun. Who was he?

    a. Wilhelm Keitel

    b. Isoroku Yamamoto

    c. Robert L. Eichelberger

    d. Tomoyuki Yamashita

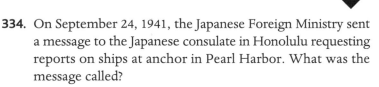
334. On September 24, 1941, the Japanese Foreign Ministry sent a message to the Japanese consulate in Honolulu requesting reports on ships at anchor in Pearl Harbor. What was the message called?

    a. Pearl Harbor Grid Message

    b. Ship Location Message

    c. Bomb Plot Message

    d. Pearl Harbor Plot Message

335. How many parts did the Sten Mark 2 machine carbine contain?

    a. Forty-seven

    b. Thirty-seven

    c. Twenty-one

    d. Forty-one

336. On what date did Great Britain and the Belgian government in exile sign an agreement to incorporate Belgian pilots into the Royal Air Force?

    a. August 18, 1940

    b. June 4, 1942

    c. September 28, 1941

    d. January 5, 1941

337. Various steps were taken by individual Allied powers to normalize their relations with Germany. On December 13, 1946, President Truman proclaimed a cessation of hostilities between the United States and Germany. However, the United States continued to maintain an official state of war because they wanted to retain a legal basis for keeping a U.S. force in West Germany. At a meeting for the foreign ministers of France, the United Kingdom, and the United States in 1950 it was stated that, among other measures to strengthen West Germany's position in the cold war, the Western Allies would end by legislation the state of war with Germany. The United States signed a peace treaty on October 19, 1951. The state of war between Germany and the Soviet Union was ended in early 1955. Finally, the Four Powers renounced all rights they formerly held in Germany, including Berlin, and Germany became fully sovereign on:

a. May 7, 1968
b. March 15, 1991
c. June 4, 1998
d. August 8, 2001

GENERAL ANSWERS

1. c.	**15.** b.	**29.** d.	**43.** a.	**57.** d.
2. c.	**16.** c.	**30.** c.	**44.** b.	**58.** b.
3. c.	**17.** a.	**31.** b.	**45.** d.	**59.** d.
4. b.	**18.** c	**32.** a.	**46.** d.	**60.** d.
5. b.	**19.** c.	**33.** c.	**47.** d.	**61.** b.
6. d.	**20.** b.	**34.** d.	**48.** d.	**62.** a.
7. b.	**21.** d.	**35.** a.	**49.** d.	**63.** d.
8. a.	**22.** d.	**36.** c.	**50.** c.	**64.** c.
9. b.	**23.** b.	**37.** d.	**51.** a.	**65.** c.
10. b.	**24.** a.	**38.** a.	**52.** d.	**66.** a.
11. a.	**25.** b.	**39.** a.	**53.** a.	**67.** a.
12. b.	**26.** b.	**40.** c.	**54.** d.	**68.** a.
13. a.	**27.** b.	**41.** b.	**55.** d.	**69.** a.
14. d.	**28.** c.	**42.** c.	**56.** c.	**70.** d.

71. a.	108. c.	145. b.	182. c.	219. d.
72. d.	109. a.	146. d.	183. b.	220. b.
73. c.	110. b.	147. d.	184. d.	221. c.
74. b.	111. b.	148. c.	185. c.	222. c.
75. b.	112. a.	149. a.	186. d.	223. b.
76. a.	113. c.	150. c.	187. a.	224. b.
77. a.	114. d.	151. b.	188. d.	225. b.
78. b.	115. b.	152. c.	189. a.	226. c.
79. a.	116. d.	153. d.	190. c.	227. b.
80. d.	117. d.	154. d.	191. c.	228. d.
81. c.	118. d.	155. d.	192. b.	229. b.
82. b.	119. d.	156. d.	193. b.	230. d.
83. d.	120. c.	157. a.	194. d.	231. b.
84. d.	121. d.	158. d.	195. d.	232. d.
85. b.	122. c.	159. d.	196. d.	233. a.
86. c.	123. a.	160. b.	197. d.	234. b.
87. b	124. a.	161. c.	198. d.	235. b.
88. b.	125. c.	162. a.	199. d.	236. a.
89. c.	126. a.	163. a.	200. b.	237. d.
90. c.	127. d.	164. d.	201. c.	238. d.
91. d.	128. b.	165. a.	202. c.	239. d.
92. c.	129. d.	166. b.	203. d.	240. c.
93. b.	130. d.	167. a.	204. a.	241. b.
94. c.	131. d.	168. d.	205. a.	242. a.
95. c.	132. d.	169. d.	206. d.	243. d.
96. c.	133. d.	170. a.	207. a.	244. c.
97. b.	134. d.	171. c.	208. a.	245. a.
98. c.	135. b.	172. a.	209. b.	246. a.
99. d.	136. a.	173. c.	210. b.	247. a.
100. a.	137. b.	174. d.	211. c	248. d.
101. c.	138. b.	175. d.	212. d.	249. c.
102. c.	139. d.	176. a.	213. b.	250. b.
103. a.	140. d.	177. d.	214. d.	251. b.
104. d.	141. a.	178. c.	215. d.	252. d.
105. c.	142. d.	179. d.	216. d.	253. b.
106. d.	143. d.	180. c.	217. d.	254. c.
107. c.	144. b.	181. d.	218. b.	255. c.

256. b.	273. b.	290. b.	307. a.	324. c.
257. d.	274. d.	291. c.	308. d.	325. a.
258. d.	275. a.	292. a.	309. d.	326. d.
259. d.	276. a.	293. b.	310. d.	327. d.
260. c.	277. d.	294. d.	311. a.	328. b.
261. a.	278. b.	295. c.	312. a.	329. c.
262. b.	279. b.	296. a.	313. b.	330. c.
263. d.	280. d.	297. b.	314. b.	331. b.
264. d.	281. a.	298. d.	315. d.	332. c.
265. d.	282. d.	299. b.	316. a.	333. c.
266. a.	283. b.	300. c.	317. b.	334. c.
267. d.	284. b.	301. b.	318. b.	335. a.
268. a.	285. a.	302. c.	319. b.	336. b.
269. c.	286. d.	303. d.	320. c.	337. b.
270. b.	287. c.	304. c.	321. a.	
271. d.	288. b.	305. a.	322. a.	
272. a.	289. a.	306. b.	323. b.	

WITHDRAWN